Hollywood's
Children

Also by Diana Serra Cary

THE HOLLYWOOD POSSE: *The Story of a Gallant Band of Horsemen Who Made Movie History*

Hollywood's Children

An Inside Account of the Child Star Era

Diana Serra Cary

Illustrated with photographs

Houghton Mifflin Company
Boston

For Roberto,
who resurrected my sense of humor,
and Mark,
who restored the missing childhood

Library of Congress Cataloging in Publication Data

Cary, Diana Serra, date
    Hollywood's children.

    Bibliography: p.
    Includes index.
    1. Cary, Diana Serra, date   2. Moving-picture
actors and actresses — United States — Biography.
3. Children as actors. I. Title.
PN2287.C32A34   791.43′028′0922 [B]   78-12585
ISBN 0-395-27095-2

Printed in the United States of America

V 10 9 8 7 6 5 4 3 2

Preface

MUCH OF THE STORY that follows is based on my own childhood experiences as one of Hollywood's earliest child stars, Baby Peggy. This insightful, but necessarily limited, viewpoint has been greatly expanded by the valuable contributions of Hollywood professionals who had occasion in their careers to work with movie children at all levels of the industry, from talent scout and assistant director to studio teacher and cameraman.

I am also indebted to many childhood friends and associates, several of them former child stars themselves, who gave generously of their time to provide me with an accurate picture of their careers, their families, the town, and the times in which we lived. My debt to all of the above required the detailed acknowledgments found later in this book.

In addition to interviewing people, I have consulted such primary sources as letters, autobiographies, and articles in those magazines and newspapers of the period whose reporting was most trustworthy. The work of both theater and film historians have proved invaluable, as the bibliography indicates. I would also like to assure the reader that whenever dialogue is used in a scene to which I was not a witness, I have been careful to rely on a primary source — newspaper interviews, tapes, or autobiographies. In this connection I am particularly indebted to Charlie Chaplin, Lita Grey Chaplin, Elsie Janis, June Havoc, Lillian Gish, and Mickey Rooney, whose memoirs have been invaluable to me in preparing this book. A detailed list of these and other works on which I have drawn is in the bibliography.

While neither a memoir nor a history, what follows is, I believe, the very first such account written by an insider who knew most of the children discussed. Because the evolution of the child star phenomenon affected us all, it is presented in the form of a group portrait. A primary goal has been to gather into a single narrative the widely scattered and fragmented accounts of those children whose special gifts established the "child star cult," for better or worse, in American theatrical history. However, I make no pretense at having written the definitive work on the subject. Some very important and talented children whose careers fell outside the time frame or the mainstream of my narrative had to be reluctantly passed over.

While our collective story contains much heartbreak and even tragedy, it is important to note that children were not the only victims. Even today, with modern economic, legal, and psychological safeguards, parents who knowingly enter into this inverted relationship with their child should not expect to come through it emotionally unscathed. By its very nature, such a wrenching reversal of roles between responsible provider and helpless dependent invites devastating consequences for both.

I hope the light shed on little-known aspects of our experiences will prove instructive to students and historians of the cinema as well as to those parents, from whatever walk of life, who may have considered a theatrical career for their children. Lastly, this undertaking satisfies a personal commitment of my own to make available to child psychologists and family counselors the raw material of our collective lives as performing infants and children. With rare exceptions, all of the children described in this book, including the writer, suffered such severe psychological traumas as a consequence of our early careers that most of us were obliged to seek professional help in some form before we could begin to function as emotionally stable adults. Some of us met with such a tragic lack of insight along the way that our problems were, in fact, compounded by the very people whose help we needed most. Perhaps with a deeper understanding of the grave psychological risks inherent in the child star experience, both counselors and parents will become better qualified to help today's children than were those to whom we turned in our time of need.

Like any other social innovation, the child star–stage mother formula had its historical precedent. Certainly a study of the documents singles out one nineteenth-century pioneer as deserving the dubious honor of being the original American stage mother. Without question she provided the dauntless prototype for all those ambitious parents who, knowingly or not, followed her example and the perilous trail she blazed. In desperation, she gambled her way into a game she did not know how to play. Precisely because she won, the childhoods of countless youngsters were destined to be lost.

Diana Serra Cary
Encinitas, California
June 1978

Contents

Preface   v

1. Blazing the Trail   1
2. A Pride of Precursors   15
3. Mother Knows Best   29
4. Kid Fever   45
5. The Children's Hour   56
6. In the World of Five-Day Wonders   71
7. At the End of the Sunset Trail   88
8. Pilgrims and Strangers   106
9. The Child's-Eye View   119
10. The Merchants of Childhood   130
11. Women and Children First   148
12. High Noon in Fort Worth   163
13. Comeback Country   180
14. Dancing Will Make It So   197
15. Growing Pains   209
16. Under the Hollywood Sign   222
17. A Child's Garden of Reverses   236
18. Rites of Passage   249
19. On the Golden Stair   264

Acknowledgments   275
Bibliography   277
Index   281

Illustrations

(following page 114)

Cordelia Howard as Little Eva, 1853. *Theatre and Music Collection, Museum of the City of New York.*
Lotta Crabtree as a child in the 1850s. *Harvard Theatre Collection.*
Mary Ann Crabtree with her son John Ashworth and Lotta, around 1879. *Estate of Lotta Crabtree.*
Mary Ann Crabtree around 1900. *Estate of Lotta Crabtree.*
Jenny Bierbower Janis and Little Elsie, Buffalo, 1897. *Author's Collection.*
The Smith family with Baby Gladys, later Mary Pickford, 1898. *Bob Cushman Collection.*
Mary Pickford, "America's Sweetheart," and mother, Charlotte Smith. *Bob Cushman Collection.*
Baby Gladys on the "kerosene circuit," around 1900. *Bob Cushman Collection.*
Hollywood's "Poverty Row" studios on Sunset Boulevard, 1921. *Bruce Torrence Historical Collection.*
Jackie Coogan and Charlie Chaplin in *The Kid*, 1919. *Author's Collection.*
Baby Peggy with Brownie the Wonder Dog, 1920. *Author's Collection.*
Baby Peggy on set with director Fred Fishback, 1921. *Author's Collection.*
Baby Peggy and the Montgomery family on location in Yosemite National Park, 1921. *Author's Collection.*
Franklin Delano Roosevelt at 1924 Democratic National Convention and Baby Peggy as mascot. *Author's Collection.*
Baby June Hovick (later June Havoc) at age two and a half. *Courtesy of June Havoc Collection.*
Century's Julius Stern, Baby Peggy, and censorship czar Will Hays, 1922. *Author's Collection.*
Mickey Rooney in a Mickey McGuire two-reeler, mid-1920s. *Larry Edmunds Bookstore.*

Hal Roach and his *Our Gang* regulars, 1929. (Photo courtesy of Richard W. Bann, reprinted from *Our Gang: The Life and Times of the Little Rascals.*)

The Parrish children, 1928. *Robert Parrish Collection.*

Dainty June (June Havoc) and older sister Louise (Gypsy Rose Lee) in their vaudeville days. *Courtesy of June Havoc Collection.*

The Johnson clan in a casting directory photo. *Dick Winslow Collection.*

A full-stage Famous Meglin Kiddies production. *Ray Sperry Collection.*

Jackie Cooper with Wallace Beery in *The Champ*, 1931. *Eddie Brandt's Saturday Matinee.*

Dick Winslow and Jackie Coogan in MGM's *Tom Sawyer*, 1932. *Dick Winslow Collection.*

Shirley Temple in an early *Baby Burlesk* two-reeler. *Eddie Brandt's Saturday Matinee.*

Shirley Temple with James Dunn in *Stand Up and Cheer*, 1934. *Courtesy of Loraine Burdick.*

Shirley Temple with her parents at a Hollywood première. *Courtesy of Loraine Burdick.*

Frances Gumm (Judy Garland) singing at age eleven, 1934. *Wayne Martin's Judy Garland Collection.*

Schooltime for child stars at Universal Studios, early 1930s. *Dick Winslow Collection.*

Freddie Bartholomew with his Aunt Cissie during filming of *Captains Courageous*, 1934. *Ray Sperry Collection.*

Deanna Durbin, 1935. *Eddie Brandt's Saturday Matinee.*

Darla Hood, star of *Our Gang*, with her mother, about 1936. (Photo courtesy of Richard W. Bann, reprinted from *Our Gang: The Life and Times of the Little Rascals.*)

Jane Withers in a typical bouncy pose. *Eddie Brandt's Saturday Matinee.*

Edith Fellows in Paramount's *Mrs. Wiggs of the Cabbage Patch*, 1934. *Eddie Brandt's Saturday Matinee.*

Jackie Coogan with his mother, Lillian, and his business manager, Arthur Bernstein, at the funeral of Jack Coogan, Sr., 1935. *Academy of Motion Picture Arts and Sciences.*

Mickey Rooney playing himself as Andy Hardy, 1938. *Larry Edmunds Bookstore.*

Margaret O'Brien with Robert Young in MGM's wartime film *Journey for Margaret*, 1942. *Eddie Brandt's Saturday Matinee.*

Hollywood's
Children

I

Blazing the Trail

*It is a dangerous thing
to confuse children with angels.*
— David T. Fyfe

STANDING ON THE STOOP of a ramshackle boarding house, her small daughter hugged to her skirts, Mary Ann Crabtree watched another day burn itself out in an orgy of color beyond the looming sierra that held her captive on the flats of Rabbit Creek. Not unlike the weather-blasted building at her back, prime lumber only twelve months earlier and now, to all appearances, ravaged by decades of sun and snow, Mary Ann looked old beyond her thirty-two years.

The birth of three children, the long voyage out, and a harrowing passage through the fever-ridden Isthmus of Panama had whittled away at her evanescent English beauty. Capping it all, for two years past she had borne alone the crushing load of operating a boarding house in two of the rawest gold camps in all California.

The fingers that fluttered upward from her little daughter's bright red curls to catch a wisp of her own faded auburn hair were callused and chapped. Her thin shoulders sagged under the remembered weight of iron cauldrons lifted many times a day and uncounted armloads of split wood, fetched and fed into the cookstove's ravenous firebox. And always off when she needed him most, forever trailing some new bonanza or waiting for one to overtake him in the nearest saloon, was Crabtree, as Mary Ann called her feckless mate.

"Nothing would do but he had to go dig gold in California," Mary Ann told anyone who would listen, and having said that she always added tartly, "He never got any." Those two statements might have summarized John Ashworth Crabtree's entire life and been etched as the kindest of epitaphs on his tomb but for the landslide of remarkable events that his wife's desperation shortly set in motion. Bone-weary she may have been, but Mary Ann was far from vanquished; her profile silhouetted against the bright, bannered sky seemed carved of granite. It was not in her nature to waste precious time wondering how she had wound up in a dead-end camp like this on the downhill side of the Gold Rush. What counted was escape, for as surely as a trail led into this godforsaken flat, she would find another leading out.

By now Mary Ann was past regretting how she had been drawn into the snare of Rabbit Creek, decoyed out to California, and, for that matter, beguiled into marrying Crabtree in the first place. It was all of a piece to a poor working girl who had emigrated from London to New York with her widowed mother two decades earlier. Despite seamstressing long hours in the family upholstery business, Mary Ann's youth had not been without promise. Wide brown eyes, sorrel hair, and a vibrant voice had all been attractive features, while a gift for mimicry had prompted friends to urge a career, though all agreed the theater posed an awesome threat to virtue.

Mary Ann's modest talents carried her instead into the arms of a fast-talking dandy who dealt in visions of opulence and ease. John Crabtree painted their future together as an effortless glide up the grand staircase of success. In fact, marriage had proved a downward flight of small but certain failures. Mary Ann, still toiling in her mother's shop, had financed scheme after scheme out of her own slender purse, only to see each one die of neglect while her husband pursued his twin passions for idleness and conviviality.

Following the death of her firstborn and the birth of a daughter in 1847, Mary Ann's concern for the future mounted. She would not have little Lotta, the apple of her eye, doomed to a life of empty promises. But then, just when it seemed that Crabtree was fresh out of rainbows, destiny served up the biggest one yet, the California Gold Rush. John was all for setting out at once, but a stern Mary Ann snapped the coin purse shut. Only after two years of wrangling did she relent, apparently convinced that John would never make anything of himself in the normal course of life; if she let him play for higher stakes, perhaps his luck would change.

As subsequent events proved, Mary Ann's proper, conservative façade cloaked the instinct of a born riverboat gambler. Perhaps it was inherited from her father who, with three of his sons, vanished while on a fortune-hunting voyage to India. It explains why she so often found John's chimeric schemes attractive if not always irresistible. She was a prude, but one quite capable of staking her life on the turn of a card, not merely through an innate love of hazard but because her heart burned at the very thought of gold.

In the spring of 1852, with his wife's blessing and the better part of her bankroll, John left by wagon for the mines. Mary Ann did not hear until the following spring, when, with typical grandiloquence, he wrote that she must join him at once, for their long-awaited fortune was all but in his hands. She lost no time booking passage for herself and little Lotta on the first ship out. Indeed, a fortune did await them in the California wilderness, but it would not be won through any help from John.

Five years after the first cry of "Gold!" San Francisco was still a roaring camp. When their steamer nosed into the wide and crowded bay, Mary Ann guessed it must contain every ship there was in all the world, and the wharf its entire population. Entire, that is, except for Crabtree. She felt her long-contained anxiety reach near-panic as she and Lotta scanned the multitude for John's familiar face. To her vast relief, family friends with whom she had arranged to stay broke from the crowd in a welcome burst of recognition. But their news of Crabtree was far from reassuring: he was last seen heading inland for a new camp whose whereabouts he had not bothered to divulge.

This disappointment might have stopped Mary Ann if at the very same moment she had not herself been caught up in the wild Gold Rush adventure that, until then, it had been only

Crabtree's privilege to enjoy. Suddenly she and six-year-old Lotta were part of a world such as Mary Ann had never dreamed existed. To the very end of her long life she would recount in vivid detail those first exciting hours in San Francisco: her initial sight of miners' tools in a hardware store, that electrifying glimpse of real gold dust, a mound of it, gleaming in a jeweler's window. And then their carriage turned into Portsmouth Square, where before her lay all the gaudy splendor of the city's center of revelry: there Mary Ann would lose her heart to the secret passion of her life — the theater.

Hotels, gaming houses, theaters, and saloons lined the square, their doors open day and night to ruby-bright interiors, emitting a siren song of music and merriment that invited the passerby to take his pick of monte, minstrels, Edwin Booth as *Hamlet*, or plain bar whiskey. Portsmouth was also the sporting ground of young Bohemians, actors, writers, artists, and assorted hangers-on whose sole qualification for membership was a constitution impervious to the combined assaults of alcohol, loose women, and bad cards.

Haughty tragedians, with brooding eyes and chronic stage pallor, strode about in wide-brimmed hats and full Spanish capes. Boldly painted actresses, swan-necked and magnificently gowned, flashed ample views of ankle and calf as they stepped from sidewalk to street. In this splashy crowd Mary Ann found she missed Crabtree not at all. While carefully shunning the square's saloons and gaming halls, she seized every opportunity to attend its theaters. With black-eyed Lotta bouncing at her side, she slaked a lifelong thirst for plays, minstrels, and hilarious burlesques. Years later, seriously arguing her preference for comedy over tragedy, she observed with her usual thrift for words, "It's life."

She hoarded stage-door gossip and justified scandal on the grounds that both were more instructive than vain. For example, was it not prudent to know that most producers of plays were richer than most owners of mines? And when Lola Montez, of the blue-black hair and marvelous violet eyes, fresh from her tour of the royal boudoirs of Europe, performed her outrageous "Spider Dance" and took the town by storm, Mary Ann savored the controversy that hung about her like exotic perfume. Restated in proper terms, it spelled success. While taking care to seem scandalized by what she heard, Mary Ann managed to remember every word.

But the single most impressive theatrical fact Mary Ann did not have to learn by hearsay, for she saw it with her own eyes every day. This was the phenomenal popularity of children, a commodity in very short supply throughout that overwhelmingly male, bachelor Gold Rush society. Nor was this public passion for toddlers lost on the veteran stage families of the square. The prolific Chapmans hailed from a Mississippi show boat tribe, and every one of their many children trouped. The pride of the Bateman family were two daughters, aged eight and eleven, who were well received playing everything from Portia and Lady Macbeth to vapid roles in a homespun piece entitled *Mother's Trust*, written, not surprisingly, by their actress mother.

Most formidable of all the clans were the Robinsons. As one of the city's leading producers of minstrels and plays, Dr. Robinson made certain his well-drilled brood was rarely off the boards. One daughter, now going on eight, was already an established "fairy star." Billed as "Little Sue," she was a solid favorite, especially in remote mining camps, where her resourceful father saw to it she appeared

Mary Ann's pretty, red-haired Lotta drew crowds simply by driving through the streets in their carriage. Miners young and old ran alongside, reaching out to touch the little girl's hand, drinking in the presence of this child who symbolized the home and family forsaken in their lonely quest for gold. A mere smile from Lotta brought tears to the eyes of otherwise manly strangers, a response that Mary Ann noted without displeasure.

By now convinced there was more gold to be mined behind the footlights than in the fields, Mary Ann still hesitated to stake her claim in territory belonging by prior occupancy to seasoned troupers. Although she had placed her own and Lotta's destiny in less than capable male hands, she knew that in Victorian America there were precious few options for a woman to go it alone and remain respectable. With her mother's shop three thousand miles away and her own funds dwindling, she felt helpless and afraid.

As though timing his letter to match her mood of dependency, Crabtree wrote to his wife at last. He was in still another camp,

farther inland than the first, and she must join him at once to con-
summate the finest moneymaking venture yet. After a terrifying
journey up the Sacramento River and an equally fearful overland
jaunt by stage, when their mud-splattered coach finally rolled to a
stop in Grass Valley, Crabtree was actually on hand to meet his
family.

Leading the way up a dusty trail to their "fine new home,"
Crabtree unveiled his latest plan. Two of the richest miners in
the mountains were presently without a place to live. It was the
Crabtrees' good fortune to provide a hospice for such well-heeled
travelers, who in gratitude would pass on to the inn's proprietor
valued tips of new bonanzas before rumor reached the rabble's
ears.

And so Mary Ann found herself tricked into operating a boarding house, an enterprise that became solely hers when Crabtree
drifted on to more promising frontiers. At this low point in her
fortunes chance intervened: a celebrity came to town who was not
entirely a stranger to Mary Ann. Leaning demurely on the arm of
a brand-new gold-rich husband, beautiful Lola Montez picked her
way up the mountain path to a white cottage just down the slope
from the Crabtrees' boarding house. As luck would have it, little
Lotta had to pass the cottage twice a day on her way to and from
the camptown school.

Lotta was now almost seven, but very small for her age. She
was a bright, good-natured little girl, with flashing black eyes,
a piquant, dimpled smile, and hair as coppery red as a newly
minted penny. Reflecting her three months' constant exposure
to the theatrical confections of Portsmouth Square, Lotta loved to
imitate the songs and dances she had seen, and she performed
with an innate sense of grace and timing that delighted Mary Ann.
It was inevitable that this petite and outgoing child, skipping past
her door, would one day catch the discerning eye of a lonely
Lola Montez.

Accustomed to entertaining and being entertained, Lola soon
ached with boredom in this high and barbarous camp, and Lotta
provided a perfect outlet for her pent-up energies. The child's
natural curiosity and eagerness to learn, coupled with her incredible store of talent and application, won Lola's heart. Mary

Ann, who would scarcely let the child out of her sight with any-one else, encouraged Lotta to pass entire days with her new mentor. In an outpouring of sheer exuberance, the Irish-born courtesan and toast of a dozen Continental courts passed on to little Lotta everything she knew about stagecraft, and Lotta absorbed it with alarming speed. Soon Lotta was dancing hornpipes, Irish jigs, and clogs. With seeming ease she mastered the exacting *cracovienne,* a *tour de force* of Lola's own considerable repertoire.

Lola also taught the child to ride, and the two remarkable friends were often seen galloping across the valley's grassy floor. On one such outing they stopped to rest in a blacksmith's shop in the nearby camp of Rough and Ready. There, on an impulse, Lola swept the little girl into her arms and stood her white-stockinged legs atop the smithy's anvil. Clapping her hands and singing the now familiar melodies, Lola coaxed Lotta to go through her routines for the miners standing around.

As though a flame had been kindled inside her, Lotta's face suddenly shone with delight. She bubbled with the excitement and pure gaiety of sharing her weeks of hard work with this impromptu gathering. Spinning on the anvil in her lively jigs and reels, Lotta looked for all the world like a tiny porcelain doll atop a black enamel music box. The miners went wild, throwing their hats in the air and declaring they had never seen the likes of "our Lotta" anywhere. Lola's black-lashed eyes sparkled with pride. One day she would take this wonderful child with her to Paris, London, Madrid!

Impulsively, Lola terminated her short-lived marriage and resumed her title of Countess Landsfeldt, converting the honeymoon cottage into a fashionable salon. With the unerring instinct of their breed, the dilettantes who haunted Portsmouth Square quickly found their way to Lola's open door in far-off Grass Valley. Inventing excuses to call on her neighbor, Mary Ann discovered that Lola's friends brought theater gossip more regularly than the stage brought the mail. While the Countess took every opportunity to introduce Lotta as her protégé, boasting that she could outperform even little Sue Robinson if given the chance, Mary Ann was anxious to pick their brains for genuinely portentous news. Beyond such local rivalries as the Chapman and Robinson clans, what were the wider trends affecting children in the mid-nineteenth-century theater?

All agreed that children were, for the very first time, coming into their own on the American stage. It was not simply a local craze but part of a universal vogue that had brought Little Sue and a bevy of "fairy minstrels" to fame. Credit Charles Dickens, whose novels were enjoying an even greater reception here than in his native England. His solicitude for London's workhouse waifs had grown into a one-man crusade against child labor in all its guises. Nor did the great man spare the theater in his campaign, for in *Nicholas Nickleby* he exposed a real-life stage family who had long exploited their perennially ten-year-old daughter on the London circuits as "the infant phenomenon." Ironically, the parents profited from being satirized, and the girl, now an adult actress, was this very moment in San Francisco reaping her rewards.

But recently there had arisen an American infant so genuinely phenomenal that she was setting the pattern for generations of stage families yet unborn. Even in Lola's small coterie, there were those who had seen the amazing Little Cordelia Howard in one of her hundreds of performances since her remarkable debut in 1852.

The Howards of Troy, New York, were a family steeped in thespian tradition. Mrs. Howard had acted since infancy; her parents and those of her husband had all grown up barnstorming. In Troy, Mr. Howard trod the boards of the family-owned theater and doubled as its manager. In both roles he noted that business was bad. Instinctively he sensed the dramatic potential of Dickens's popular books as plays, and in bringing one to the stage he also tapped the box-office magic of another midcentury craze: the American public's obsession with childhood death.

Scarlet fever, diphtheria, pneumonia, and a host of other unchecked plagues carried off thousands of children every year. Countless more perished in such everyday fatalities as scalding, lockjaw, snakebite, and drowning in cistern, well, or pond. Death had emptied a cradle in virtually every household in America at a time when a mother needed to bear thirteen children if she hoped to see six reach puberty. On the fringes of Catholic doctrine, the cult of the guardian angel had such appeal that many of the faithful taught it as gospel. Popular piety went further, declaring that these babes, gathered to the bosom of God in the bloom of innocence, were transformed into "angel children," powerful intercessors before the heavenly throne for parents, brothers, and sisters still caught in this vale of tears. While no playwright had yet built upon this widespread morbid fixation, George C. Howard, facing a nearly empty house every night, decided to bring the hypnotic anguish of infant mortality to the stage. Unwittingly he made it possible for parents who repressed their grief at home to express it vicariously in a darkened theater.

Howard wrote a play based on Dickens's masterwork of childhood grief, *Oliver Twist*. But with opening night almost upon him, the key role of Little Dick, a four-year-old consumptive inmate of the workhouse Oliver was fleeing, had yet to be filled. In desperation he substituted a girl, his own four-year-old daughter, Cordelia. Powdered to a sickly pallor, dressed in rags, and provided with a little spade, the child was set down beside a pile of earth and told to pretend she was digging another poor orphan's grave. She only had to learn four simple lines.

> OLIVER: I'm running away Dick.
> DICK (Cordelia): Won't you come back anymore?
> OLIVER: I'll come back and see you someday.
> DICK (Cordelia): Goodbye, Oliver.

But on opening night, with her parents watching nervously from the wings, Cordelia responded to Oliver's "I'll come back and see you someday" by bursting into loud, unrehearsed sobs. Then, in a heart-rending voice, she delivered one of the greatest ad libs in theater history: "It won't be any use, Olly dear! When you come back I won't be digging little graves. *I'll be in a little grave myself!*"

She had the trouper's instinct for driving home a point. An echoing gasp of sorrow swept the audience, and a thrill went down George Howard's spine. By God, the child was an actress!

She deserved more than Little Dick's two paltry lines of dialogue. Casting about for a popular story that would challenge Cordelia's talents and capitalize on the public's penchant, he hit upon *Uncle Tom's Cabin*. The book had an appealing child in Little Eva and an angelic, redemptive death in her untimely passing.

The first "Tom show" in a long and venerable tradition opened in Troy on September 27, 1852; it was a family triumph and went on to New York City and fame. Four-year-old Cordelia was a star. In what amounted to an embarrassment of riches, Howard discovered his play also qualified as a genuine religious drama, thereby breaking the long-standing preachers' ban on "Satan's palace," as the faithful referred to the theater. Attending a performance of *Uncle Tom's Cabin* became an obligation of conscience for thousands of devout Christians who had formerly shunned the proscenium as the very gate of Hell.

To her everlasting glory, Little Cordelia had succeeded where such giants of the stage as Jefferson, Forrest, and even the Booths had failed. She compelled entire congregations to pay for the privilege of witnessing on stage what was commonplace and gratis at home — namely, grown men being brought to their knees by the edifying death of an ethereal "angel child."

Notwithstanding the enthusiasm Lola's friends showed for Little Cordelia's melodramatic skills, Mary Ann still chose comedy. And yet, ironically, despite her favorite definition "It's life," her own life did not reflect her preference; now, just when she was fired up with tales of other children's successes, she was stopped dead in her tracks by the appalling discovery that Crabtree was more than a memory. She was pregnant.

When a boy was born in midsummer, she dutifully named him John Ashworth. At this same time, his namesake chose to break his long silence with another fateful letter. Mary Ann must join him in a camp called Rabbit Creek. Once arrived in her new home, a place so remote they traveled to it by mule train, she discovered that a second boarding house awaited her. Undaunted, her first concern, even in this obscure pocket of Creation, was to find a dancing teacher to continue Lotta's lessons. His name was Mart Taylor, a raven-eyed, long-haired Italian, a cobbler by trade and a saloonkeeper by necessity. He also ran and rented out a small log theater for touring companies who braved the trail, and he danced and played guitar.

When Lola Montez rode over from Grass Valley to ask that Lotta go with her on tour to Australia, Mary Ann refused, and the two friends parted in anger. But Mary Ann knew she was right when, a day or two later, Taylor came breathlessly to her door, bearing the great news that Dr. Robinson himself was in camp: he had come all the way just to see Lotta dance.

Mary Ann and Lotta found Robinson with Little Sue in Taylor's saloon, seated by a crude table the cobbler had set up as a stage. The two little girls eyed each other solemnly. If not exactly sworn enemies, they were certainly opponents committed to an exacting competition not of their own choosing. In what might be construed as a friendly overture, Little Sue offered to turn the hand organ for Lotta while she danced.

As Lotta whirled through her routines, Mary Ann watched the veteran showman expectantly. If only Dr. Robinson would put her in his troupe! If only he would say she was as good as Little Sue! When Lotta finished, the producer seemed noncommittal but not displeased. He was preoccupied, it seemed, about putting on a performance that very night, featuring both little girls. Suddenly his genial mood vanished as he and Taylor fell to arguing over the log theater's rental fee. Pompously declaring that the charge was outrageous, which Taylor denied, Robinson vowed to rent the hall across the trail and stalked out with a meek Little Sue at his heels.

Why not stage our own show? Taylor proposed to Mary Ann. Why not star Lotta on her own in open competition with Little Sue? Why not? Mary Ann echoed. She was still a wizard with a needle and could make a professional costume in no time at all. Taylor set about cobbling a tiny pair of authentic Irish brogans. Why, together they would give Lotta the chance to prove herself a true "fairy star" — let the miners themselves make the choice!

Now at sundown, the costume completed, Mary Ann stood for a long time on the front steps of the boarding house, clinging to the little girl on whom so much depended. She felt a cold rage rising up within her, directed partly against her wayward husband for his cruel and mindless neglect, partly against Dr. Robinson, on whose aid she had secretly counted from the very beginning, back in Portsmouth Square, to help launch her daughter's career. He, too, had failed her. Now, silhouetted against a blazing sky, she made a silent vow that she would not let another sun go down on her as a helpless, dependent woman. She would place her bets, win or lose, on her own Lotta's artistry. And at this point there was precious little left to lose.

As the mountain twilight deepened, music began pouring out from both crude entertainment palaces into the dusty trace dividing them. From all over camp the miners drifted there, nuggets and gold dust exchanging hands as extravagant bets were placed on the two contending "fairy stars."

With tablecloths for curtains, candles in bottles for footlights, and Taylor accompanying on the guitar, Lotta highstepped out onto the rough-hewn stage. She was dressed in bright green silk breeches with matching long-tailed coat and high-buckled shoes. Part leprechaun, part old-country Irishman of legend and song, she carried a small shillelagh tucked under one arm and with her free hand lifted an audacious little stovepipe hat in salute to her audience. With a roguish smile, she launched into a rousing series of jigs and reels that brought the miners to their feet whooping wildly.

Through wreaths of smoke from candle wick and cigar, Lotta seemed a human sparkler, ablaze with energy and light. When she exited to change for her next number, pandemonium broke out, and the pro-Lotta ranks were swelled by defectors from the show across the way.

Dressed in a long white gown with low neck and demure puffed sleeves, Lotta moved like a chaste and luminous taper to center stage. The mood changed dramatically from merriment to melancholy as she lifted her clear voice in a familiar ballad, freighted with bittersweet memories for her homesick audience. When she finished and bowed, the men rose, stomping and screaming, chanting "Our Lotta! Our Lotta!" in a wild display of total adoration. And to make their sentiments more tangible, they began showering the stage with half-dollars, quarters, Mexican silver dollars, a hailstorm of gold nuggets, and one fifty-dollar gold piece. The hall across the trail had been completely emptied, leaving Robinson and Little Sue alone in their defeat.

Amid the ensuing riot, in what would in time become a ritual in itself, Mary Ann swept onstage, oblivious to everything except the gold and silver littering the floor. Almost piously, she set about gathering the loot into her large gingham apron. Seconds later she had vanished into the wings, leaving Lotta the center of every miner's eye.

Later that night, as she counted out the take, Mary Ann marveled. In this single night's performance she had got her hands on more money than she had seen since her arrival in California almost two years earlier. But it was more than the money that stunned Mary Ann. It was the irrefutable proof that Lotta was a "fairy star" at last. Now all that she needed was someone who would put the child where she belonged, heading her own company, so that she could repeat tonight's bonanza in every camp with a stage, a bar, or a table that could echo to her clogs.

Mart Taylor, too, respected Lotta's gift for separating miners from their gold. He knew a good fiddler, he said. He himself could dance, play the guitar, recite, and do imitations. He would teach Mary Ann to play the triangle, that quaint and lowly instrument that was not hard to master and was welcome in the camps. Mary Ann understood well what he was saying: they would form their own traveling company around Lotta. Suddenly the trail leading out of Rabbit Creek was sharp and clear, and Mary Ann was game.

Crabtree, of course, was away, but Mary Ann, dutiful wife to the end, baked several loaves of bread, prepared a crock of beans, and against this provender she leaned a tersely worded note, the import of which was that she and the children were gone, she knew not where, and this was her last goodbye.

Mary Ann came out of the boarding house as Taylor pulled up in a wagon drawn by four mules, their harness jauntily trimmed with blue and yellow tassels. This touch would help proclaim to every camp they entered that "the show" had come to town. Stoically she handed up their portmanteaus, to be stowed beneath the canvas top. Gathering her skirts, she climbed onto the spring seat beside Taylor, her eyes straight ahead as he clucked to the team and the big mules plodded forward.

With Lotta on the seat beside her holding the baby in her arms, Mary Ann was profoundly aware of the enormity of the course she had taken. She knew what John would think, what others in the camps and towns ahead would say of her. She would be branded a faithless wife, a doubtful mother, but necessity and chance were on her side. Securely in her lap sat her "plunder basket," holding those very personal and precious treasures a lady did not entrust to trunks and bags. In it was the fifty-dollar gold piece and her small trove of gold dust and nuggets. Ambition had finally triumphed over propriety. The saga of Lotta Crabtree was about to begin.

2
A Pride of Precursors

My Mother bids me bind my hair,
And not go about such a figure:
It's a bother of course, but what do I care?
I'll do as I please when I'm bigger.
                    — Lewis Carroll,
                        "Those Horrid
                        Hurdy-Gurdies!" 1861

NO CHILD IN THEATRICAL HISTORY ever made a more arduous and literal climb to fame than Lotta Crabtree. Mary Ann and Taylor chose the outermost camps, mere clusters of men spurned by other players as not being worth the risk and toil of reaching them. Starved for diversion and loaded with gold, these very patrons made the Crabtree efforts pay. Higher into the pine-sweet Sierra they spiraled, more and more loot their reward. Scrapping the cumbersome wagon, they took to mules, the sure-footed mounts tied bridle and tail for even greater safety. To her other accomplishments, eight-year-old Lotta now added the art of sleeping in the saddle. Years later she told of waking one night as her mule picked his way along a thread of canyon trail to see, far ahead, a lone horse and rider plunge soundlessly over the ledge into the purple mists below.

Just outside each tiny settlement, the weary troupe would quietly dismount, to rest briefly and freshen up before making their deliberately ostentatious entry. At the head of the parade pranced the wild-maned, gypsylike Taylor, shattering the sylvan hush as stridently as a scolding mountain jay, shrilling out his invitation to "Come see the show" while pounding a large drum he carried before him. Behind, on her festooned mule, rode little Lotta, every inch the "fairy star," beaming smiles and blowing kisses as though hailing multitudes. Next came the fiddler, scratching out a sweet-and-sour reel as he danced along between the tarps and shanties, and last, coaxing an occasional timorous chime from a triangle held firmly aloft, a prim Mary Ann brought up the rear.

The handful of scattered miners, jolted from their preoccupation with pick-ax and pan, would straighten up and stare in disbelief as this cacophonous and hallucinatory company filed past. Could that have been a child they had just seen go by, a real little girl dropped from Heaven into this forgotten outpost of Christendom?

The perils and hardships of touring this transalpine circuit took their toll of Lotta. Overwhelmed by the frightening strangeness and insecurity of her surroundings, the little girl often became deeply despondent just before a show. These depressions struck terror in Mary Ann's heart, underscoring the little troupe's total dependence on that seemingly fathomless well of energy and verve that generated Lotta's distinctive style and its lucrative rewards. Working frantically to lift her drooping spirits, Mary Ann told Lotta jokes, did imitations, primed her with favorite stories and songs. The instant Lotta seemed to brighten, Mary Ann pushed her gently out onto the platform or bartop that served as a stage: Taylor and the fiddler struck up their thin accompaniment. For one heart-stopping moment the child would appear to falter, then her incredible buoyancy returned and she launched into her routines, playfully shouting her songs at her audience as though she had known these rough, bearded strangers all her life.

When the performance ended with the usual hail of offerings, Mary Ann went about her ritual of harvesting them into her wide gingham apron, finally cinching it snugly about her waist, a ready-made money belt. On a good night the Crabtree apron might yield up to four hundred dollars.

Impending winter and the urgent demands of a fourth pregnancy drove Mary Ann and the company down out of the mountains. But not before Crabtree, having learned that his daughter had become a traveling bonanza, sold the house in Rabbit Creek and rejoined his suddenly precious family. While Mary Ann went into confinement, Crabtree farmed Lotta out with another band of touring players to keep the money coming in. When Mary Ann found out, she notified the sheriff of Humboldt County to take her daughter from the actors and place her with a good family in Eureka until she could fetch her home. The sheriff's in-laws took her in.

During Lotta's brief stay in Eureka, her sympathetic hosts often asked her to perform for company. One visitor, a young army captain who was billeted nearby, was enchanted by the child's spirited routines. Twenty years later Ulysses S. Grant was still a devoted fan, applauding her from the President's box when she played Washington's National Theater at the apogee of her fame.

With newborn George added to her brood, Mary Ann gathered up her scattered family and descended upon San Francisco, determined to conquer Portsmouth Square. The results were discouraging. Impresarios like Dr. Robinson and Tom Maguire, with entire battalions of talented children waiting in the wings, remained cold to what they regarded as just one more aging youngster in from the mines. A scheming Lola Montez rediscovered them and, according to Mary Ann, tried to shanghai Lotta for a European tour, but eventually the Countess drifted out of their lives. Not so Crabtree. He had come to stay, and he threatened to abduct his daughter bodily unless he were cut in on the take. A furious Mary Ann found herself compelled to share the spoils.

Unable to crack the square, Mary Ann settled for bookings in the low "bit" theaters, areas cleared for entertainment in the backs of stores. Admission was fifteen cents a head, the acts considered risqué, and the audiences even rowdier than those in the camps. After another season of touring the Sierra with Taylor, Lotta renewed her campaign, even playing such places as the Bella Union on San Francisco's notorious Barbary Coast. Patrons entered the "Belly Union" via the well-stocked bar and continued to sample its delights throughout the show. Still, Mary Ann saw to it that all swearing ceased during Lotta's turn, no small feat in itself. Willing to pluck her gold from the fires of Hell, Mary Ann whisked the child in and out of these unsavory dives, content in the knowledge that Lotta was not singed.

During this period, the legend began to grow that Mrs. Crabtree was drawing a ring of fire around her daughter. A certain Mr. Gedge of San Francisco, who as a youth had lived next door to the Crabtrees, in later years recalled being deeply smitten with twelve-year-old Lotta. After gathering the prettiest rose in the neighborhood each day, the boy would wrap it carefully and toss it into Lotta's back yard, "for if her mother saw the act, woe to me!" Less persevering swains were permanently driven off by Mary Ann's protective wrath; it was small wonder that the erstwhile fairy star came to be known as "Lotta The Unapproachable."

In a city whose theaters had a disconcerting habit of burning to the ground every other season, the bond between actors and volunteer fire companies went beyond mere camaraderie. And for an actress to be chosen mascot of a certain battalion could, and often did, insure her fame. So it was with Lotta; after three years of playing benefits, road shows, "bit" theaters, and melodeons — the lowly forerunner of vaudeville — she became the pet of a local fire company. Rebilled by Mary Ann as "Miss Lotta, the San Francisco Favorite," she became just that: an irresistible confection of wicked innocence, flirting her skirts in a walkaround as she sang such show-stoppers as "The Captain with His Whiskers Gave a Sly Wink at Me." By then, too, she was a first-rate banjoist, blackface artist, soft-shoe dancer, melodramatic actress, and comedienne, her many skills learned backstage, often from the famous innovator of each specialty.

A solid success at last, hailed by her adopted city as "the California Diamond" and the "Pet of the Miners," Lotta began to listen to Mary Ann's suggestions that it was time to take on the rest of the country — New York, Chicago, Philadelphia — perhaps even London itself.

In April of 1864, with Portsmouth Square a priceless trophy safe at last in her "plunder basket," Mary Ann, Lotta, and a very respectable-looking John Crabtree set sail for New York via Panama. Only eleven years earlier Mary Ann and Lotta had landed on California's golden shores.

New York was not easily won over by a country girl's charms, but Chicago audiences quickly found Lotta their cup of tea. Gradually Gotham critics and those in such staid eastern cities as Philadelphia and Boston began praising Lotta's comic witchery, referring to her as a "dramatic cocktail." Before she was twelve, Lotta had received no less than a dozen costly watches from her admirers. At seventeen she was almost as rich as she was popular. At twenty-one, when thrifty Mary Ann presented her daughter with her very first silk dress, the girl was well on her way to a fortune. Still, Mary Ann made sure that Lotta never had more than ten cents' spending money at one time. "She has everything she wants," her mother explained to anyone who questioned her frugality. "She has no need of money."

The rest of the family did not apparently share Lotta's modest tastes. Her two brothers attended only the finest schools, both in America and abroad, while Lotta made do for life with a brief six months of formal schooling in San Francisco. His daughter's wealth enabled Crabtree to support his drinking habit in considerable style. On Lotta's spectacularly successful cross-country tours he appeared, a conspicuously well-dressed and affluent figure, lounging in the lobbies of those posh theaters where Lotta was starring, living the role of proud papa to the hilt.

After a patient search for just the right vehicle to show off Lotta's witchery, Mary Ann hit upon *The Old Curiosity Shop*. Heeding the lesson she had learned so well in Lola's Grass Valley salon, that Dickens and "fairy stars" are a potent mix, Mary Ann even saw to it that Lotta doubled as the comic Marchioness and ethereal Little Nell. In the latter role she melted audiences by ascending into Heaven at least once a day. Debuting in Boston in 1866, she later took the play to England, where Charles Dickens the younger touched up the script, took a curtain call with Lotta on opening night, and showed mother and daughter the high spots of London. Other Dickens adaptations foundered, but Lotta's lasted for twenty-five years.

Lotta remained a hard-driving professional — her dances the most exhausting, her roles the most demanding of any in her large troupe. At thirty-five she still looked (and acted) like a child onstage, her roguish black eyes and coquettish smile as delectable as ever. Envious actresses marveled that she had only to stick her leg through a velvet curtain and waggle an ankle in the spotlight to bring down the house. But after the last performance she was often seen driving her carriage furiously through a town's deserted midnight streets, trying to work off the tremendous tensions built up onstage. She was not close to her company, had no special friends, and not infrequently was found at dawn curled up alone on a bench in a railroad waiting room, smoking the black cigars it was rumored Lola Montez had taught her to enjoy.

Mary Ann, on the other hand, drove her carriage through town by day. Her "plunder basket" and apron had been replaced by a leather money bag in which she carried Lotta's growing hoard of jewels (nearly all gifts from her fans) and the weekly box-office receipts, which in those days were paid in cash. Fellow troupers described the satchel as "clanking like a plumber's kit." Mary Ann's increasing distrust of theater managers, bankers, and Crabtree alike finally prompted her to design an iron-clad trunk, constituting an impregnable portable bank, to which she alone possessed the key.

Driving through the towns where Lotta played, Mary Ann inquired of the natives which way "the right address" was moving. Before the engagement had ended, she would have purchased — for hard cash from the trunk — another city block or prime country parcel. These land speculations, reaching from coast to coast, constituted the cornerstone of the $4 million fortune Lotta left to a variety of charities upon her death.

But for all her miserly ways, Mary Ann remained a gambler and sometimes lost money, too. Once, the temptation to play a hunch and her abiding passion for raw gold cost her every cent of the $27,000 her son, John Ashworth, persuaded her to sink in a bogus mine in, of all places, Rabbit Creek.

On another occasion, in Cincinnati, while Lotta and Mary Ann were absent from the hotel, an overpowering thirst drove John Crabtree to take a crowbar to the hallowed money trunk and force the keyless lock. A large sum was irretrievably lost to several bartenders in as many saloons before Mary Ann caught up with her wayward spouse in New York and demanded his arrest. After an uneasy truce, the Crabtrees finally cut the deck for the very last time and John was dealt out of their lives. He asked for a pub of his own, but gladly settled for retirement to a house in Cheshire, England, with a trotting horse, an American carriage, and five pounds a week for life. Once arrived abroad, he let his aristocratic neighbors know he was a gentleman of independent wealth who had made a killing in the California gold fields — as indeed he had.

While most theatergoers found in Lotta Crabtree the ultimate diversion, for one young matron of Columbus, Ohio, catching Lotta's performance represented a solemn obligation, the fulfillment of a vow. Jenny Cockrell Bierbower was an avaricious woman, with piercing black eyes, pompadoured chestnut hair, and a profile described by herself as patrician. Her proud, high-bosomed figure seemed to have been made for the corseted, hourglass fashions and millinery plumage of the day. Where less aggressive ladies sauntered, Jenny strode; where other women dreamed, Jenny acted; and what other females deemed beyond their sex or reach, Jenny set her cap for. Once her falcon's eye fixed upon an object or a goal she made straight for it, her inflexible will and razor-sharp ambition the very talons needed to carry off whatever she seized upon for herself or her young.

It is not surprising then that, in the late 1880s, when Lotta played Columbus for the last time, Jenny bought a single ticket, but saw to it that two took in the show — she and her unborn child. It is highly probable that she went backstage to meet Lotta and questioned Mary Ann on how she had put her daughter where she was. The two women would have gotten on well, for Jenny, too, came from a family in which women were the survivors. When young, Jenny had also shown a dramatic flair, and when friends suggested she might be destined for the stage she had brazenly responded, "Yes, I know."

But for perhaps the first and certainly the last time in her life, Jenny's ambitious plans misfired. Instead of center stage in a rose-colored spot, she found herself married to an obscure railroad clerk in benighted Marion, Ohio. The full import of her plight did not register until a year later, when the first baby came. Then, on being told it was a boy, she had wept for two whole days before saddling him, as if in spite, with what she considered the baleful name of Percy.

Her second pregnancy was different. A firm believer in prenatal exposure, she mapped out a careful month-by-month campaign. This child would be a girl, a beauty, an actress, everything "that pretty Cockrell girl" had so narrowly missed becoming. Jenny attended every minstrel show and play that came to town, studying the stars and their individual styles, satisfied that each performance had left its special mark of genius. As a consequence, her unborn daughter would one day possess "all the eloquence of Modjeska, the versatility of Maggie Mitchell and the elfin alertness of Little Lotta," as she told the story in later years. When, in the spring of 1889, a baby girl was laid in her arms, Jenny was of course not surprised. She named her Elsie Janet Bierbower, but a photographer friend later changed it, saying that "Elsie Janis" would fit better on a theater marquee.

Curiously, John Bierbower and John Crabtree were alike as two potatoes, although Bierbower at least held down a steady job. This gratuity enabled his wife to ignore him and their son while focusing the burning glass of her zeal on her all-important daughter. As soon as she could toddle, Little Elsie was bearing rings at weddings, lisping poems at teas, and gracing every church, school, and county festival. When Elsie was four Jenny landed her the part of Little Willie in a road-show version of *East Lynne* that came to town. Little Willie, who died even more grievously and at greater length than Little Eva, was a plum role for any child (boy or girl), but somehow Modjeska's eloquence had failed to rub off on Elsie as planned. She loved being onstage, but she did not like to act. Unfortunately, too, not a shred of Lotta's elfin alertness came through onstage.

At five, Elsie was a rather old-looking child, with dark circles under her woebegone hazel eyes and little of her mother's patrician beauty. Nevertheless, Elsie was not without talent, and her strong suit proved to be impersonations. She imitated well-known stars, did an astonishing number of them, and did them all exceedingly well. Although her singing voice remained throughout her life on the brassy side and her dancing was more ragged than smooth, Elsie possessed a rare comedy sense and what would eventually ripen into a positive genius for the saving ad lib.

With *East Lynne* and a few other local triumphs behind her, Jenny told John that the time had come to launch Elsie's vaudeville career. In a surprising show of mastery he absolutely forbade her to take the child on the road, whereupon Jenny obtained one of the fastest divorces in Ohio history, won custody of both children, and set out on her own.

Not yet knowledgeable about show business, she decided to start at what she guessed must be the top — the White House. A former Ohio governor's wife and Jenny's long-time friend was now First Lady, and Jenny contrived to get herself invited to tea. There is no record of President McKinley's reaction when Little Elsie was unexpectedly trotted out to perform, but her song, "Break the News to Mother," could hardly have qualified as ideal escape entertainment. The country's "splendid little war" was turning into a nightmare of yellow fever and mass ptomaine poisoning, a secret debacle the President would have preferred to forget, however briefly. But Jenny, seated grandly in the Blue Room, beamed as her pride and joy wrung every possible tear from the maudlin lyrics of the Spanish-American War's hit tune:

> *Just break the news to Mother,*
> *For she knows I love no other,*
> *And tell her not to wait for me*
> *For I'm not coming home.*

When it was over, McKinley gamely kissed the prodigy on her brow and, with the politician's customary wizardry for coining a phrase, pronounced her "destined for great things." That was enough for Jenny.

Pocketing this presidential endorsement as her first leg up the ladder, Jenny decided to challenge the well-known gambling instincts of a certain Buffalo theater owner, Mike Shea. Out of the blue she wired the man, declaring he could have the services of the wonder child, Little Elsie. The salary she demanded was an unheard-of $125 a week, "but," Jenny added temptingly, "*only if she makes good. If not, you don't pay her a dime!*" In an era when entire stage families were grateful to get thirty-five dollars a week for the lot, Mike Shea was intrigued by Mrs. Bierbower's brass. Besides, his reputation as a gambler was at stake. When Jenny received Shea's cryptic reply, "Bring her on," she crowed in triumph.

From that day forward, "Mother marched head up, eyes front," Elsie recalled, "my hand in hers, her life in mine. Men meant nothing to her unless they were interested in me, and if they were not, it was unfortunate for them, as I was ever present."

Seated across the table from her nine-year-old daughter in the elegant dining room of Buffalo's Iroquois Hotel, Jenny outlined the act and the imitations Elsie was to do. Remembering that day in later years, Elsie wrote: "Mother was wearing a tight-fitting broadcloth gown with a train, and a large velvet hat, slightly Gainsborough, with plumes that waved and beckoned in friendly fashion. I hear her voice, vibrant and low, as she planned our attack on the vaudeville front."

Nearly three decades later, on the Orpheum circuit in the late 1920s, I came to know Jenny Bierbower of the beckoning plumes and vibrant voice very well indeed. By then she was notorious, wherever footlights shone, as Ma Janis, the scourge of agents, theater managers, and producers everywhere, the incarnation of what show people meant when they referred to a bona-fide stage mother. By this time, too, Elsie was a thirty-eight-year-old spinster who somehow still emanated a youthful, tomboyish aura, belying her many years as a top-flight star. If Mary Ann had drawn a ring of fire around her Lotta, Jenny Janis had surrounded Elsie with a moat that no man had yet had the temerity to cross.

And yet, despite the power and wealth with which Elsie's talent, submissiveness, and uninterrupted income had endowed her, Ma Janis was not entirely her own woman. John Bierbower had refused to take his daughter's good fortune lying down, demanding and ultimately wresting from his former wife what he considered his rightful share. Now, not unlike Crabtree, he too could bask in outer lobbies, dressed like a lord, traveling with his family when it pleased him to do so, being supported in luxurious retreats when it did not. In all fairness, however, it must be said that John and Elsie's rudderless brother, Percy, were only two in a veritable cloud of relatives and parasitic supernumeraries that

Elsie carried with her on the road or supported at home throughout her long career. But a great deal happened before our paths crossed in big-time vaudeville in 1927.

Jenny was not the only American mother to take her cue from Mary Ann Crabtree. In 1898, when Elsie Janis was nine and playing in Toronto, another child was appearing on the same bill in a one-act play entitled *The Littlest Girl*. Billed as Baby Gladys Smith, she was a pretty thing, Elsie thought, with her great brown eyes and honey-colored curls. Her mother, Charlotte Smith, had lost no time coming round to Elsie's dressing room to inquire peevishly why her baby was making only $15 a week while Elsie was drawing down $75. She had been in show business a scant few months while Jenny was now an old hand of three years' experience.

Unlike Jenny — or Mary Ann, for that matter — Charlotte Smith had not walked away from *her* John. John Smith had died from a blow on the head and left twenty-four-year-old Charlotte nearly destitute with three small children and a ferryboat candy concession on the Toronto–Niagara Falls run. When that project failed, she sold sweets in a Toronto fish market, took in sewing at night, and even rented out the master bedroom of her home in her struggle to make ends meet. The manager of the local Cummings Stock Company and his wife rented the room and brought her luck. The company needed extras for a schoolroom scene in a play, and the pay was $10 a week for each child. To her astonishment, Charlotte realized she had three breadwinners for hire.

By the time Charlotte encountered Jenny and Elsie, five-year-old Baby Gladys was a veteran of sorts. Vain and painfully insecure, Gladys cast her envious gaze on the row of fancy gowns that hung on the pipe rack in Little Elsie's dressing room. "Do you suppose I will *ever* have pretty dresses like those?" she asked her mother. Elsie would never forget that question, for when Charlotte Smith died in 1927, she left an estate of $3 million in her own right. In the meantime, however, Baby Gladys had been gloriously transformed into Miss Mary Pickford.

It would be fascinating to know what Mary Ann Crabtree thought of the rise of these young hopefuls, although it is unlikely she would have been very interested in their achievements. After all, what was it to her that a child actress named Baby Gladys was playing Little Eva in yet another version of *Uncle Tom's Cabin*? Hadn't she seen Little Cordelia Howard herself grow to womanhood in the role, graduate to playing Topsy, Mrs. St. Clair, and, so the legend went, retire at last as old Aunt Ophelia? Had she not indeed lived to see the greatest fairy star of them all — her own adorable, darling Little Lotta — grow old?

By century's end, Mary Ann's show business bonanza had been thoroughly mined out. She dwelt mostly in the past, her memory and ability to recreate the Gold Rush days in words a marvel to all who knew her. Although both Crabtree boys had started life on the back of a mule, they now rode the best-blooded racehorses Lotta's money could buy. When the younger died at thirty-five, "lost at sea" on one of his many Atlantic crossings (falling overboard, either drunk or a suicide), an actor who knew him well remarked, "All he left behind was an empty bottle."

In 1892, on her forty-fifth birthday, Lotta retired. She was not only the most popular actress in America but the richest as well. In the established family tradition of giving Lotta a piece of her own cake, Mary Ann's birthday gift was a horrendous architectural pile she had built on the shores of a fashionable lake in New Jersey. This mansion she named Attol Tryst: "Attol is Lotta spelled backwards," the old lady informed visitors without fail.

In the grand reception hall, above the fireplace, she had enshrined an enormous oil painting of Lotta in her prime. The windows looked out on stately hills and parks. Although she forgot to include a parlor in her plans, the poor immigrant lass who had once delivered slipcovers to the mansions of Park Avenue now boasted her own manor house complete with English butler, French maid, wine cellar, and a private launch on the lake.

Lotta in retirement became a melancholy woman. She still rode spirited horses, but she always rode alone. She counted many acquaintances and visitors, few if any close friends. She remained fickle in her relationships, a rolling stone to the very end. She had of course never married, never had a serious male companion, and, although there were many men who aspired to courting her, she had never had a real beau.

Lotta hated growing old, although at fifty she still looked scarcely thirty, while Mary Ann could have passed for her great-grandmother. The old lady wore her silver-gray hair in crimped tight ringlets that one visitor likened to new dimes, and she always dressed in black, usually taffeta. She wore an old-fashioned bonnet, dating back to the style of her youth, and she spoke of Lotta most of the time as though she were still a little girl. Seated by the window, she would content herself for hours with an all but silent game. On approaching more closely, visitors were astonished to discover that she was playing with a lap full of silver coins, passing them steadily from hand to hand, seemingly soothed and reassured by the gentle clinking sounds of the familiar metal.

Mary Ann died at eighty in 1905, with many thousands of dollars stashed away in teapots and other favorite hiding places. A heartbroken Lotta moved into the Brewster Hotel in Boston, which she owned and where she would cater to theatrical folk. There in 1917, herself now seventy, she attended a performance of *Dear Brutus* in which a promising young actress played the ingénue. Going backstage after the performance to congratulate the cast, she assured the girl that she was "a born comedienne." The young lady's name was Helen Hayes.

By this time Lotta's world had vastly changed. Nearly all the forty-niners of her singular youth were gone. The terrible war in Europe was casting shadows over her own America. By this time, too, Little Elsie and Baby Gladys Smith were no longer children but young ingénues. The movies, which had been born not far from Lotta's own Attol Tryst in New Jersey, were the newest entertainment rage.

Film was a strangely impersonal medium, and one that so intimate an artist as Lotta must have had difficulty relating to. She knew well what adulation and applause in very close quarters could mean to an entertainer. Surely audiences would never be so moved by film that they would feel compelled to throw money and gold watches at the mere shadowy reflection of a child on a cold and distant screen.

Remarkably enough, Lotta would live to see how movie fans expressed their affection for a new crop of child favorites that film would bring to fame.

3
Mother Knows Best

*How my dear Mother endured it, I don't know.
My days were filled with flowers, candy, presents
and praise! . . . On my poor Mother's slim shoulders
rested all the worry and real labor. Literally, all I
did was give my performance. Everything else was
done for me.*

— Elsie Janis,
So Far, So Good, 1932

As EARLY AS 1898 Charlotte Smith was ready to take to the
road with a vengeance. Emboldened by her backstage brush
with the Janis juggernaut in Toronto, she began goading her three
small breadwinners — Baby Gladys, Lottie and Jack — toward her
twin goals of immediate solvency and eventual security. But, although she was armed with such powerful natural weapons as
the one, true faith, an inborn Irish feistiness, and enough gall for
three women her size, the widow Smith entered the child-star
sweepstakes a poor second to Little Elsie's mother.

Ma Janis, queenly in bearing and with an awsome gift for
crowning the outrageous proposal with the imperious command,
was a truly formidable presence. While both Mary Ann Crabtree
and Charlotte Smith admitted they were green to show business,
Jenny behaved as though she had invented it. Through sheer
magisterial bluff she commandeered top billing, star dressing
rooms, and unprecedented salaries for Elsie, at the same time
bringing a record number of redoubtable impresarios to their
knees in stunned capitulation.

By contrast, Charlotte was neither statuesque nor stylish. To

Jenny's strident peacock she was a scrappy bantam hen. Dark-eyed and brunette, with a square face and wide, pugnacious jaw, she was buxom and stood barely five feet tall. The ankle-length gowns of the time only served to convert her into a small, square crate, belted in the middle and mounted on stout spool heels. Pugnacity aside, Charlotte had been more at home imploring strangers to buy her fudge than expecting favors from anyone. But her long novitiate in Toronto's fish market and aboard the Lake Ontario ferry would serve her well in the contract skirmishes that lay ahead. Years of elbowing and outshouting fellow vendors had made upstaging others second nature and rendered her impervious to insult or chagrin. While more discreet matrons felt themselves too well bred to grow shrill in public over money, Charlotte was unencumbered by such vain restraints. Since fine manners usually spoiled a good fight, she took pride in her belligerence and made up in aggressiveness what she may have lacked in self-esteem. As a consequence, she quickly perfected the stage mother's art of sharpening her claws on every flinty circumstance, obstacle as well as opportunity, that fell her way.

After marking time at home with only Baby Gladys on the local boards, Charlotte's first break came in 1902, when Baby Lillian Gish, another child actress from a fatherless family, fell ill while touring in *The Little Red Schoolhouse*. The producer knew that Baby Gladys was up in the part and sought her as a replacement. Already aware that sporadic and conflicting runs only split up the family and duplicated expenses, Charlotte saw her chance to consolidate. Hire the four of us, she wired back, or no Baby Gladys. Pressured to keep the curtain rising and his actors paid, the man complied, repaying Charlotte's impertinence by restricting the family fee to $25 a week.

Living out of the common purse — as they would do for years to come — the Smiths hoarded every cent against the omnipresent threat of layoffs and the ultimate calamity — being stranded on the road. Charlotte soon recognized that she stood outside the theater's aristocracy; to these proud, old, floating dynasties, acting was a time-honored profession, no matter how sorry the play or miserable the pay. To Charlotte, the theater was just one more handy raft for her economically shipwrecked brood, a cut above taking in washing, sewing, or boarders and with a far greater windfall potential than its alternatives.

However, to the average turn-of-the-century small-town American, all show people were tarred with the same brush. Traveling entertainers might be tolerated, even welcomed, as a temporary palliative for the almost universal boredom that oppressed the natives. But an actor still remained taboo, something most Americans prayed no son or daughter either married or became. Like transient Negroes of the same era, derelict actors were encouraged not to let the sun set on them in most God-fearing communities.

Young Lottie and Jack were hardly taxed by their roles as extras, while Charlotte, having boldly passed herself off as a seasoned understudy, was grateful that all the women in the troupe remained in robust health. The full workload fell, as usual, on the real trouper of the family, nine-year-old Baby Gladys.

A proud and sensitive little girl, Gladys was not preoccupied by what possible horrors might befall them on the road; the daily road-show grind itself was misery enough. To her, the "kerosene circuit" constituted a kind of perpetual Purgatory as opposed to New York's Great White Way, which she equated with the beatific vision. She loathed the run-down theaters they played and the rank theatrical hotels with their scuttling roaches and invisible but ubiquitous bedbugs. When not bedded down in such quarters as the local townsfolk deemed proper for greasepaint pariahs, they were rocked to sleep in springless daycoach seats and rattled over an endless maze of complaining rails to the following one-night stand.

After months and finally years of this brutal barnstorming existence, Gladys became obsessed with the desire to escape. But it was not in her nature to jettison her family or run away. Instead, during a brief layover in New York City, she saw her chance and seized it. David Belasco was searching for a little girl to play the part of Betty Warren in his forthcoming Broadway production of *The Warrens of Virginia*. Without her family's knowledge, Gladys walked into the producer's office and won an interview.

The silver-maned Belasco, who affected a clergyman's black garb and collar, was impressed by both the youngster's talent and her candor. "I'm the father of my family," she told him forth-rightly when the conversation turned to salary, "and I must earn all the money that I can." Belasco was so pleased with her performance on opening night that he made her a present of her very first doll. He also changed her professional name from lackluster Gladys Smith to the more genteel sounding Mary Pickford. The name having been plucked from a lofty branch of the Smith family tree, Charlotte, Jack, and Lottie also became Pickfords overnight.

Thirteen-year-old Mary Pickford was in her element at last. She adored her pretty costumes, every one as lovely as those in Little Elsie's dressing room that night so long ago. She found Broadway's cultured patrons a blessed change from the gamy rubes she had played to in the sticks. But, although the production enjoyed a long, successful run, no play lasts forever and, at sixteen, Mary found herself and her family right back where they had been at the outset of her career as Baby Gladys, nearly ten years earlier: out of work, with no future bookings, and behind in their rent at the boarding house.

For a time, to help make ends meet, the impoverished Pickfords shared a flat with the Gish girls and their mother. Mrs. Gish was a gentle soul from Urbana, Ohio, whose spouse had vanished years earlier into that limbo of irresponsibility where poor providers hie themselves, leaving his wife neither decently widowed nor divorced. She, too, had been in the candy business, hawked her wares in amusement parks, and finally, in desperation, had sunk to intermittent employment on the stage. Her two young daughters, Lillian and Dorothy, though not yet in their teens, were already as tremulously beautiful as two camellias. The girls also worked, occasionally modeling children's wear (their mother made all their own clothes by hand) or touring with various nonrelated "aunts," actresses who befriended their mother and agreed to act as chaperones while drilling them in what was fast becoming their profession. Road shows were popular and children still very much in demand. Most melodramas called for a younger brother or sister of the heroine: if the heroine was married and truly worthy of that noble role, she had to boast at least two or three children to make the part believable.

Baby Lillian shared Mary Pickford's hatred for the hardships of the road. In one typically bug-infested theatrical hotel, when Lillian knelt down one night to say her prayers, she burst out impulsively, "And please, God, don't let us wake up in the morning!" Through it all Mrs. Gish, who had herself been raised with fine linens, silver, crystal, and servants, strove mightily to erect a wall of grace, good manners, and an exquisitely sewn wardrobe between her lovely daughters and the rude, gypsylike existence in which they found themselves.

Lillian was in frail health. Suffering from anemia, she had dropped out of the cast of *The Little Red Schoolhouse*. While the child's delicate constitution naturally worried her mother, it positively alarmed Charlotte Pickford. One day, out of earshot of the girl, Charlotte shook her head solemnly and in the pious phrase of the day advised Mrs. Gish, "My dear, I'm afraid that child is *just too good to live*." It seemed that even veteran "angel children," who died edifying deaths onstage (and Lillian had played her share of Little Willies and Little Evas in her time), were in equal danger of being found ripe for Heaven offstage as well. Not wishing to be present at Lillian's real-life deathbed scene, Charlotte chose to move her family out. After all, in show business, where chance and superstition reigned supreme, one couldn't be too careful; there was no sense in being cursed by someone else's broken mirror.

The year 1909 was a slack season on Broadway, and one day Mary Pickford, obeying strict orders from her mother, found herself in front of 11 East Fourteenth Street, looking for a quite different kind of job. The place was a dingy old brownstone, in a neighborhood that New York's better families had abandoned years before. The once elegant Victorian homes had been partitioned into small tailor shops, piano showrooms, and other fly-by-night businesses. Although everything about the district depressed her, necessity drove her on. Casting a furtive glance to make certain no one saw her entering this disreputable address, Mary darted up the stairs and into a dark entry hall pungent with the unfamiliar scent of film.

What had been the grand ballroom back in the mansion's salad days now served the Biograph Company as a large indoor set. Mary was ushered in, and the more sophisticated players stared in disbelief at her long, honey-gold curls. The leading man, a handsome black Irishman named Owen Moore, was immediately struck by her beauty. So, too, was the director, a tall man in his early thirties with heavy-lidded eyes, a high-beaked aristocratic nose, and the fine manners of a southern gentleman. In a gesture of welcome he came forward and asked, "What may I do for you?"

Mary, striving to look every inch the Broadway star, replied nonchalantly, "Well, I thought I wouldn't mind working in pictures for a while, that is, if the price is right."

David Wark Griffith, himself a refugee from the stage, recognized the contempt in which actors held what they termed "galloping tintypes." He realized that only hunger drove most of them to his door, and this girl was obviously no exception. Griffith had been looking at the world from behind a camera for the past three years, and he understood film and the mentality of the moviegoing public perhaps better than any man then alive. While originally joining Biograph for the money, he had become a convert to moving pictures and now was wholly absorbed in developing new narrative and dramatic techniques for the medium.

Sizing up the child-woman before him, he thought her features too pretty, her height inadequate, and her voice too reedy for the stage. But he surmised the camera would turn every minus into a plus. Her luminous beauty, far more than her experience and acting ability, interested Griffith. He offered her the standard five dollars a day and a job if she came back the next day.

The girl surprised him. Drawing herself up to her full sixty inches, she explained that she was "an actress and an artist" and must be paid "twice what ordinary performers" received. Inwardly amused but impressed by Mary Pickford's first Biograph performance, Griffith agreed to meet her terms. Mary was relieved to learn from the other players that her name would not appear on any of the movies in which she performed. No one's did. How merciful, she thought; in total anonymity she could earn a living from this grubby underside of her profession until Broadway came alive again, and the great Belasco need never be the wiser.

As he directed Mary in film after film, Griffith discerned an elusive quality about her that came across on the screen through all the translucent backlighting and sentimental silks. It was an unsuspected inner toughness, a hard edge to her beauty, which had at first seemed marshmallow soft. Stubborn, willful, ambitious, Mary's soul was scarred by hard work and privation, and it showed. Here was a heroine with whom the moviegoing poor — and there was scarcely any other kind in 1909 — could identify. Mary personified youthful America on the threshold of a century of promise, peace, and scientific progress. She was a spunky girl, someone that the immigrant, the country folk, and the self-made man could all believe in: everything was possible for Little Mary and the land in which she pursued her happy endings. Obviously, both America and the girl who became America's sweetheart were born to win.

Although Mary never intended movie work to be anything but a stopgap, a year later she was still with Griffith, and the old place on East Fourteenth Street had become a second home. With the darkly handsome Owen Moore most often cast opposite her, Mary had become a well-known personality to moviegoers even without her name appearing on the film. People wrote in to ask about the marvelously beautiful actress with the expressive eyes. What was her real name? Where had she come from?

Not only was Mary becoming famous, she had overcome her shame; she was actually writing movie scripts, selling them to Biograph for $25 each, and acting in them as well. Unlike the stage, film work proved unbelievably steady — Biograph players were almost never laid off, even for a day — and the opportunities for financial advancement seemed limitless. Mary defected to Broadway only once, returning to star for Belasco in *A Good Little Devil*, a play in which Baby Lillian, still very much alive, played Golden Fairy and hovered overhead on wires in the best "angel child" tradition. At the end of the run, Mary returned to

Biograph, followed by both Gish girls, who soon became full-fledged members of Mr. Griffith's stock company.

Charlotte never forgot that it was she who had insisted Mary try the movies. Although Charlotte had become something of a trouper herself by then, even working with Chauncey Olcott in a play, the compass needle of her ambition had never veered from Mary. Before anyone else in the family recognized the full financial possibilities of films, Charlotte had been alert to them. Now she sensed that the miracle she had been praying for these many years had, for all practical purposes, already transpired. Thrilled by a generous salary increase, Mary vowed she would be making as much as $500 a week before her twentieth birthday. To that Charlotte said "Amen." Properly handled, her daughter could earn thousands — who knew, even millions. And since Mary weighed in at only ninety pounds, Charlotte reasoned the best way to market her was by the ounce, like gold.

In 1910 Griffith took his company to California for three months, and thirteen-year-old Jack Pickford went along as seventeen-year-old Mary's chaperone. Living like church mice in the cheapest lodgings they could find, while Jack worked as an extra and Mary played leads, as usual, opposite Owen Moore, the two saved up the munificent sum of $1000. Triumphantly they took it back to Charlotte, who deposited it, as always, in the family purse.

Charlotte had stayed home, but she had not been idle. Persuading Carl Laemmle, the wily president of IMP Films, that her daughter was the most sought-after actress in films, she had wrung from him a contract guaranteeing Mary a whopping $75 a week. A second powerful motive lay behind her eagerness to move Mary out of Griffith's orbit: Owen Moore. She suspected that propinquity was working its expected magic, and that Mary was beginning to reciprocate the affection that the actor had shown toward her from the very first. The contract with IMP would break them up, both on screen and off, and not a minute too soon.

As always, Charlotte was right, but the capricious demands of the nascent star system conspired against her. When Laemmle's company sailed for location in Cuba, with it went Charlotte, Mary, Lottie, and Jack. Not until they were at sea did Charlotte learn that Laemmle had cast Mary's long-time screen lover opposite his newest star, for box-office reasons. The black Irishman was back inside the fold, and Charlotte increased her vigilance.

In Havana, Jack and Lottie obediently stepped into their customary roles as extras while their highly paid sister held the limelight. Still, their earnings were not insignificant to Charlotte. The Pickford purse was growing fat and the future looked bright when, like a sword through her mother's heart, Mary broke the awful news: she and Owen Moore had been secretly married before leaving New York. (Indeed, it was Moore's insistence on enjoying his connubial rights that compelled Mary to confess her treachery.)

Charlotte took it like a death sentence. For days she was, in Mary's own words, "apoplectic, but helpless." Hysterical with grief and rage, she cried for three whole days and nights, while on the painful voyage home neither Lottie nor Jack would so much as speak to their perfidious sister.

But if Owen Moore believed that he, like one of the heroes in Griffith's melodramatic screen plays, had cleanly purloined the fairest jewel ever to grace a mother's crown, he found himself tragically mistaken. Charlotte's swift and unexpected blessing proved more lethal than her wrath. On reaching home, she smilingly declared herself reconciled to the match and moved in permanently with the newlyweds. From that day forward, she presided over Mary's life and career with a will of iron. As Mary phrased it, "Until the day she died, Mother's word was law."

Helpless to escape his mother-in-law's abrasive presence, Moore sought comfort in bottled spirits and high-spirited friends, an escape that backfired by further estranging his wife and driving her into the arms of an increasingly sympathetic and understanding Charlotte. It was some time before he realized he was fighting a losing battle, both with his marriage and the bottle. Mother and daughter had everything in common — Mary's career — a bond, indeed, that only death could break.

In 1913 the tireless Charlotte announced another new contract, this one with film producer Adolph Zukor, who agreed to pay $500 a week for the services of Mary Pickford. Charlotte had helped Mary keep her vow: it was exactly one week before her twentieth birthday. (Although it seemed an astronomical sum to the family then, two years later Charlotte forced Zukor to raise the weekly take to $4000.) By that time Charlotte might have been forgiven for seeking an opportunity to brag to Jenny Janis on her own not insignificant show business achievements in the years since they had last met.

Not surprisingly, Jenny and Elsie had done extremely well. Elsie was one of the highest paid musical comedy stars and vaudeville headliners in the world. She was as popular in London and Paris as in her native land, and the two dashed back and forth across the Atlantic as though an ocean voyage were an inexpensive overnight jump. In Paris, Jenny made a point of taking her daughter to every risqué nightspot there was. No man could ever say to Elsie: "If you can get away from your mother, I'll take you to places you have never been!" Between her eighteenth and twenty-first birthdays Elsie admitted that "several well-meaning friends tried to break the combination," but, as Elsie put it, "Some optimist tried to chisel his way into the Bank of England once!" Still, Elsie had dozens of handsome, wealthy, even titled escorts, which Jenny could afford to note with pride as she tagged along.

Tragedy had also cast its shadow with the death of brother Percy. En route to England alone, to play his first lead on the stage, he had inexplicably shot himself and fallen overboard. If what the old actor had said about Lotta's brother Ashworth — "All he left behind was an empty bottle" — did not entirely apply to Percy (who also nipped), the parallel was striking. Elsie remembered the time as one of almost unbearable anguish for her mother, who suffered paralyzing remorse over her lifelong neglect of this unwanted child. Instinctively, Elsie realized that the only cure was: "the show must go on." The following Monday she opened in vaudeville at a salary of $2500 more per week than she had ever earned before. She and Jenny rejoiced, grieving only that poor, dear Percy could not share their good fortune.

In 1913 Elsie was offered a movie contract by the Hobart Bosworth Studio in Hollywood. Jenny, with her usual genius for going first class, wangled $30,000 per picture, plus the use of a private parlor car to and from the Coast for themselves, their servants, dogs, caged birds, relatives, and friends. When Elsie learned that Owen Moore might be her leading man, she wired her erstwhile friend, his wife, "Will you please lend me your husband for one picture?" to which Mrs. Moore responded magnanimously, "With pleasure!" Elsie did not fully understand Mary's generosity until later, when she played a key role in the final unraveling of the Moores' unhappy union.

After four films, Elsie was recalled from Hollywood to London to fulfill her contract with *The Passing Show of 1915*. She had long been deeply in love with Basil Hallem, her British leading man, a romance that grew more serious with the increasing threat of war. Jenny and Elsie crossed on the *Lusitania*, sailing on January 31, 1915. Submarine warfare was not yet a reality to Americans, and when the engines stopped at midnight in a storm-lashed sea, Jenny tied her chair to the cabin door and herself into the chair, sewing fiercely to keep calm. For two hours the ship's engines were soundless; then, at dawn, they began to throb again. Rushing up on deck, Jenny and Elsie were astonished to see the American flag flying from the stern of Great Britain's proudest liner. For this act the *Lusitania*'s captain, "Paddy" Dow, was severely reprimanded despite the fact that his strategy for dodging prowling German submarines had undoubtedly saved the lives of everyone aboard. His successor did not escape so lightly.

On May 15, 1915, when Elsie awoke to the devastating news of the sinking of the *Lusitania* in the Irish Channel, it spelled the end of her innocence and youth. The list of casualties read like a social roster of every party she had attended over the past five years, and many of the dead were long-time friends. She and Basil "walked out" on the show, he to enlist in the British Army, she to return to a homeland steeling itself for its first European war. The lovers were inseparable and vowed to marry before tragedy tore them apart, but Mother knew best, and Jenny's firm counsel to wait until the war was won prevailed. Hand in hand, Elsie and Basil stood onstage at the final encore, and in a rain of tears, Basil recited in ringing tones the poem a stricken Elsie had written for this hour:

> *Where are you God,*
> *In whom I have believed?*

Are you in heaven?
Have I been deceived?
With poison gas and crucifixion
Battles have been won,
And yet upon this earth of yours
There still exists The Hun.
Where are you God?

Tears and cheers mingled as the audience of Americans and Britons rose from their seats, proclaiming their undying comradeship in arms and their blind faith in an already outmoded chivalry of war.

Jenny and Elsie shared, with many Americans of their era, the commoner's worship of English royalty and those special blessings that flowed from it — castles, pageantry, titles, and handsome country manors with spacious grounds. Only the last could be duplicated in democratic America if one had sufficient wealth — and Elsie had. After living abroad for several seasons in cottages on the Thames and in the shadow of Windsor Castle, Elsie and Jenny had a raging case of British fever, augmented by observing that doughty race at war. The only cure proved to be a rambling old house in Tarrytown-on-the-Hudson in the heart of Sleepy Hollow country. Built in 1683 by Frederick Philipse, who had married a Dutch aristocrat's daughter, the venerable estate bore the good manor approval of no less than the Colonial Dames. What Jenny referred to as Manor House may not have been exactly a castle, but it was certainly the next best thing.

At first they merely rented, but when the sad news came that dear Basil had been killed in an observation balloon over France, Jenny bought the place, perhaps as much to stifle her own feelings of guilt for having kept the lovers apart as to assuage Elsie's grief. Jenny felt her decision had been best for everyone, of course, but that was cold comfort in the presence of her daughter's broken heart. In the long view, however, Philipse's manor house and what it stood for transcended the times. Like Attol Tryst, it lent the patina of age, lineage, and respectability to what was at best a well-barnacled but anchorless existence. Show business offered precious little elegance and even less stability, however rich stardom might have made one.

Since Elsie and Jenny were virtually never alone, it was hard to mourn for long. Irving Berlin lay on the white polar bear rug and wrote a song especially for his hostess: "Don't Wait Too Long," he warned in his bittersweet title, while Jenny chattered busily with guests about the aviary she planned to install the full length of the veranda. Elsie was bigger than ever in vaudeville, and Manor House became a haven for celebrities. Here Elsie's close friends Irene and Vernon Castle gazed sorrowfully into each other's eyes while they waltzed, knowing he must soon follow Basil's lead. Here, too, on a golden Sunday afternoon late in 1915, Mary Pickford and husband Owen Moore were introduced by their vivacious hostess to another attractive couple, Beth and Douglas Fairbanks. Young Doug was rising fast in the theater, and already films were beckoning. Beth, heiress to a southern fortune, had been an actress briefly but was now content to decorate her handsome husband's arm.

After lunch and an hour or so of lighthearted songs, Elsie proposed a hike along the Hudson. As they tramped the full eleven acres of Philipse's estate, the ranks grew thin until only Elsie, Mary, and Doug were left. Coming to a stream with a log for a bridge, Fairbanks swept the diminutive Mrs. Moore into his muscular arms and carried her across. By the time he set her down tenderly on the opposite shore, he had fallen in love.

Charlotte was gleeful, as was Fairbanks's mother. Neither woman liked her child's present spouse, so they conspired to stage little teas at the Algonquin Hotel and other hideaways where the two famous young people could carry on their courtship behind at least a scrim of privacy. Predictably, Mary succumbed to the two mothers' machinations and the Fairbanks charm. He would prove to be the great love of her life.

The entry of the United States into the war in 1917 provided the lovers with yet another legitimate façade behind which they might pursue their increasingly reckless affair: Liberty Bond tours. With her burning patriotism and the timely success of her latest film, *The Little American*, which dramatized the sinking of the

Lusitania, Mary was a potent propagandist. "I'm only five feet tall," she told the thousands who thronged the rallies, "but every inch of me is fighting American!" She traveled with a galaxy of world-famous movie stars, prominent among them Douglas Fairbanks.

Charlotte went along on these passionate and patriotic junkets, buying thousands of dollars' worth of Liberty Bonds on her own and investing thousands more in Canadian War Loans. (Later they would all come in handy, when Owen Moore refused to step aside for Fairbanks and named an undisclosed sum as the price of his pride. Mary, fearful of alienating her fans if word leaked out that she was buying off one husband for another, turned to her mother for help. Charlotte withdrew a great bundle of her own bonds and, with genuine relish, personally handed over the specified sum to her archrival. Moore's price can only be gauged by what it reportedly cost Fairbanks to let Beth divorce him — between $400,000 and $1,000,000.)

By now, too, Charlotte had fully come into her own. In sharp contrast to the dynastic, structured theater world, the Hollywood of 1918 was nearly as wide open and hardscrabble as any gold camp of Mary Ann's time. If the earliest Yankee settlers had set up social elites, they were never honored by the motion picture people who flocked there after 1912. Success was high society, money substituted for good family, and stardom, not charity, covered a multitude of sins. While other newcomers to Beverly Hills might have mistaken it for a high-class neighborhood, Charlotte knew better and felt at home; she recognized it for what it really was — the fish market all over again. Here she was free to deal with vendors of flesh and film who until yesterday had been ironmongers, glove merchants, druggists, cloth spongers and buttonhole makers. They were all born hagglers, and one thing Charlotte knew how to do was haggle. In her negotiations with Mary's long-suffering producer, Adolph Zukor, a Hungarian immigrant who had formerly dealt in furs, she was ruthless. When Mary and Charlotte learned that an upstart comedian at Mutual was making $650,000 a year, they renegotiated their contract with Zukor, demanding more money because the comic was making only two-reelers while Mary's films were full-length features.

"Mary, sweetheart," Zukor groaned, "I don't have to diet. Every time I talk over a new contract with you and your mother, I lose ten pounds." Samuel Goldwyn later complained that "it took longer to make Mary's contracts than it did to make her pictures." But Charlotte railed until she got her terms. In 1917 she squeezed $10,000 a week out of the harassed Zukor, along with a $300,000 bonus, just to put Mary ahead of her sole competitor, the comedian who was still making two-reelers. For a lagniappe and to keep her mother pacified, Zukor tacked on free parlor car transportation to and from the West Coast for Charlotte plus another $150,000 for such contractual vagaries as "Ma" Pickford's "standing by" and "good will." Charlotte was rapidly becoming one of the highest paid unphotographed movie stars in the industry.

When peace was proclaimed on November 11, 1918, Charlotte won a victory almost as total as that of the Allies. Having bled the poor man white, she abandoned Zukor for First National, a company that she made fork over $675,000 a year, against 50 per cent of the gross, to get Mary's services, plus another $50,000 to herself for her mysterious but indispensable "good offices."

Paradoxically, at this time, when Mary was living a highly sophisticated and unconventional private life — a professed Catholic and a married woman, carrying on a doubly adulterous affair with another woman's husband — her public image became drenched in innocence and began a singular retrogression into childhood. With Griffith, Laemmle, and Zukor she had played fairly typical ingénues, young women with special problems but who, once they were overcome, were unquestionably headed for marriage and maturity. Now, perhaps as a subconscious desire to give the lie to her very adult off-screen actions or in response to the widespread postwar preoccupation with childhood and youth, she entered a new "Little Mary" decade. Between her twenty-fourth and thirty-fourth birthdays, she starred in a baker's dozen of famous films in which she played children twelve years of age or under.

Another young Hollywood star who was soon preoccupied with the renewed popularity of children was Mary's nemesis, the comic whose overnight success she had used as a lever in forging her own contract demands. While she had been in movies a total of seven years, not to mention her long stage career, he had been making films for only three. The two were already rivals; they would soon become business partners, inseparable friends, and, in the end, once again bitter enemies. His name was Charlie Chaplin.

4
Kid Fever

Today is the day
They give babies away,
With a half a pound of tea.
Just lift up the lid
And out pops a kid,
With a half a pound of tea.
— Popular song, c. 1918

IF NINETEENTH-CENTURY AMERICANS projected their preoccupation with infant mortality onto the dramatic stage, twentieth-century parents focused their anxieties on the motion picture screen, and wartime posters set the pattern for the films that followed. Although the nation's propaganda mills were in their infancy between 1915 and 1918, Liberty Bond and Enlistment posters bloomed on every wall. Their impact went far beyond their initial purpose, which was to make a tight patriotic fist of a singularly disparate and unconsolidated population. The burden of their message, both conscious and subliminal, was nothing less than "motherhood is sacred and children the salvation of the world!"

MUST CHILDREN DIE AND MOTHERS PLEAD IN VAIN? asked one poster depicting Belgian war victims. The sinister nature of submarine warfare was symbolized by a single drowning woman, her babe at her breast, both going down to a watery grave behind the inescapable summons ENLIST! Not since Herod's soldiers bathed the stones of Bethlehem in the blood of the Holy Innocents had history served up a more heinous child slayer than the Hun of propagandists' brush and pen.

American filmmakers were quick to transfer the tragedy of

war from static poster to animated drama, at the same time being careful to capitalize on this new facet of the durable cult of childhood. D. W. Griffith, a man who all his life had brooded over peace, inexplicably succumbed to a combination of Kaiser and kid fever by throwing himself wholeheartedly into the creation of an unabashed propaganda film entitled *Hearts of the World*. His obligatory genuflection to childhood was writing in Little Benny Alexander, a dolorous four-year-old who had debuted a year earlier as Cupid in *Every Pearl a Tear*. Little Benny's gift for turning out torrents of tears won him the professional's ultimate compliment: he made Charlie Chaplin cry! (The very incarnation of the suffering wartime child, he wept even more copiously for director Cecil B. De Mille in *The Little American*, the war film that was Mary Pickford's spunky rejoinder to the Kaiser's affrontery.)

Nothing would do but Griffith must shoot his epic against authentic European backgrounds. In 1917, at the peak of his power and at the height of American involvement in the war, he and his ever-loyal company braved the now doubly perilous Atlantic. The unsinkable Gish family made the crossing under heavy convoy aboard the same ship that carried General John J. Pershing to his overseas command.

In London, Griffith's patriots defied German air raids and visited hospitals that were filling up with wounded men, pouring in by the trainload from France every day. When the Gish girls, who were starring in the film, begged their mother not to join them in the company's hazardous Channel crossing to French locations dangerously close to the front lines, Mrs. Gish delivered what deserved to be a second-act curtain line. "There are only three of our family left," she declared in ringing tones. "If one of us is going to die, *all* of us are going to die together!" And off they went with Mr. Griffith to face the needless perils of wartime France.*

---

* In Los Angeles in 1973 I saw the venerable Lillian Gish hold an audience of American booksellers spellbound as she told how two property men drowned in an icy river on one of Mr. Griffith's authentic locations for *Way Down East*. "But," she declared by way of giving meaning to the tragedy, "our dedication to Mr. Griffith and to making movies was so great, their deaths only made the picture *that much more important!*"

Partly because of the impact of such propaganda films, partly because such catastrophic loss of life cried out for propagation of the race, Americans entered the postwar world with two conflicting attitudes toward children. On the one hand, a high birth rate secured the future; on the other, modern economics militated against big families. The late nineteenth century had brought unprecedented waves of immigrants to America. Industrialization and the phenomenal growth of urban centers had eroded the land-based family. Increasingly, farm fathers and sons were being forced into factory jobs while mothers and daughters now purchased from the general store those necessities that they had made by hand at home not long before. Traditionally, on frontier and farm, sons or daughters were valued as unpaid hired hands and a large family welcomed as a gift of God. But children in the city meant an added financial burden, even a luxury, which the working class and especially the jobless immigrant poor could ill afford.

In this transitional period, however, there were still two broad areas of American life where the attitude toward children remained stable and where child-rearing flourished as a prosperous cottage industry: the solvent homestead, ranch, or farm and the family-owned business. Veteran stock actors and touring vaudevillians qualified as one of the latter.

These rootless families were tightly knit, self-contained units, in which every member — usually even the dog — worked in the act. "My mother thanks you, my father thanks you, and I thank you" was a time-worn curtain speech long before George M. Cohan made it his own. Family members tended to be short-tempered and combative, taking out on each other the anxieties and frustrations of their insecure existence, yet closing ranks with savage loyalty against any challenge from outsiders.

Unable to accumulate those comforts and possessions that make a settled home emotionally supportive, show people reinforced their identity by putting all their money on their backs. The men, compensating for the lack of recognition and respect that might have been theirs in a stable community, indulged in flashery — checked vests, spats, gold-tipped canes, real diamond stickpins (how they glittered in a white spot!), and showy finger rings. They saw to it that the "little woman" had her share of diamonds, too, and not just for the pleasing dazzle; gems provided these high-risk professionals with their only form of insurance on the road, and a conveniently portable one as well.

The women were given to dressing any way they pleased, which was eclectic, since no one dictated style to them. They usually dyed their hair and were artists with a hot iron, a toothpick, and a tin of melted black wax. Most of them wore full make-up, including beaded eyelashes, offstage as well as on, and the saucy black droplets gave these worldly women the curiously innocent expression of wide-eyed, bisque-headed dolls. With their diamond-hard egos and cast-iron constitutions, these quarrelsome Pullman gypsies seemed a merry, carefree lot: the families close and effusive, as emotionally interdependent as the flesh-and-blood components of a human pyramid, that familiar vaudeville phenomenon so often used to open or close a bill. Sometimes they grew giddy at the thought of enjoying such perpetual freedom. At other times their glance conveyed a look of loss and loneliness, the heart-piercing gaze of some lovely zoo creature, dying of confinement while providing a festive outing for the crowd.

Baby Lillian Dolliver grew up in one such typical show business family. Born in San Francisco in 1892, she made her stage debut at six, adding her dramatic bit to the family effort as naturally as a farm child churned butter or gathered eggs — simple, useful chores scaled down to the worker's age and size. Touring with the California Stock Company, the Dollivers covered an arduous circuit that took them annually from mist-veiled Seattle to sunny San Diego, from the arid wastes of Nevada to the palm-shadowed sands of Waikiki. Although it was far from being the big time, the Dollivers, born to the buskin, took it all in stride. They loved their profession and were careful to pass on to Baby Lillian its skills, traditions, and taboos.

Growing up on the road, it was expected that when it came time to think of marriage, a girl would build her nest with a similar bird of passage. Predictably, at twenty-one, plump, pretty Lillian Dolliver turned her chocolate-brown eyes toward a dapper young hoofer who had just joined the troupe and lost her heart.

Although born and reared in Syracuse, New York, Jack Coogan had showed the good sense, while still in his teens, to renounce the family drugstore business and strike out for the stage. His dream of becoming a musical comedy star eluded him, probably because he lacked the boyish good looks that were then so much in vogue. A practical youth, he decided to exploit what he had — a long nose, narrow face, brush mustache, and a lean, loose-jointed body — becoming what was known as an eccentric dancer, a blend of feather-light soft-shoe artistry, exaggerated bodily movements, and droll delivery of standard comic patter. Despite his orthodox origins, Jack was brash, ambitious, and egocentric enough to qualify as a genuine born-in-a-trunk vaudevillian. He was also an Irish Catholic, as was his bride.

Lillian left the Dolliver family act, and in classic stage family style, the newlyweds worked up a new one of their own, in which she sang and served as a foil for her mate. Their first child, born in Los Angeles in 1914, was named after his father, and briefly his parents succumbed to the abiding temptation of their kind, placing the infant with settled relatives to spare him the rigors of the road. But instinct and custom soon prevailed, and in 1917, when little Jack was three, his parents picked up their "excess baggage" and commenced their son's apprenticeship in the family trade.

The vaudeville child's world was entered by the stage door only. Home, such as it was, consisted of a small and musty dressing room. In a thousand and one ways, he was taught that the only place authentically alive and counting for something was that brightly lighted slice of stage he could view from the wings. Steeped in an ambience where performance was the supreme purpose of existence, the boy picked up everybody's act, mimicking those he liked, but making his own the material and nuances of his special favorites. This pleased everyone from the stage door man to his parents, for it meant the pup was learning to swim and could survive in their precarious floating social world.

Like every other vaudevillian, the boy's father carried in his head a map of the nation on which each major city was flagged

as either hot or cold. In backstage parlance, Kansas City and Los
Angeles, for example, were infamous for being cold, while New
York and San Francisco got high marks for being warmly responsive show towns. Therefore, in 1919, when Jack and Lillian joined
the act of Annette Kellerman, a former aquatic record-setter
turned headliner, they naturally looked forward to opening night
in San Francisco. And they were not disappointed.

A packed house gave Jack's eccentric specialty an ovation, and,
taking bow after bow, he glowingly carried the cherished tribal
fire of adulation with him into the cold, dark wings where his
little son watched adoringly. In a gesture as instinctive as it was
impulsive, the father picked up the boy and carried him onstage,
setting him down before the footlights, much as a trainer might
set a wobbly young coonhound on his very first trail.

Momentarily stunned by the spot, the five-year-old boy turned
his great brown eyes toward the front, trying to find the audience
in the vast, black void beyond the familiar foots. Then, almost
automatically, he threw himself into one of his spirited imitations,
which won a storm of applause. Taking his father's silent cue,
he then launched into the recitation of David Warfield's classic
speech from *The Music Master*. It stopped the show.

While some stage veterans deplored the old trick of "bringing
on the kid," equating it with bearing the American flag across
the stage as the cheapest way to milk an audience for more applause, Annette Kellerman only knew what she saw and heard:
the people liked it. As a consequence, she offered the proud parents an extra $25 a week to keep their little boy in the act.

The torch was being passed, the dynasty assured; still, it was
depressing to know that come the next week, they must exchange
San Francisco's glowing audience for the small-town hicks of Los
Angeles, who "sat on their hands" in the worst tradition of "a
Kansas City supper show." But then, moving on was life for Jack
and Lillian Coogan, and at least after L.A. they could look forward
to a week in good old San Diego. The pattern was as familiar
and dependable as the sunrise and the tides. But on opening
night in Los Angeles something would go wrong, very wrong,
with the seemingly predictable future of this tight little family,

obviously destined to sing and dance their way through life together. A stranger in that audience would steal the bright gypsy
ribbon of their promising tomorrows, put it in his pocket, and,
in exchange, leave them only money and a tenuous foothold in
an alien world.

At twenty-nine, Charlie Chaplin had virtually everything that
would have sent most of his male contemporaries into deliriums
of joy — good looks, success, fame, fortune, health, friends, his
own studio, a pretty (and patient) mistress, and a beautiful, blond,
movie star wife. And yet, on this particular evening in 1919, he
considered himself the most miserable of men. Nothing was
going right. Nineteen-year-old Mildred Harris, whom he had married in such prudent haste, had turned out not to be pregnant
after all. She had also turned out to be an insipid bore. Their
first child, conceived to salvage a shaky marriage, had died only
hours after its birth. Now his wife was threatening to turn her
divorce into a professional windfall for herself and a financial
disaster for him. Still worse, his career was at a dangerous
crossroads, for the reliable font of comedy ideas, the very hallmark of his genius, had chosen this critical time to dry up
completely.

Having established his reputation with Mack Sennett in short
comedies, Chaplin felt the time had come to move into longer
and more ambitious vehicles. Against almost everyone's advice
he had produced *Shoulder Arms,* a comedy about the war, which,
when it was made in 1917, had seemed a tasteless contradiction
in terms. Nevertheless, his instinct had been right, and the movie
(which ran three reels instead of the usual one or two) had been
an artistic and financial success. A sensitive and exacting artist,
Chaplin had seen other movie comics ruined by tiresome and
repetitious material and style simply because they were unable
or unwilling to grow and change. He was determined not to let
this fate shackle his career, even if it meant taking risks with
his familiar image and with his fans. And so, day after day
throughout the late autumn of 1918, with his stock company on

full salary, the famous comedian joined them on the set to discuss plans for his new production breakthrough. And day after day, theme, plot, and story continued to elude him.

In desperation he returned from one such unproductive day at the studio and decided it was time to prescribe for himself the tonic he was always dispensing to others — a good laugh. The Orpheum Theater in downtown Los Angeles offered first-rate vaudeville, and being himself a child of the theater, he felt an evening spent in that familiar environment might prove restorative if not a total cure.

Chaplin watched the show with mild amusement until the eccentric dancer with the wry face and rubber legs finished his act and, as an encore, brought on his four-year-old son. The little blond boy executed a shimmy, which was the daring dance of the era, and, strangely enough, the usually restrained Los Angeles audience was not offended by it. Instead they asked for more. The child obliged with a lively imitation, for which he was rewarded by a round of applause.

Chaplin felt himself responding to something almost nostalgic about the child. Little Jackie may have quickened into life the long-dormant child that Chaplin himself had been. He could see five-year-old Charlie backstage in London, with his handsome father, a vaudeville baritone, and his mother, a modestly gifted music hall soubrette. Clearly he could recall standing in the wings one unforgettable night, witnessing, not the triumph, but the downfall of his mother's career. Her voice, never strong and long abused, had given way in the middle of a song, and the rowdy patrons had begun hooting and peppering her with vegetables. In a last-ditch effort to save her pride and her livelihood, she had fled to the wings and shoved five-year-old Charlie onstage in her place. He had done a pint-sized version of a grownup performance — much as the vaudevillian's little son was doing now — and was rewarded with a shower of coins. He had wondered why his poor mother cried when he gave them all to her.

Then the backstage childhood had vanished. His father, while still a young man, died of drink. His mother, her mind crumbling under the repeated blows of failure, poverty, and despair, went insane. Charlie and his older half-brother Sydney were incarcerated behind the high walls of fearful Lambeth Work House in London, where they spent two terrifying years. Not even Dickens himself could have conceived a blacker childhood. And yet, by dint of optimism, chance, and talent, Charlie had found salvation in the same profession that had destroyed both parents. In his late teens he became an entertainer with the Karno Company, which toured England and eventually America. Mack Sennett caught his imitation of a drunk during Karno's New York run and brought him to Hollywood. Now, five years later, he was one of the highest paid performers in the motion picture industry, his nearest rival being Charlotte Pickford's little girl, Mary.

Although the Coogan child had touched a highly responsive chord, Chaplin later admitted in his autobiography that he let an entire week go by without thinking of him again. Then, one morning on the set surrounded by his company, he inexplicably remembered him and began telling them how cute the boy had been. Someone mentioned having seen in the paper that Jackie Coogan had been signed by the Mack Sennett comic Roscoe Arbuckle. Suddenly Chaplin thought of the Coogan child as a marvelously attractive screen personality who had been snatched from under his nose by his chief competitor. While his company looked on, completely mystified, Chaplin paced up and down the set, describing all the situations in which his own famous screen character of the Little Tramp might have worked wonders with a winsome kid who went about breaking windows so the Tramp could mend them for a livelihood. Why had he allowed Arbuckle to steal away the boy and a dozen appealing plots in which he could have shone! One of the group, in an effort to calm the overwrought comedian, suggested finding a cute little Negro boy for the part he had in mind, but Chaplin shook his head. He was about to leave the studio for the day when his publicity man burst onto the set. "It's not Jackie Coogan that Arbuckle's signed up," he cried, "it's the father, Jack!"

Chaplin dispatched the man to find the elder Coogan and bring him to the studio at once, charging him not to say a word about the reason. Two hours later Coogan appeared, bewildered and surprised.

"He'll be a sensation," Chaplin enthused, grabbing the vaudevillian by his arm, "the greatest thing that ever happened." Coogan continued to stare at the comedian uncomprehendingly. "This story will give your son the opportunity of his life!"

"My son?" Coogan echoed, beginning to get the drift.

"Yes, your son — if you'll just let me have him for this one picture."

"Why of course you can have the little punk," Coogan replied, as if to say, "Is *that* all you wanted?" The important thing to Coogan was getting a few days' work with his old friend Roscoe Arbuckle and picking up small change in films while they played L.A.

He found Chaplin in dead earnest. The comedian really wanted the boy, and later that evening, when the Coogan family met with him at the Alexandria Hotel to discuss details, the seemingly casual offer began to take on more solid dimensions. Still, for a millionaire, Chaplin's offer could hardly be considered grandiose — $75 a week for one picture only to practically costar with the most famous comedian in the world. Old Hollywood hands could have told Coogan that shooting on a Chaplin film might easily run into months of steady work, because he usually went through three times as many feet of film as he finally used. However, Jack Coogan was already making $100 a week on his own in Kellerman's act, and Jackie $25. But Jack Coogan's ego was not easily overshadowed, and he knew how to drive a bargain when his own career could be advanced. He managed to obtain Chaplin's assurance that if he agreed to let him have Jackie, he would be written into the script wherever possible, making certain he did not take a back seat to his son.

Years later Jackie claimed that his father wound up playing six parts in *The Kid,* moved up to being Chaplin's assistant, and, by the time the film was finished a year and three days later, that the elder Coogan was earning $150 a week to his son's $75.*

---

* "Jay Rubin Interviews Jackie Coogan," *Classic Film Collector,* October 1976.

But that night in the Alexandria Hotel, little Jackie fell asleep in a big lobby chair while the blueprint of his own and his family's life was being redrawn. He awoke to find himself in another world, where he, the hoofer's son, had been transformed into a veritable angel child, complete with luminous spirituality and truly awesome redemptive powers.

5
The Children's Hour

It's a great life for a kid. It's wonderful to be someone before you're old.
— Jackie Coogan,
in the Los Angeles
Herald Examiner, 1962

CHAPLIN FOUND LITTLE JACKIE an intelligent youngster, but also surprisingly timid and shy. The sudden wrench from his self-contained backstage nest to the complex studio world proved — even to such a precocious child — a severe cultural shock, although neither the term nor the trauma had yet been recognized by parents or psychologists. Having graduated from the wings' crescent view of the stage to actual over-the-footlights contact with an audience, Jackie had already become dependent on that distinct orientation and sense of place that a curtain at one's back and an exit on either side gives the stage performer. Securely positioned, he was free to direct his full attention "out front," toward that fixed but highly malleable material, the audience. Much as a sculptor works his clay, the vaudevillian shaped and molded audience response to match the model already set up within his mind. A child of Jackie's age would have acquired these skills and concepts wholly unconsciously, but that would have made them no less real and supportive, nor their sudden withdrawal less traumatic.

By contrast, a studio set was theater in the round, the audience consisting of director, cameraman, crew, other actors, and occasional visitors, with a tangle of black cables and fuse boxes underfoot and a half-seen shadowy corps of electricians working the lights on the catwalks overhead. There was no reassuring backdrop to shoulder up to, no responsive but pleasantly faceless "out front." Instead, strange, demanding personalities and faces pressed in upon him from every side. In the vortex of this distracting pool of activity, Jackie was expected to distill the very essence of himself and project it like a powerful beam of light into the camera's bleak, unblinking eye, all the while making sure not to commit what was regarded in movie circles as a mortal sin — and a common perversity of new child actors: staring long and directly into the lens.

After a few fruitless attempts to work Jackie with his stock company, Chaplin realized that the boy would have to acquire some form of camera sense before they could even attempt the exacting scenes he had in mind for *The Kid,* as the ambitious tragicomedy was to be titled. Ready to shoot was a lightweight script entitled *A Day's Pleasure.* A family outing and its pitfalls provided the theme; a small, undemanding child's part would serve to break in the skittish Jackie.

Actress Babe London starred with Chaplin in this two-reeler and remembers Jackie as "being very confused by it all." Chaplin, however, impressed her as the soul of patience in his direction of the child's earliest scenes. "Chaplin seemed to adore Jackie. I think he really loved him." Whether Charlie was in love with the idealized child-self he was projecting onto the little boy or was unwittingly using him as a vicarious means of releasing his own long-repressed childhood anguish is a matter of speculation. But it is well known that during the filming of *The Kid,* Chaplin seemed consumed by a feverish preoccupation with childhood innocence, vulnerability, and love. It was also noted by many besides Miss London that the comedian seemed enraptured with the boy.

Between takes his father prompted Jackie to dance his popular "shimmy" and do other bits from his old act for the entertainment of the company. Perhaps the elder Coogan was unconsciously trying to prove that, while he might still be inept at movie work, the kid was a real showstopper when you got him on his own turf. Aside from carrying his dad through the ordeal of an embarrassing apprenticeship, these interludes gave Jackie a much-needed touchstone with that other world in which it had been so easy for him to shine, thus reinforcing his own badly shaken ego between challenging bouts with chalk marks, Chaplin, and the camera.

By the time Chaplin felt that Jackie was ready to start work on *The Kid,* the child had developed a working rapport with him and the company and had begun to take the unsettling mechanics of the work in stride. Still, he was fortunate to be working for the industry's archperfectionist: if a scene was not exactly so, Chaplin thought nothing of shooting it twenty or seventy times, until it satisfied him. This gave Jackie ample opportunity to polish his own skills, and it protected the sensitive child from those cruel outbursts of scornful disapproval that low-budget directors were capable of heaping upon children who did not master their bit of business in the very first take.

"Mood music" was provided by a portable organ, a violin, and a base viol, to help Chaplin's players develop and deepen the emotions they were striving to portray. Visitors to a Chaplin set were carefully screened; most often they were world-famous artists, writers, musicians, or minor British nobility, for whom Charlie shared the Janis women's weakness. Compared to most movie factories, Chaplin's studio exuded the hush of a Romanesque cathedral, while the scene being celebrated moved with all the stateliness and grace of a solemn high mass. Jackie was discovering that once the movement, placement, and other bodily distractions were memorized, he was free to devote his entire attention to the emotions that informed a scene and gave it purpose and life.

But as Chaplin retold the story years later, just when Jackie's confidence was building, they came to the scene in which the workhouse officials drag the child away. This episode, lifted out of Chaplin's own dreadful London past, was to be the high spot of the film, the final proof that Charlie's genius had indeed carried off the unprecedented blend of comedy and tragedy in equal parts, which skeptics were already claiming could not be done. To build the mood, Charlie took Jackie aside and graphically described the horrors of life in a London workhouse. He painted all the pain and loneliness that lay ahead for the Kid once he was torn from even those minimal comforts supplied by the Tramp.

Almost as if he meant to spite the man to whom this scene represented so much, Jackie had come to work that day in exceptionally high spirits. Nothing Chaplin described could douse his cheerfulness. After appealing to every possible childish fear and phobia, Chaplin despaired. Declaring even his inexhaustible patience at an end, the comedian threw up his hands, and instantly tension began to build on the set. If Jackie was too good-humored to sense it, his father was not.

Coming forward, Jack Coogan assured Charlie, "I'll make him cry."

"Don't frighten or hurt the boy," Chaplin cautioned guiltily.

"Oh, no, no," Coogan replied. Not wanting to know what means brought on the indispensable tears, Chaplin disappeared into his dressing room. Moments later he heard the broken-hearted wail of a child. Rushing back onto the set, he was met by the elder Coogan, who informed him calmly, "He's all ready."

Without delay the cameras turned, the officials came to drag the boy away, and the Tramp rescued him. While the Kid continued to sob inconsolably, Chaplin picked him up, hugging and kissing him in an almost genuine effort to restore Jackie's own plundered happiness. The scene ended and a beaming cameraman signaled the perfect take.

Walking out of the set, a shaken Chaplin asked Jack Coogan, "How did you get the boy to cry?"

"Nothing to it," Coogan replied, barely restraining his satisfaction at his son's performance. "I just told him that if he didn't, we'd take him away from the studio and really send him to the workhouse."

Turning to Jackie, who was just beginning to settle down and whose cheeks were still streaked with tears, Chaplin ventured a tentative consolation. "They're not going to take you away," he smiled.

"I know it," Jackie replied tremulously, and then, turning his great melancholy eyes on his father, he added, as though explaining away a parental embarrassment, "Daddy was only fooling."

With the release of *The Kid*, the durable myth of the redemptive child was once more let loose upon the public. But this time, because the screen was larger than life and silent films were exported to and understood in every corner of the world, the phenomenon was no longer merely an American one. What Dickens and Harriet Beecher Stowe did for Little Cordelia Howard and Lotta Crabtree, Chaplin did again for Jackie Coogan, but on a global scale. Polish peasant and Russian serf, Chinese coolie and French diplomat, Sicilian immigrants and middle-class American parents, Catholic, Protestant, Moslem, and Jew, were all equally exposed to, and captivated by, childhood. And curiously enough, the most avid consumer of this suddenly fought-over product was the man who had packaged and marketed it, Charlie Chaplin himself.

When interviewers descended upon him with questions about little Jackie, he delivered incredibly cloying and sentimental asides.

> Ah, Jackie, wonderful Jackie! Jackie is inspiring and inspired. Just to be in his presence is to feel inspired. His personality is beautiful, lovely. It's spiritual. You feel close to his spirituality.

Chaplin went on record as being primarily concerned that Jackie's purity of mind, heart, and soul remain unsullied by adults and other evils of this world.

> The essential thing is to keep his little mind clear of all opinions, prejudices, creeds, religions and manufactured thought. It is such a fine, sensitive mind, it mustn't be twisted. I don't like seeing him attending Chamber of Commerce banquets, press luncheons and such, sitting at the head of the table receiving homage and applause.

Of course, even this rhetoric would pale beside the gilded praise which Jackie's presence brought gushing from writer Herbert Howe in the same lengthy article.*

---

* Herbert Howe, "What's Going to Happen to Jackie Coogan?" *Photoplay Magazine*, December 1923.

After meeting him several times with his serious little manner, his courtesies and profound remarks, you wonder, "Am I hypnotized? Is he genius or child?" We talked, he danced for me and recited with a reverence close to holy, the words of "My Madonna." I thought of the Young King who stood in rags at the steps of the altar . . . and lo! through the painted windows came the sunlight streaming upon him, and the sunbeams wove round him a tissued robe . . . he stood there in king's raiment, and the glory of God filled the place, and the trumpeters blew upon their trumpets and the singing boys sang, and the Bishop's face grew pale and his hands trembled. "A greater than I hath crowned thee" he cried and he knelt before him . . . I thought of Jackie as the Young King. And I went away wondering. For me Jackie is a masterpiece of life. Can the world change or time alter such a masterpiece?

The only cleared-eyed appraisal of Jackie's career, which seemed almost hard-boiled by comparison to Herbert Howe, Chaplin, Fairbanks, Harold Lloyd, and other Hollywood prophets, was made by Mary Pickford, who was qualified by experience to evaluate a child star's gifts. Quoted in the same article, she said:

I do not see why he cannot continue as an actor right through. It's quite possible. I did. I wasn't much older when I started my career than Jackie was in *The Kid.* And of course, we mustn't forget in our appraisal of Jackie the wonderful genius that has inspired him.

Jackie, however, was not Chaplin's only inspiration and chaste symbol of childhood innocence during the making of *The Kid.* One afternoon an assistant, Chuck Reisner, brought around to his bungalow a pretty, olive-eyed little girl named Lilita McMurray. She was half Mexican, her mother being descended from early Californios, and Reisner introduced her as his little son's neighbor and playmate. When the shy twelve-year-old shook hands with the world-famous star, on whose set she was working as a mere child extra, she blushed to a deep copper, and Chaplin's eyes widened with interest. He confessed himself completely enchanted — she looked for all the world like the girl in Sir Joshua

Reynolds's famous painting, *The Age of Innocence* (an early-nineteenth-century English favorite that, in print form, was standard equipment for every well-decorated child's bedroom in America at the time). Chaplin later repeated his observation to a studio artist; then, caught by his own flight of fancy, he ordered the man to paint Lilita's portrait in the identical dress and pose.

A week or so later, when the painting had been duly executed and delivered to his dressing room, Chaplin invited the girl in to see it. Lilita was shocked to find her portrait hanging on this great man's wall, and she was both flustered and flattered when he whispered to her softly that she had "such mysterious eyes." Would she like to be a movie star? Having grown up in Hollywood, stardom did not seem an entirely attractive prospect, but she knew that her mother would find it so. Afraid to answer no, she nodded her assent. Splendid! Very well then, he would make her dream come true! The make-up man would pile her long black curls atop her head and make her up to look at least eighteen years of age. Then he would order that she be given her very own screen test.*

A few days later, having viewed the test, Chaplin pronounced his new discovery, "exquisitely lovely" and immediately wrote a dream sequence into *The Kid* to feature the child's ineffable charms. In this scene the Tramp would fall asleep on his doorstep and dream he is in Heaven, where the streets are paved with gold. Lilita was cast as the Flirting Angel, a theological monstrosity that, if anyone but the great Chaplin had conceived it, would have been declared in poor taste if not downright sacrilegious. The burden of Lilita's peculiar role was to flirt with and "sweetly tease" the Little Tramp, supplying a love interest that however bizarre, had indeed been missing from *The Kid*.

Completely enthralled with Lilita's performance, Charlie decided to banish from her star dressing room his long-time leading lady and long-suffering mistress, Edna Purviance, and ensconce Lilita in her place. Overnight the child extra who had been playing games with little Jackie between scenes on the set found

---

* Although Chaplin remained silent in his autobiography regarding his relationship with Lilita, in her own book Lita Grey Chaplin goes into considerable detail about the early phase of their association, the version I have followed here.

herself under contract at the same $75-a-week salary that Chaplin was paying the Kid.

But Chaplin was to be rudely jolted out of his preoccupation with childhood. The time had come, at last, to cut the picture, and several very real problems loomed before him, not the least of which was that his wife, Mildred Harris, and her pack of lawyers were in full pursuit of his millions. While Mildred could legally claim only $25,000 under California Community Property Law, Charlie was more than willing to pay $100,000 just to be rid of her.

The Kid had been made to sell to First National, but when they offered a mere $405,000 Chaplin refused, countering that he had already spent half a million dollars on the picture. He suspected First National of trying to attach the film by working through Mildred Harris, who, without explanation, now spurned his generous settlement. He decided to cut the picture in another state, where he would be safe from both his adversaries. With two experienced cutters he fled to Salt Lake City, where the three men holed up in a hotel room and set to work.

An unbelievable 400,000 feet of film — 500 rolls — had to be cut and reduced to a manageable, not to mention salable, motion picture. Working day and night, they sorted out the more than two thousand single takes. Without any facilities and against infuriating handicaps they draped film over bathtubs, sinks, bedposts, and the backs of chairs. Entire sequences got lost under the bed. When they were finished, they sneak-previewed it in Salt Lake City, and the Mormon audience found everything about *The Kid* warmhearted, touching, and fun. It was given its formal première in New York City in January of 1920, and, except for a few critics who took offense at what they considered unnecessarily "vulgar" touches, it was hailed widely as a masterpiece.

In the end, Chaplin sold the rights to First National for a $1.5 million, with payment to him of 50 percent of the profits once their purchase price had been recouped. Moreover, after five years all rights to the film would revert to him. Mildred helped herself to her $100,000 and everyone seemed satisfied.

The Coogans emerged from this welter of wealth as poor as Job's turkey by comparison. But then, thanks to *The Kid*, Jackie

Coogan had become a household word. The elder Coogan, having watched Charlie's half-brother Sydney at work, had already decided to guide Jackie's career in similar fashion. Sydney was to Charlie what Charlotte was to Mary; probably no other layman in Hollywood, with the possible exception of Charlotte Pickford herself, knew more about money and how to make it multiply than Sydney Chaplin, the financial Merlin behind the throne that the Jester now occupied. None of this awed Jack Coogan, who was content that he had learned from Syd all he needed to know to cash in on the unprecedented publicity and exposure that *The Kid* was garnering for Jackie every day.

Chaplin now set about making one more movie, *The Idle Class,* before closing down the studio, putting his company on vacation, and making a nostalgic pilgrimage to London. He had left ten years before, an unknown entertainer. He would be returning in triumph as the undisputed King of Comedy. One to whom he would extend an even longer holiday was winsome Lilita McMurray. Her mother had earned Chaplin's displeasure by suggesting that his intentions had not been entirely honorable when he had invited little Lilita, alone and unchaperoned, to spend an evening at his home. Piqued, and temporarily sated with childhood and childish things, Chaplin deliberately cast mother and daughter as unattractive maidservants in *The Idle Class,* cancelled Lilita's contract, and put her out of his life forever — or so he thought.

Some twenty blocks east of Chaplin's timbered, Tudor-style studio at La Brea and Sunset stood a very different, far less presumptuous film factory. Century Studio occupied a full city block on the southwest corner of Gower Street and Sunset; it had been built in no style at all except what might be described as Early Hollywood. The buildings were mostly made-over barns dating from when it had been a humble farm. Remodeled frame California bungalows served as offices, relics of a slightly later period when L-KO (Lehrman's Knock-Out Comedies) had operated on this site.

The product here was called exactly that — the product. At Century no one spoke in hushed tones of genius at work or extolled the everlasting greatness of any film. Film was shot to sell, and when no longer salable it was unceremoniously burned to retrieve the silver nitrate it contained. After all, two dollars was two dollars, for Century stood in the heart of what the industry referred to as Poverty Row, a string of the poorest studios in town.

The studio launched its unpretentious operation in 1918, featuring comic animals in short comedies. The owners, president and vice president in charge of churning out the monthly blizzard of two-reel comedies and serials, were Julius and Abe Stern. The Sterns were brothers of Recha Stern, who had married Carl Laemmle, the legendary head of Universal Pictures. The Stern brothers had emigrated from their native Germany and gone to work for relatives at Stern's Department Store in Oshkosh, Wisconsin. Here Carl Laemmle got his start in America and later married Recha, the boss's niece. But in 1905, disenchanted with the clothing business and anxious to strike out on his own, Laemmle took his life savings of $5000 and moved to Chicago. His wife's brothers followed him.

There, with Julius and Abe Stern at his side, Laemmle took his stand before a storefront nickelodeon for one full day, his coat pocket filled with dried beans. For each patron who paid five cents and went inside to see the show, Laemmle moved a bean from the full pocket to an empty one. At the end of his ten-hour vigil he counted the number of beans that had changed pockets. That many nickels in so short a time indicated a lucrative business and a fantastic return on a minuscule investment. Still, they hesitated. Never had these veteran merchants seen a piece of merchandise quite like movies. The moviegoer paid good money for his purchase, but all he ever did was *look* at it. After that, he walked out of the store empty-handed, leaving his purchase still in the hands of the man who had sold it to him. The merchant was now free to sell it over again to another customer. It was like no other retail business; it was insane, but who *shouldn't* get into it? Julius and Abe flipped a coin to decide if they would join their brother-in-law in the nickelodeon industry or buy a five-and-ten-cent store. The dime store came up tails, and the family empire was launched.

After 1915, when Laemmle built Universal City in the heart of California's sunny San Fernando Valley, Julius Stern often took over as head of the studio during the chief's frequent absences to visit New York bankers and family back in Germany. Keeping Universal's budget on anything resembling an even keel was an almost impossible feat for anyone — Laemmle was not called "Uncle Carl" without reason. Because the lot swarmed with relatives, competent and otherwise, and time-servers to whom he felt he owed the debt of regular employment, Universal was referred to even by Uncle Carl himself as the Bottomless Pit. Laemmle vacillated between largesse and a parsimony prompted by guilt, causing the budget to float free or fetch up on the shoals of debt, depending on the owner's prevailing mood.

Understandably, then, when Julius bought his own studio, he was determined, as both captain and pilot, to run a tight ship. He did. The sails were trimmed, the crew was small, and, at times, it seemed even the water was rationed. Accordingly, their Hollywood detractors claimed that the Stern brothers had mounted the first nickel Century ever earned and the rest was kept in the studio vault. Be that as it may, Julius recognized talent and had a knack for hiring away from his competitors some of their best people. One such prize, stolen from Mack Sennett himself, was the top-flight comedy director Fred Fishback, lured to Century by an offer of $150 a week, twice what he was earning at Keystone. Julius knew when it paid to relax the purse-strings.

Fishback, a native of Bucharest, Rumania, had come to America with his widowed mother and brother. Working as an electrician, he drifted west from New York to Detroit and thence to Hollywood. Upon his arrival in 1909 he was fifteen, and on an impulse he answered an advertisement in a Los Angeles newspaper for movie extras to report to a nearby railroad depot. He was hired and subsequently found steady employment as a property man with producer-director Thomas Ince. In the following decade he rose to become one of Sennett's best comics and directors, acting with and later directing such stars as Roscoe Arbuckle, Ford Sterling, Mack Swain, Polly Moran, Ben Turpin, and Marie Dressler. Fishback, a tall, handsome man with bright blue eyes and dark hair, was innovative, and at Century he quickly capitalized on the wide latitude Julius gave his directors. They quarreled often over money, but that was not unusual on Poverty Row.

One trend that Fishback felt was due to crest once more was the exploitation of children in comedy. Before Chaplin had caught the Coogans' act at the Orpheum Theater, Fishback had seen little Jackie perform and had taken him to Century for a test. He had in mind doing something with Jackie along the lines of the popular "Little Billy" series, in which an appealing five-year-old named Paul Jacobs had starred for Keystone back in 1913. That series had run dry, but the concept had been a sound one, and Fishback felt it had never fully realized its potential. Julius and Abe screened Jackie's test, but they were not impressed with his performance and lost him by default to Chaplin soon thereafter.

Now, some fourteen months later, the boy Fred Fishback had envisioned as a comic was almost six years old and irreversibly type-cast as a tragic waif. What Fishback was still looking for was a much younger child, under three if possible, who possessed a combination of spontaneity, good bodily coordination, personality, the willingness and ability to take direction, and, above all, an un-self-conscious comic appeal that audiences would find irresistible. He already had his story in mind and an established actor to play the lead — a popular Century star, Brownie the Wonder Dog. Fishback was realistic enough, however, to appreciate that even in such a happy hunting ground as Hollywood his dream child was not going to be easy to find.

He was seriously considering advertising in the local newspapers when lightning struck. One day as he finished a scene, he was called aside by an extra girl who had worked on his set the week before. It seemed that the studio had not yet paid her and, as was the informal custom of the time, the genial Fishback obligingly peeled off five single bills from the roll he always carried. Then his glance strayed beyond the extra girl, and there, seated on a property man's stool, sat his dream child. Like a birdwatcher who fears he may frighten away his quarry with a too-sudden move, he slowly slipped the roll of bills into his trouser pocket, gently pushed up the green-lined white felt visor that shaded his eyes, and moved softly toward the child.

His precautions proved unnecessary, for the little girl appeared to be neither startled nor alarmed by his presence. He guessed she was about two years old. She was very small, compactly built, dressed in a simple cotton dress and matching bonnet. Her eyes were dark brown but as marvelously merry as Jackie Coogan's were sad. She had a turned-up nose and a whimsical crooked smile, all set in a square face under a fringe of short black bangs. Without a doll or any other toy to cuddle or occupy her, she seemed remarkably composed for a tot her age. Fishback tried engaging her in the usual baby talk that passed for communication between most toddlers and adult strangers, but she merely smiled in response as though she found his language quite amusing. He tried to coax her off the stool, but while not intimidated, she made it clear without words that the stool was where she intended to remain.

Somewhere nearby there had to be the mother, Fishback reasoned, and sure enough, he noticed a pretty but obviously unsophisticated young woman starting to walk anxiously toward him.

"Is she your little girl?" Fishback asked disarmingly.

"Yes, she is," the woman said, her blue eyes clouding over with concern. "I do hope she hasn't done something she shouldn't have. I told her not to move or leave the stool, and usually she's very good about staying put."

Fishback shot the woman a quizzical glance. "No, she hasn't done a thing wrong," he assured her, "but isn't she a little young to understand and obey like that?"

The woman relaxed and laughed, "Of course not. She understands. She's been brought up to do exactly as she's told. Both our children have."

Fishback, who was listening with growing interest, began circling the stool, studying the little girl from every angle, as though she were an intriguing piece of bric-a-brac he could not resist investing in.

"You see, I've been searching for a child exactly like her. By the way, how old is she?"

"Not quite nineteen months. But she's small for her age. She was very sick as a tiny baby. She almost didn't live."

Someone near the camera called the director and his attention was pulled back to the set. "I have to return to work now, but my name is Fred Fishback. Please leave your name and address at the reception desk in the front bungalow. I am very interested in using your little girl in a picture I plan to make soon."

Movie-struck mothers were the only kind Fishback had ever seen lugging small children through studios. None of them had ever needed any more encouragement, if as much, to nail their feet to the front-office floor until the promised job materialized. But my mother was different.

The extra girl to whom Fishback had just paid her overdue $5 was Mother's only friend, a fellow resident of the Beaudry Arms apartments. Mother had accompanied Margaret to the studio simply because she had not been out of the apartment in the three months she had lived in Los Angeles. While movie studios as such did not especially intrigue her, she was so anxious to escape her drab four walls that she would have almost welcomed an invitation to a public hanging. She took along her two little girls because she had no one with whom to leave them.

As the two friends left the made-over barn where Fishback was shooting, Margaret was bubbling over with excitement. "See! Didn't I tell you studios were exciting places? Imagine, being discovered sitting on a stool — just like that!"

Mother tried to mumble something intelligent in reply, but her heart was pounding, not with excitement but fear. What would Jack say?

"Jack is going to be furious if he finds out we were even here," she said aloud.

"But, Marian, don't be silly. Think of Peggy's future. She can have money, a college education, world travel — how can you deny her the chance at all that just because you're afraid of what your husband is going to say!"

"But I've told you how he feels about me even going near a studio, let alone taking the children to one."

"I know, but he's just old-fashioned. Doing stunts and falls out at Mixville isn't like being in Hollywood. What do Jack and his cowboy friends get to see of the really *big* opportunities waiting on every corner in this town?"

Mother suddenly felt a violent tug of war commence within her, a struggle between the solid midwestern precepts by which she had been raised and the limitless opportunity beckoning on every side in this strange community where all the time-honored values seemed irrelevant. After only three months' exposure to the world of movie-making (and until today even that was secondhand), she already felt herself reacting to the uncanny sense of urgency.

Hollywood seemed to operate on the premise that everyone should take a hearty bite out of every golden apple that came around. Success, like ripe fruit, had to be picked if the tree were to bear again next year. It was very much like the Garden of Eden in reverse.

As she approached the front office, Mother felt convinced that the Hollywood genie had indeed materialized before her eyes in the person of Fred Fishback. What he had asked her was only the first of three magic wishes. It was not in her power to say no. She gave her name and telephone number to the receptionist at the desk, just as the director had told her to do. It was her very first defection from her grandmother's conservative nineteenth-century principles. It would not be her last.

6
In the World of Five-Day Wonders

When you find fortune favorable, stride boldly forward, for she favors the bold, and, being a woman, the young.
— Baltasar Gracian,
The Art of Worldly Wisdom, 1647

HAVING GROWN UP in the home of her paternal grand-mother, Marian did not remember her own mother, who was variously said to have died young, disappeared mysteriously, or simply run off with another man. Grandmother Baxter, for reasons best known to herself, raised Marian on the early-death version. Her father was a railroad man who rarely took the time to visit with his child. The rest of the family was staid and prosperous. Aunts and uncles owned businesses in the small Wisconsin town, their homes surrounding the spacious Baxter residence and their lawns merging to form a vast, maple-shaded familial domain.

When she was eighteen, Marian left this sheltered world to join her father and stepmother in Chicago. There she met Jack Montgomery, the son of neighbors in fashionable Villa Park. A sensitive youth with a strong romantic streak, Jack had run away from home at thirteen and gone west to become a cowboy. During the intervening dozen years, he had ridden for some of the West's greatest spreads until the collapse of the cattle empire forced thousands of adventurous young men like himself to seek their livelihood in less picturesque occupations. In Jack's dark eyes and stern, craggy profile Marian saw her ideal knight errant.

In Marian Jack saw the perfect wife — pretty, docile, at home on the pedestal where he would place her, yet plucky enough to rough it on a ranch of their own if and when that undying dream of his materialized. Six weeks after they met they were married. Marian was nineteen, Jack was twenty-four.

When America entered the war two years later Jack was all for enlisting, although by then he had a year-old daughter, Louise, as well as a wife to think of. The recruiting officer refused to sign up a family man and suggested he apply for work with the army at Camp Kearny in far-off San Diego. The little family migrated to California, where he was hired as a construction foreman and where Marian immediately consulted a physician about a suspected second pregnancy. The old doctor was kind but concerned. "I only wish you were pregnant," he said gravely, "but what you have is a dangerously advanced tumor and it must be removed at once." That was Friday. The surgery was set for Monday morning. On Sunday the doctor was stricken with a heart attack. His young assistant, after reexamining the patient, paled, apologizing for his colleague's near-tragic diagnosis. Marian was indeed far along in pregnancy, and the narrowly averted surgery would have taken the life of her unborn child. The overriding element of chance that seemed to enter my family's lives upon my arrival had made its first appearance.

I was born two weeks before the armistice of 1918, the latter event terminating Father's employment with the army. Having heard that the National Park Service was recruiting men to serve as rangers, he applied, was selected, and for eighteen months served as a park ranger — first at Yosemite and later at Grand Canyon National Park in Arizona. Then, recognizing that he had freelanced too long to adapt to a government bureaucracy, he turned in his resignation.

Mother was dismayed. Although she had no love for the hard life of a pioneer ranger's wife — living in a tent, summer and winter, with two tiny babies and only rattlesnakes, wild bears, and fierce-looking Havasupai Indians for company — at least it was the devil she knew. The uncharted future seemed still more frightening and insecure. All she really wanted out of life, as she would often say, was to be able to pay her bills and call her soul her own. But it was becoming daily more apparent that her husband would only be happy in a job that placed a high priority on horsemanship, a skill that in an increasingly urbanized society was rapidly becoming an anachronism.

Having gained some carpentry skills at Camp Kearny, Father's next move was to Los Angeles, a city enjoying a postwar building boom. He found work on a downtown building site and settled his family in the Beaudry Arms, grateful to be earning a living, but still far from happy. Then one day he met an old cowboy friend who told him of a clandestine saloon in nearby Hollywood, where cattlemen from all parts of the vanished open range were said to gather.

The two men took a trolley into Hollywood and discovered the Waterhole, a combination bar and café that served up a genuine chuck-wagon reunion of long-lost cowboy friends. The Waterhole also proved the open sesame to a unique line of work that seemed tailor-made for grounded horsemen like themselves — riding in Westerns. Riders simply hired out to different studios, much as they had done on western ranches, except the pay was three times what the average cowhand ever earned. Many of the Waterhole's regulars were already engaged in the work, and with typical western generosity they offered to help their two old friends get on.

Father was hired by the first studio to which he applied, and a few weeks later, due to his fine horsemanship and a strong resemblance to the western star Tom Mix, he was selected as his double. The pay was an unheard-of $7.50 a day, plus a studio horse and a box lunch. But far more important to Father was the chance to be with his own kind once more, men whose companionship, moral code, and rough-cut chivalry had formed his character during the years he had grown to manhood "riding the river" with them.*

Although Hollywood had provided Father with this Heaven-sent solution to his singular employment needs, it did not follow that he would find movie studios a suitable, let alone desir-

* For the full story of the introduction of authentic range cowboys into Hollywood films, see the author's *The Hollywood Posse* (Boston: Houghton Mifflin, 1975).

able, environment for his innocent, wide-eyed wife. Jealous and protective, he intended to keep her as far removed as possible from Hollywood's seductive moral climate. Mother, knowing this, and dreading his anger when he was deliberately crossed, sensibly kept silent about her business at Century. Her second defection from her grandmother's counsel was to secretly withhold $5 from the weekly grocery money to buy me a new bonnet and dress and to return surreptitiously to Century for the promised interview with Mr. Fishback's assistant.

The encounter was a disappointment. After questioning Mother about my theatrical experience, the man unexpectedly released Brownie into the office. Startled by the dog, who licked my face without invitation, I backed up and burst into tears. Satisfied that I would never do, the man dismissed us and the matter seemed closed. But later Fred Fishback himself telephoned, asking Mother to please bring the baby for a final interview the next day.

Realizing that she had reached the end of her secret mission, Mother gamely confessed everything to Father when he returned home from Mixville that night. Having weathered his first reaction — which was, as expected, total outrage — Mother engaged in a calculated divertive action by remarking offhandedly, "It seems too bad that Peggy was afraid of the dog."

Afraid of a dog? Father's anger was extinguished by his pride. Although I could barely walk, he had never exempted me, nor my sister Louise before me, from the code by which he measured himself and other men. At three months he had placed me in the saddle before him while he made his rounds at Yosemite, and I had not registered a flicker of fear. Big Jim, the ancient, wrinkled, fearsome-looking patriarch chief of the Grand Canyon's Havasupai tribe, had marveled when his ranger friend's year-old daughter reached out to him affectionately. "First white papoose ever, not scare, never cry, always laugh when see Big Jim!" he would repeat delightedly as he carried me around in his arms. Backing away from a gentle studio dog cried out for a second chance to prove, if only to himself, that I was indeed my father's child.

Father's uncompromising attitude involved more than the cowboy's traditional respect for courage. As a small boy, he had come under the influence of his British-born paternal grandfather, a strict disciplinarian and himself the son of a Crimean War veteran. This upright gentleman demanded that all Montgomery progeny over whom he wielded any authority must grow up "keeping form." Children, he declared, should be seen and not heard, idleness is the devil's workshop, obedience is the crowning virtue, and an erect, soldierly bearing (in girls as well as boys) is the hallmark of a child properly reared according to "the old school." It was a hard school, one against which Father had violently rebelled, running away from home to elude its farthest reach. But, in spite of his resistance, those rules of conduct had formed his character and, while never as tyrannical as his grandfather, he *was* a strict disciplinarian. From my earliest memory, a sharp look from Father or a snap of his fingers across a crowded room signaled that a breach of comportment had been made or was imminent, and I reacted accordingly.

At the same time, he made it clear that obedience also spelled self-preservation. When a rattlesnake had coiled under Louise's swing outside our Grand Canyon tent, Mother ordered her to "come inside this minute!" Without stopping to question why, Louise jumped from the swing just as the rattler struck. Her split-second obedience had undoubtedly saved her life, as it would mine on several occasions during my eventful film career. Father further contended that children who understood rules and limits were happier, while those who threw tantrums and demanded bribes for performance or good behavior were being criminally spoiled or neglected. No one could accuse Father of either indulgence or indifference. Bribery was unheard of in our house and even baby talk discouraged, the reason, no doubt, I had found Mr. Fishback so amusing when he attempted to communicate with me in that oddly foreign tongue.

"I'm sure Peggy would not have cried if *you* had been with her," Mother ventured, and of course Father agreed. "*I'll* take her to see Mr. Fishback tomorrow," he announced by way of settling the question. "He told you it was for one picture only, and certainly there'll never be two for a baby her age. Anyway, he'll see that she's not afraid of the dog — or anything else that wears hair!"

It had taken the careful Charlie Chaplin fifty-two weeks to film his six-reel masterpiece *The Kid.* It took Fred Fishback exactly five days to shoot the two-reel comedy *Playmates.* Fishback was ecstatic with the rushes. Not only was Baby Peggy treating Brownie like a trusted pal, she was proving to be everything he had hoped to find in his discovery: responsive, curious, outgoing, and with an inborn sense of humor that was an asset if not a necessity at Century. She was also obedient to a degree the director considered phenomenal. Best of all, she possessed a clownish quality, which, when honed by confidence and experience, he felt sure would make her a popular comedy star who would keep moviegoers coming back for more.

Riding herd on his baby daughter's five-day venture into movies certainly posed no great threat to Father's pride or his own film career. At week's end he was ready to return to work for Mix when an announcement from the Stern brothers threw his uncomplicated but hardscrabble world into confusion. Julius and Abe told him they wanted to put "the baby" under contract at once. They recognized that a child star's life expectancy was roughly equivalent to that of a dog. At the expiration of a seven-year contract, a two-year-old like me would be pushing ten and, professionally speaking, ready for the grave. There was no time to lose.

Subconsciously, most movie parents bring to the child star trap the very bait that both attracts and ensnares them. In Father's case, my career was made doubly attractive by his lifelong dream of buying a cattle ranch of his own. His earnings at Mixville had made such a prospect appear remotely possible Now, however, from a totally unforeseen source, he could quickly realize enough money to put that neat little spread almost within his grasp. Century was offering $75 a week for seven long years — the same salary Chaplin had paid Jackie Coogan for one picture only and exactly twice what Father was making with Mix. In the spring of 1920 that was a great deal of money for a very poor man. Still, the cowboy Jack Montgomery, like the hoofer Jack Coogan, hesitated, reluctant, even fearful, of handing over his career, ego, and freedom to his own small child.

At that time there may have been a dozen psychologists in the world capable of putting into words the nameless fears, conflicts, and doubts that came rushing into Father's mind. On the one hand, he weighed the injuries he had already sustained doing stunts; being crippled for life or even killed were not unlikely prospects. On the other hand, what if he did pass the reins of his family's destiny to Peggy? What were the possible consequences of such an extraordinary relinquishment of power and control? An unsophisticated man of action with an eighth grade education, he could only evaluate this windfall in terms of money and material benefits.

The Hollywood genie had appeared again, and this time both parents were being asked to make the second wish. "All I want is to be able to pay our bills," I can hear Mother saying. And Father? "Well now, there's a sweet little spread out in Montana with tall grass, timber, and a river running through . . ." By temporarily pawning his pride, he could one day boast of a ranch that would constitute an imposing family estate, to be handed on to generations of Montgomerys. This mixture of inherited and cultivated values proved the irresistible bait entrapping Father in my child star career. It also formed the foundation of our working relationship for years to come.

Unlike four-year-old Jackie Coogan, when I reported, at twenty months, for my first day's work at a movie studio, I had no stage techniques to remember or forget. Unlike Little Elsie, I had never memorized or recited so much as a nursery rhyme in my life. But I had been a rolling stone since birth and had experienced a far greater variety of living conditions — most of them primitive — than most vaudeville children. I had learned to crawl on rustic tent and cabin floors. A daily parade of cowboys, Indians, and tourists pouring through the ranger's station had made me highly tolerant of strangers. I would find the Stern brothers' heavy German accents no more surprising than Big Jim's pidgin English. I was outgoing and friendly, but was also content to play alone for hours at a time with only a kitchen pan and wooden spoon for toys. This talent for making do with less than perfect tools would prove the ideal survival kit for the movie years ahead.

The Stern brothers' little clap-trap fun factory had been humming along with pratfall and pie-in-the-face prosperity for nearly three years when Baby Peggy first toddled into their lives. Wartime restrictions and the shutdown of European studios had given Century and others on Poverty Row a golden opportunity to provide the sole comedy product for a world population that was virtually starved for diversion and entertainment. Their product was silent and visual, their market global, and they were making money at an unprecedented rate. Except for adding considerably to their revenues, my arrival hardly caused a ripple. Century did not adjust to me. I adjusted to it.

The studio proved to be a combination opera house, barnyard, film factory, and winter quarters for a circus. Once beyond the gateman, we passed a made-over gray frame bungalow that served as cutting room, laboratory, and storehouse for films. Through its heavily screened windows drifted the smoky-sour aroma of raw film, soon the most familiar and, second only to saddle leather, the sweetest scent I knew.

Although the lot was not yet ten years old, including the brief reign of L-KO, it was in an advanced state of decay. Once-gaily-striped awnings hung in sun-bleached shreds over windows fogged with grime. The owner-producers toiled in cubicles euphemistically referred to as offices, but their raw lumber walls, door jambs, and windowsills had yet to be framed, painted, or sealed. A dressing room at Century was nearly as bare as a jail cell. My own — despite the star on the door — was windowless, uncarpeted, and all of ten feet square. It was equipped with a rough-hewn make-up bench and mirror framed in wire-caged light bulbs, an unyielding army cot (for the naps I would never have time to take), two straight chairs, a curtained pole to serve as a closet, and an antique kerosene stove for chilly dawns and nights when we worked overtime. These spartan quarters bespoke the studio's philosophy of total commitment to the product. Everything and everyone had been stripped for action, every needless creature comfort jettisoned to insure expediency, speed, and profit. At Century time

was money, and one always had the uneasy feeling that both were
running out.

When I was introduced to my new employers, Julius Stern's
first concern was to ask, "Is she housebroken?" Being assured I
was, he took me in his arms for our first publicity still. Julius
was a bland, oval-faced man, with shrewd eyes, a high forehead,
a prominent nose, and a puckish smile. Like his brother Abe, he
was never without a derby (de rigueur in California from October
to May) or a straw hat (May to October) clamped firmly on his
head. Both brothers favored stripes, worked in shirtsleeves most
of the time, and dressed up this undress with a high collar, a tie,
and sleeve garters.

The Sterns had a good sense of what was funny on film, and
some of their two-reelers ranked among the best ever made in
that golden era of comedy. But they possessed little sense of
what might seem ridiculous about themselves. In consequence,
both men are among the most quoted pioneer figures in Hollywood. Julius is said to be that producer who was trying to coin
a catchy name for his studio and an equally good slogan to go
with it. Hitting upon the logo Miracle Pictures, he came up with:
"If it's a good picture, it's a miracle!" No one could convince him
it was a bad choice. When a competitor referred jokingly to the
quality of the Stern brothers' slapstick two-reelers, Abe burst out
indignantly, "Century comedies are *not* to be laughed at!" And
when one of my directors wanted to go to a distant mountain location because the story called for spectacular scenery, Julius delivered the oft-quoted "A rock's a rock. A tree's a tree. Shoot it in
Griffith Park!"

Century ran a weekly one-column ad in the *Saturday Evening
Post* announcing its forthcoming films over the signature of its
distributor, Carl Laemmle. "Look for Baby Peggy," read a classic
example of pure Sternese. "She is only three years old but she is
a better actress than a lot of older people who draw aristocratic
salaries. Exhibitors are booking her right and left; and there isn't
a pretentious theater in the country that doesn't regard her as a
great drawing card." My own aristocratic salary, paid to me by
one of the least pretentious studios in the industry, later became a
bone of contention, but at the beginning everyone was happy.

The studio maintained its own menagerie, for Julius, always fretful of the budget, reasoned that it was cheaper to keep his four-legged stars and extras in pens and cages scattered about the lot than it was to hire them by the day from such competitors as Gay's Lion Farm. Reading from the bottom up, in order of their earning power and popularity, were two toothless old lions; a mangy tiger; one brown bear in fair condition; a billy goat; several aging deer; a hoary old elephant called Charley; Teddy, a dignified Great Dane; Brownie the Wonder Dog; and an exceptionally ugly, clever, and world-famous chimpanzee, Joe Martin.

Joe's yellow-toothed grin was his trademark; he starred in his own two-reelers and enjoyed a box-office following that many a human comedian of the day might have envied. He sometimes appeared in comedies with me, but usually he was too busy working on his own, for which I was secretly grateful, for I dreaded working with Joe.

The trainer for the tiger, the lions, the chimp, and the elephant was a muscular blond man named Curley Stecker. Although he was said to have an explosive temper when aroused, Stecker seemed good-natured enough, was a veteran animal handler, and got on well with most of his charges.

"But I hate working with old Charley," Stecker confided one day to Father and me when we met in the hayloft of the old barn overlooking the elephant's corral at the far end of the lot. We had chosen the loft as a quiet place to work on my diction. Although my films were silent, I nevertheless had to learn my lines, and Father had no patience with my childish lisping. As he plunged his pitchfork into the hay and tossed samplings down into Charley's corral, Stecker continued: "Old Charley turned on me once, some twenty years ago, and I had to beat him off with a chain. He never forgot it. Mrs. Stecker can work with him just as easy as she does with the big cats and Joe Martin. But he'll have no part of me."

He leaned on his pitchfork, looking down as Charley lifted wisps of hay into his mouth with his trunk. "I always make it a point to throw him his hay from up here, or over the gate into his stockade. He don't like me inside, and when I have to go in I always carry that." He pointed to a high-powered elephant gun leaning against the wall. After we left the loft, Father cautioned me never to go near Charley's pen alone. I hardly needed his warning, for everyone at Century harbored a secret fear that the elephant would one day break out of his corral and run amok across the lot.

If Julius kept animals against the day when the script rained tigers, in the prop department he hoarded enough scenery and supplies to film the history of the world. The big old building probably was not as vast as it seemed to me as a child, but it *was* crammed with painted flats of jungles, drawing rooms, palaces, and dungeons. There were jury boxes, gallows, pulpits and thrones, moose heads, cigar store Indians, African shields, carriage harnesses, medieval suits of armor, bits and pieces of castles, a drawbridge, sedan chairs — literally everything and anything that might be needed to simulate a fairly believable background on an unbelievably low budget. Every item in the prop department was familiar to me, too, for sooner or later nearly every weapon in this great arsenal of optical illusion found its way into one of the hundred and more Baby Peggy comedies that streamed off the studio assembly line on the average of one a week during my tenure at Century.

High above the working set, like giant yellow tulips in a black window box, bloomed the spots, big and little, on short stems and tall. The electricians who tended them seemed shadow people, raising and lowering the spots according to orders from below. If the first instruction I received was not to look into the camera, the second must have been to keep my eyes closed while they were setting up the lights. (Stand-ins came much later, and they never came to Century.)

Perhaps reflecting the stigma attached to retakes at Century, I soon developed into a quick study. Overhearing myself referred to by a director as "one-take Peggy" was more rewarding to me than all the effusive praise and adulation poured out upon me by visitors to the studio. From the outset, I understood that these people were "outsiders" who did not know *me* at all. It especially distressed and embarrassed me to see older and otherwise very dignified bank presidents and politicians reduced to doting grandparents by a little girl who was, in fact, a total stranger to them. They only knew her image on the screen, the same one I saw at the end of each day when I viewed the rushes with the rest of the company. "She" was Baby Peggy, who did what they saw up there, but I was the one responsible for *how* she did it, the difficult part, deserving of approval. These reactions were of course purely emotional, for I had no words to describe my feelings even to myself. But much of my uneasiness sprang from the curious first premise that I brought to my profession — that all adults had worked in movies as children. How else, indeed, had their parents survived? It came as a fresh surprise each time to discover that everyone, from my governess to the fan magazine writer, thought it a rare treat for a child to work in films.

Understandably, given the peculiar circumstances in which I found myself breadwinner for my family, I was intolerant of children who did not work. (That excepted my sister, Louise, for she sometimes worked as an extra in my comedies.) On those rare days when I stayed home and looked into the back yard of the elegant house next door and saw children playing in sand-boxes, on swings, and screaming their way down the shining slides, I was filled with a sense of bewilderment that, as the years passed, turned into a feeling of unspeakable outrage. How could they? Where was their sense of responsibility to their families, their self-respect, their *pride?* Similarly, when children who worked with me on the set staged tantrums and insisted on being primed with ice cream before they would do a scene, I suffered from acute embarrassment, feeling that my peers had somehow betrayed me. For the lazy, sandbox bums I harbored a degree of compassion because of their apparent ignorance of the way things should be. For the badly behaved studio child, however, I felt nothing but undisguised contempt.

I also picked up a protective attitude toward Mother; in fact, toward all women who did not work. Not only were they to be shielded from the labors and risks involved in our career (Father's and mine were one), they must also be protected from any un-necessary worry and preoccupation over the chances we were taking. Perhaps one reason my recollections of those early days are so vivid is that I was recording everything that was happening on two levels simultaneously: the action itself and the carefully edited version I would relate to Mother that night. Working mostly with men, I unconsciously absorbed the prevailing male attitude toward keeping "the little woman" safe at home. Throughout the rest of my life, it would be difficult to relate to other women except on a professional basis, while with men I immediately assumed that a working relationship existed by the very fact that they were men.

I worked for the satisfaction of a job well done and for the respect and approval of Father and my coworkers. It was a wordless compensation, cutting across all barriers of sex and age, because making movies was serious business and, as no one at Century could forget, a very costly one. I reflected Father's own pride in performance and, possibly through my constant exposure to him and his cowboy friends who so often worked with me, I picked up their decisive way of dealing with challenging or dangerous situations.

While different directors were assigned to my comedies, it was Father who translated their demands to me. He based his logic on what he knew about horses, reasoning that a promising green colt could be ruined if handled by different riders, while a top cutting horse could result from one man's patient training. This also gave him some small degree of control over my safety in what proved to be the very risky occupation of making slapstick comedies.

At Century (and later at Hal Roach, Educational, Mascot, and Monogram — wherever *Our Gang* and its imitators employed children), the perils sprang from carelessness of the safety factors. That, and a firm belief on the part of most adults with whom movie children worked that youngsters were physically indestructible, conspired to create potentially dangerous work situations.

Over the months I was made sick by having to work all day in a bathtub of sour whipped cream (to simulate soapsuds), I was nearly drowned in Santa Monica's ten-foot surf, and I was thrown from a speeding pickup truck together with the terrified goat to which I had been wired. A passenger train that was to be used as a prop in a railroad scene pulled out of the station minutes before Brownie and I were to work under the wheels. Hit and dragged by a speeding bicyclist, my road burns were painted with white iodine, a cosmetic concession to my career but hardly a painless remedy. In every case, when the ordeal was behind me, I faced one almost as painful — how to keep from telling Mother the truth of what had happened at the studio that day.

Years later I found that my experience was about average for a movie child. Shirley Temple claimed that the things she was made to do while filming her *Baby Burlesks* were so dangerous that directors barred the mothers from the set. And Darla Hood of Our Gang recalls spending half a day hanging onto the back of a dogcatcher's wagon, shooting the same scene over and over until she was finally overcome by carbon monoxide fumes and passed out cold.

In nearly every comedy I made at Century, some member of the studio menagerie was certain to appear. Abe and Julius instructed their writers and gag men to keep in mind, while conjuring up funny and frightful situations for their human actors, that the animals were eating a hole in the Stern brothers' pockets. And so Joe Martin was assigned to play my patient when I portrayed a youthful dentist's assistant. The dental chair, of course, was one more treasure produced from the prop department's trove.

Inured though I was to working with the animals, I feared Joe almost as much as Charley. It gave me chills to shake Joe's leathery black hand or put my arm affectionately around his scraggly shoulders. Curley Stecker assured me he was harmless and even assigned Mrs. Stecker to work on the set with me while he directed the chimp from behind the camera, but I still was not convinced.

However, I had to admire Joe's professionalism. He was a remarkably cheerful, obedient, and long-suffering creature, putting up with the discomfort of wearing clothes and working patiently for hours under the burning klieg lights and spots. But a few days after my scenes with him were finished, his patience suddenly snapped, and without any warning he turned on Mrs. Stecker in the middle of a take and sank his teeth into her arm. While she bravely tried to calm him, Curley Stecker's temper erupted. Picking up a short iron crowbar, the infuriated trainer charged into the set, beat Joe over the head until he was groggy, and then dragged him off the stage.

Alarmed by Stecker's pitiless treatment of the chimp, the director decided he had better inform the front office. Bursting unannounced into Abe's shabby cubicle, he cried, "Abe, Curley Stecker's gone berserk! You've got to get him away from the chimp!"

Abe clapped a hand on his straw hat, vaulted his desk, and set out after the director at a run. Already Joe's screeches could be heard all over the lot, setting off pandemonium among the other animals. Tracing the sound of the chimp's screams to the prop department, Abe and the director rushed in to find Joe Martin strapped down in the very same dentist's chair he had occupied a few days earlier. Bending over him was the furious and powerful trainer.

"No, no, Curley!" Abe Stern pleaded. *"Not his trademark!"* But the producer's pleas came too late. Using a pair of ordinary pliers, Stecker had already pulled out every tooth in the poor chimp's mouth!

As though suddenly coming out of a dream, Stecker realized that he had done far more than destroy Joe Martin's million-dollar smile. Looking into the animal's pain-crazed eyes, he saw that the beast had gone stark, staring mad. Even toothless, the now murderous chimp was wholly capable of tearing a man to pieces.

As Abe turned away in anguish, he heard a pistol crack behind him. With that shot Stecker mercifully put poor Joe out of his agony and one of Century's most lucrative comedy series out of business forever. As Century ads had long proclaimed, there was only one Joe Martin.

The final chapter in the decline and fall of Century's animal kingdom came late one sun-gilded afternoon when every company on the lot was getting ready to wrap up shooting for the day. I was working on an outdoor set with several studio deer when suddenly everyone froze at the sound of an elephant's trumpeting, unlike anything we had ever heard from Charley's corral before. It was followed by the piercing cry of a man in mortal terror: "Stop him! Stop him!"

"That's Stecker," I heard a prop man say. "Old Charley's loose! My God! Everybody run for your lives!"

Father swept me into his arms as panic-stricken extras, crew members, and deer scattered in all directions, toppling reflectors, chairs, and cameras in their frenzied flight for safety. Reasoning that both the prop department and the front office were too far to risk making a dash for, Father set out at a run for the hayloft in the sturdy old barn overlooking what would now be Charley's empty corral.

But when we reached the loft, Father looked down, and there, to his astonishment, he saw Charley still safe inside his pen. But he was standing over the crushed and broken body of Curley Stecker. Outside the gate a prop man found Stecker's big elephant gun, just where the trainer had left it, leaning against the stockade beside a little pile of hay. It took three blasts to lay the raging bulk of old Charley in the bloodied dust beside the man on whom he had finally taken his revenge.

Shortly after these tragedies had decimated the zoo, taken the life of its trainer, and unnerved everyone on the lot, including Julius Stern, the producer was approached by one of his directors with a problem that touched not only on the animals, but on an even more delicate subject — money.

"We've got to hire a lion for the Western serial I'm shooting," the director announced.

"Lions we've still got," Julius replied brightly, grateful the man hadn't asked for an elephant or a chimpanzee. "What's wrong with the two old cats on the back lot?"

"But they're African lions, Julius," the director replied with infinite patience. "They have big furry ruffs around their necks. What I need is a mountain lion — you know, the kind with a short, sleek coat. It would be ridiculous in a serious picture like this to show a cowboy being stalked by an African lion in Montana. We'll just have to hire a puma from Gay's Lion Farm."

But the producer's instinct for economic survival was not to be circumvented. Bringing his clenched fist down on the scarred desktop, Julius delivered a line that would pass into the unwritten folklore of Hollywood:

"Shave 'em! Disguise 'em! But goddammit, use 'em!"

Not long after that the Hollywood fire chief paid an unexpected call on Julius Stern to complain about the presence of wild animals on the lot. "My men have informed me they will refuse to respond to any fire that might break out while the cats remain on the lot. They're firefighters, not lion tamers."

Julius, threatened with cancellation of his insurance, was forced to sell the remaining animals back to Charley Gay.

A few years later came the final irony, a serious fire that broke out at Century in the middle of the night while Julius was away in New York on business. Abe telegraphed his brother that the studio had burned to the ground and asked him to send instructions. Julius wired back: "Fire the night watchman!"

Few people outside of Hollywood realized what a genuinely informal operation movie-making really was. Perhaps that explains why newcomers with extravagant dreams and plans continued to pour into town, convinced that everything was well planned, safe, and almost certain to lead to ultimate success.

7
At the End of the Sunset Trail

You know
the Hollywood sign
that stands
in the Hollywood hills
I don't think
the Christ of the Andes
ever blessed
so many ills

The Hollywood sign
seems to smile
like it's
constantly saying cheese
I doubt if
the Statue of Liberty
ever welcomed
more refugees

— Dory Previn, *"Mary C. Brown*
and the Hollywood Sign," 1971

THE WESTWARD MOVEMENT, which began east of the Appalachians in 1783 and reached its apogee when the Crabtrees turned forty-niners, enjoyed an unexpected resurgence after 1921. While land and climate were undoubtedly among the Golden State's major allurements, it was the magnet of potential movie stardom, baked like a tantalizing prize inside California's multi-layered cake, that most attracted outsiders. Every year thousands of pretty, single, and disparately talented young women migrated westward seeking the Cinderella dream. Every year newspapers and fan magazines duly mourned how only one or two emerged victorious, while the rest joined the mounting list of Hollywood casualties.*

A less well reported but more formidable contingent of American womanhood was also descending upon Hollywood in those early years. These ladies were conspicuous, not for their youth, pulchritude, talent, and grace, but ironically for their almost universal lack of these marketable attributes. They were wives, mothers, even grandmothers, fading matrons all, most of whom felt they had been betrayed by men and the false dawn of their own vanished youth. Now, disenchanted but not entirely dispirited, they were heading west on the sunset trail, reaching out for what they hoped would prove a more enduring light — reflected glory. Clutched in each woman's strong right hand was her passport from domestic oblivion to worldly fame: the small, powerless, and trusting hand of a little child.

History smiled upon these latter-day madonnas of the trail, placing at their disposal an ideal means of escape from America's hinterlands. It was the motor car. Just as the European conquest of the Americas would not have been possible prior to the perfection of the sail, so, too, the great migration of mothers to movieland could not have transpired without cheap motorized transportation. Before the war, ownership of an auto was restricted to the wealthy few. By 1920 a car was within the reach of any man or woman who could rake up the $190 it took to put themselves and their families on wheels. Tires cost $10 each; gasoline was twelve cents a gallon.

Despite the primitive state of the nation's highways, the fearful distance between fueling stations, and the almost total absence of tourist cabins, as the forerunners of motels were called, the cross-country motorist of the twenties set out with far fewer maps and a lot more nerve than his modern counterpart. Granted all the hazards of the road, most considered it a far sight safer way to

---

* Remarkably few of the failures left the area. Most drifted into local jobs as waitresses, extras, models, wardrobe women, and hairdressers, usually marrying men whose history of not making it big in movies was an echo of their own. While many successful female stars adopted their children from fashionable foundling homes back east, these couples spawned the tall, handsome, leggy race that still endures in Southern California.

go than by Conestoga, the only other cheap private vehicle they had to judge the crossing by.

More than the mode of transportation had changed since the barnstorming days of Lotta and Baby Gladys. There was a growing liberality toward entertainers and movie people in particular. Movies were a popular art, an entertainment that the public mind associated more with respectable storefront nickelodeons than the sinful stage, thus escaping some of the odium traditionally heaped upon the theater by Christian fundamentalists. As the industry's recruits were increasingly drawn from the rank and file of American youth, most of whom had no previous link with the stage, news of Hollywood people and events took on the flavor of reports from some remote outpost like the Indian territory. Its lucky strikes reminded readers more of Cripple Creek and Virginia City than of New York's Great White Way. The movie capital came to be viewed quite tolerantly by the rest of the nation as a boisterous boom town on a new gold rush frontier. (This relaxation of moral judgment prevailed until an epidemic of Hollywood sex and drug scandals brought the wrath of church groups and women's clubs down upon the industry.)

If Lotta Crabtree, busy with her watercolors and her guests at Boston's Brewster Hotel, still doubted that a child could win the hearts and minds of fans through so impersonal a medium as film, the advent of Jackie Coogan changed her mind. By 1921 the new child star craze had swept the nation. Jackie's face was on the cover of movie magazines, articles reported his every action from the cereal he ate for breakfast to the prayers he recited at bedtime. "Jackie doesn't belong to any one person," wrote a famous Hollywood director, "he belongs to the world." Humorist Irvin S. Cobb paid lip service to the fading myth of the redemptive child while endorsing the more hedonistic aspect of the new child star cult, entertainment: "Perhaps the kindly angels are responsible for Jackie Coogan. If so, they did a good job . . . if the world doesn't spoil him and God lets him live with us, he will, in his maturity, be the blithest spirit that ever gave unending joy to countless millions — indeed, he is that now." Another fan magazine writer expressed it all in a poignant sentence, freighted with tragic implications for the future: "Dear child, we have only one prayer to offer . . . *don't grow up!"*

However, Jackie was not required to carry on this twentieth-century children's crusade all by himself. By this time Hal Roach had put together his own winning formula of *Our Gang* comedies, which had shot half a dozen unknown children to overnight stardom. Meantime, too, Brownie the Wonder Dog had died, and I was now starring in my own comedies. Most of these were well-costumed and highly sophisticated satires of either classic fairy tales or modern melodramas; in them I lampooned famous films and popular movie idols. On the same program with a melo-dramatic Valentino, Mae Murray, or Pola Negri tear-jerker, audiences were treated to a hilarious Baby Peggy parody of the same star and film. These two-reelers provided a necessary comic relief at a time when moviegoers tended to lose themselves completely in the tragedy unfolding on film. As a natural consequence, Baby Peggy comedies became almost as popular with world audiences as the stars and film classics they ridiculed.

Pious nineteenth-century attitudes toward child stars were becoming conspicuous by their absence. Increasingly, when Jackie and I were interviewed, reporters wasted less time speculating on how many stars these angel children might have in their respective crowns. What gripped them were the material, even crass, aspects of the new child star phenomenon, such as how many dollars we were putting into our parents' pockets. A few journalists expressed concern that, in the process of earning their millions, these children were losing out on a normal childhood. But there was no lack of producers, publicists, and even parents to put such groundless fears to rest. In a roaring camp like Hollywood, an enterprising parent could lower his child into the mine shaft at dawn, pull him up at sundown with another full load of gold, and, in good conscience, brag about giving him a normal childhood for the rest of the day.

Jackie's own publicity man was quick to assure one editor that the child's shooting schedule had been worked out so precisely that he actually spent less than two months of every year before the camera (a fact of which I am sure his penny-wise producer must have been ignorant). The rest of the time he was tutored by the finest teachers money could buy, he read the classics, played with his little friends, and enjoyed the completely normal life that "any child of wealth would lead."

Another entirely new facet of the child star experience — and also a sign of the times — was the growing interest in the intelligence quotient, or possible genius level, displayed by movie children. Interviewing me for *Motion Picture Classic* in 1922, writer Willis Goldbeck was careful to list my psychological credentials. "In a recent mental test of the child film stars, that included them all from Wes Barry to the inimitable Jackie, Baby Peggy carried off first honors. The test, conducted by the University of Southern California, consisted of oral questions and answers and covered a wide variety of subjects."

One psychologist who examined me at three and gave me an IQ rating of 148 explained: "Most children make use of the objective mind. Baby Peggy is learning daily to make use of the subconscious mind by the mental suggestion she receives from fine adult minds." In later years I looked back and wondered if the psychologist who wrote that evaluation had any idea of the "fine adult minds" to which I was exposed at Century.

Mother gave a rare interview, in which she offered advice to the parents of would-be child stars: "Don't teach a child to act. Let them keep their natural habits, for that is what producers and directors are constantly fighting for. She [Peggy] works — if you would call it work — four hours a day, never at night and never on Sundays. She considers her work play and nothing is ever done or said to let her feel otherwise." (Apparently my campaign to keep Mother sheltered from the harsh truths of life on the Century lot was eminently successful.)

In a similar interview, Jack Coogan attributed his son's success to public acceptance and acclaim, at the same time backhandedly recognizing the inherited value of Jackie's special gifts. "I cannot say that Mrs. Coogan and I had been blind . . . to Jackie's differences. But I cannot say we saw in him what the public discovered — genius."

"Beautiful Baby" contests, with a promised screen test serving as bait, were run in every major city by photographers, dancing schools, local dairies, theater managers, and other opportunists who, like scavengers, recognized a fat herd on the move and knew how to hang on to its heels for stragglers. "Your child should be in pictures!" became as commonplace a phrase as "What an angelic-looking child!" had been a generation earlier. In 1921 the Los Angeles *Herald Tribune* headlined a thought-provoking article with: "Has Your Baby Charm?" and went on to pierce every ambitious mother to the marrow of her soul. "Baby Peggy has charm! It has opened the door of the movies to her and enabled the young lady, while still a child, *to earn a salary of a million dollars a year.* Maybe *your* child can go and do likewise!"

This was heady stuff, and women from every walk of life were reading such articles every day. As they washed the dishes and shelled the peas, they wondered how they could parlay their own penniless son or daughter into a pint-sized millionaire before another month had passed. Sometimes they did not even realize how far their plans had gone in their imagination until someone or some item in the newspaper triggered the almost ready-made blueprint drawn up in idle moments during the day's routine. A handful of such parents made the impressive jump from daydreaming of stardom for their child to putting it into action, almost without realizing what had been accomplished by their own well-defined schemes.

There was Nell Carter, for example. Nell was an end pony — the short front-line chorine as opposed to the tall back-line showgirl — in the chorus line of a third-rate burlesque troupe. Nell hailed from Kansas City, Missouri, and more recently from the outer marches of Oklahoma, where she had toured for several thankless seasons with Bobby Barker's dancers earning $14 a week. After marriage to a prop man turned burlesque comic and the subsequent birth of a son, she found herself one of Pat White's Gaiety Girls, still high-kicking and slamming her taps in a string of dirt-road theaters. Nell's boy was already in the act, but he was also in his father's way. A kid in the top drawer of a wardrobe trunk and milk bottles warming over the jet where the black wax was melted had, from Sonny's birth, brought chaos to his father's neat portable regimen. The dressing room just wasn't big enough for Nell, Joe, and Joe, Jr.

One day in the Chicago train station Nell pulled out a roll of bills from the crocheted boodle bag in which she kept the family finances. With a sigh she counted out $20 and handed it over to Joe, his share of the act. She and four-year-old Sonny would take the other $20 and make it on their own somehow. With a girl friend named Myrtle, she opened a restaurant in Kansas City, the house specialty a plate of chicken, biscuits, and a beverage for twenty-five cents. At best this venture amounted to treading water, and one afternoon, between customers, Nell spread out the evening paper on an empty table and looked for something better. Her eye was drawn to a squib announcing that Mr. Hal Roach, the famous Hollywood producer of *Our Gang* comedies, was looking for talented children for his series.

"Myrtle, how would you like to go to California?"

"Where?"

"California. I've got a feeling about Sonny and the movies."

"When do we leave?"

"How about tomorrow?"

The next day, having purchased a secondhand car, a lean-to tent from Montgomery Ward, and some groceries for the road, the trio set out. After years of concocting forbidden meals in the rooms of theatrical boarding houses, Nell had mastered the fine art of cooking over canned heat. Preparing her Sterno cuisine outdoors and sleeping under the stars would be the only innovations. As for finding Hollywood, any fool knew that California was due west of Kansas City, and if you kept steering into the setting sun you couldn't help but eventually drive into the Pacific.

The trip proved something of a lark, but the Hal Roach interview was a disaster of Nell's own making. After weeks of patiently outwaiting the hordes of other mothers and children who had seen the same notice in their local papers, Nell's name was finally called. Roach's assistant, somewhat impressed by Sonny's background, said they would try him out at $5 a day. Five dollars for her Sonny? Why, he was worth three times that! Hadn't he been onstage when he was one year old and already working as part of the act when he was two? She hadn't been starving all these weeks to accept such a miserable crumb. After all, she could always go back to hoofing in a chorus line. In so many words, the gentleman encouraged her to do exactly that and closed the interview. Nell fell back, all the way back to Kansas City, and regrouped for another run at child stardom for Sonny.

Her chance came a year later, when a local theater owner decided to lead his own assault on Hollywood, an imposing body of eleven people and two cars. Each member contributed something toward the trip, and Nell bought into the enterprise by supplying four new tires for the second car. They traveled without even a tent this time, merely spreading their blankets in an open field or beside the road. While it had taken Nell and Myrtle two full weeks to find Hollywood, this expeditionary force hit their target in ten days flat.

With her former Hollywood experience of near-starvation and false pride still fresh in her memory, Nell decided to get a job as a telephone operator. It was only temporary, she assured her son, but it would pay the rent, buy food, and make sure their all-important lifeline, the telephone, was not cut off. Besides, the Hollywood switchboard was a good place to tune in on the studio grapevine; and sure enough, Nell was among the first to learn of an important part for a child over at Larry Darmour's studio on Poverty Row.

Comedies featuring kids were all the rage, from *Our Gang* to its carbon copy, *The Us Bunch*. Darmour wanted to build his own series around a well-known comic-strip character in Fontaine Fox's nationally syndicated "Toonerville Trolley" cartoons. The lead must be a small, pugnacious-looking boy with touseled black hair. Sonny was an ash blond, but for Nell Carter there were no insuperable problems. She got out the black shoe polish, scrubbed it into Sonny's hair and scalp, then scrubbed his ears and forehead with nail polish remover to remove the unwanted stains from his skin.

At Darmour the boy was tested, and the agonizing wait began. After five days Nell could stand it no longer, and she called the studio. When were they going to decide on the test? she asked. "After all, the kid's had five other offers since it was made!" Her bluff worked. She was told to bring Sonny back for more tests.

He was naturally brash and cocky, a typical show business child who was used to fighting for the limelight against resentful adults. All he had to do was look and act a little tougher than he already was, and to do so dressed in outsize shoes, torn pants, wearing a derby two sizes too big, and chewing on a big brown rubber stogie. He made the character his own and got the part. Nell quit her job. After all, Sonny was making $75 a week.

When several comedies had been completed and the success of the series assured, the tight-fisted producers decided they could save the studio a thousand dollars a picture in royalties, paid to the cartoonist Fox, if they legally changed Sonny's name to that of the cartoon character he portrayed. As Joe had become Sonny, so Sonny became Mickey McGuire. But Mr. Fox was not fooled; he sued the studio, and the series fell on hard times. At this point Universal was interested in hiring Nell Carter's son as a child character actor, but because of the litigation over the series they insisted he find another name. Universal's publicity man thought that "Mickey Rooney" had a nice ring.

In Seattle, Rose Hovick had separated from her husband for the sixth time. She had also made several determined attempts to get rid of the unwanted child. She had tried starving it out, punched herself in the stomach, gone on bumpy rides, and in a final effort had heroically hurled herself down an entire flight of stairs, but nothing worked. When the baby finally came she was the smallest infant her mother had ever seen. "I could have put Junie's head inside a teacup" was her favorite phrase for describing the baby's size.

Rose had wanted to be an actress, but her father had forbidden her to go on the stage. Meanwhile, her first daughter, Louise, turned out to be beautiful, but she could neither sing nor dance. June was not pretty, nor could she talk at two, but she took to dancing like a cat to milk. Rose had reconciled with her husband before June's birth, and now she decided he should pay for the child's expensive dancing lessons. Her husband, a hard-working, underpaid newspaper man, flatly refused to contribute a dime to such thriftless trivia. Following a climactic quarrel, Rose burst into tears and yelled: "Marry a Norwegian, my poor mother tried to tell me, and take your place at the very last trough in the barn!" With that parting shot, Rose gathered up her frightened wide-eyed girls and moved back to her father's house on the other side of Seattle.

The girls' grandfather had been against his own daughter's career, but now Rose painted Baby June's future in colors that added luster to his own small world. Papa was a big man in the local Shriners; little June could entertain at their meetings, and think of the nice things his lodge brothers would have to say about his fairy-footed grandchild once she had mastered the lessons he would finance. He swallowed the bait and paid the bills.

Subsequently June was booked into every convention and theatrical function that came to town. At one benefit Rose and June found themselves on the same show with the great Russian ballerina Anna Pavlova, who was making her farewell tour of America.

As soon as June finished her number, Rose dragged her in her tiny tutu over to where the dancer stood in the wings.

"Ah, Madame Pavlova," Rose breathed, "did you see my baby dance? Would you say she is a natural dancer? Should I train her?"

"One cannot tell such things," the bewildered Pavlova replied in hesitant English. "She is not even yet borned. Her feets have not yet formed enough to hold her."

A week later Rose and her two-year-old daughter left Seattle with the new billing: "Baby June, the Pocket Size Pavlova." The unpromising Louise was temporarily banished to a kindergarten while Rose and June launched the first of many assaults on Hollywood.*

Rose made the usual rounds of agents and studios. At interviews, Baby June's blond curls were whisked into wild, stiff wings away from her pale narrow face by a brush that her mother carried always at the ready for such emergencies. She was trained to pinch her cheeks and bite her lips for color, all the while smiling as though her life depended upon eternal cheerfulness.

---

* In later years, Louise Hovick redeemed herself for this unproductive period by becoming the famous stripper Gypsy Rose Lee, while Baby June eventually blossomed into actress June Havoc. Both girls wrote books about what life was like with Mama Rose.

At one interview two men beckoned her forward from the crowd of mothers and their curled and painted moppets.

"Do you know any rhymes?"

June had difficulty talking, but her mother had discovered the child could sing. She had taught her a slightly bawdy song that hardly matched up with the dimpled darling in the lacy party dress. Responding the only way she knew, June sang:

> *Nobody knows me number,*
> *Nobody knows me name,*
> *Nobody knows*
> *Where I gets me clothes,*
> *But I gets them just the same.*
> *See?*

The song ended with a come-hither wink. The men looked at each other. "She'll do," the director said. And instantly they began dismantling the party-child image. "Brush those curls out of her hair, and stop slapping her cheeks for color. She's okay as is. She plays the part of a hungry, beat-up street kid."

Rose was speechless with disappointment, but a job was a job. Unfortunately, it only lasted a few days, but meanwhile Rose, always on the lookout for new opportunities, had met a baker who was catering a very important celebration at Pickfair, Hollywood's version of Windsor Castle for visiting European royalty and American dignitaries, which Mary Pickford and Douglas Fairbanks had set up after their long-delayed marriage. June was to be hidden inside an enormous confection, emerge unexpectedly from it, and then perform a toe number before the cream of Hollywood society.

On the afternoon of the scheduled banquet, June broke out in red blemishes all over her body. Rose summoned the hotel doctor, who pronounced the rash a blue-ribbon case of chicken pox.

"But she can't have chicken pox!" Rose cried indignantly. "Not tonight, she can't!"

When the doctor left, Rose got out the greasepaint. "Don't you worry, lambie," she cooed. "Tradition is religion, the mail must go through, and the show must go on."

Over the greasepaint went powder, mascara, and lip rouge. Examining her handiwork by the light of the desk lamp, Rose was satisfied. "You're my little trouper, baby," she told her proudly. "No one could guess by looking at you that you've got a temperature of a hundred and three."

Dressed in her spangled tutu, a silver cap, and a tulle pompom perched on her bleached-blond curls, June crouched inside an enormous hollow meringue. On cue she lifted the top over her head, pushed it to one side, unfolded in the spotlight, and flashed into her showiest toe number, entitled "Destiny." The heat of the spot, the exertion of the pirouettes, and her own high temperature made June feel dizzy, but she carried herself through to the spectacular finale.

Mary Pickford, pretty as a princess, her long golden curls glowing against a pink chiffon dress, came forward, gathered the child into her arms, and carried her back to her table. Staring around, June realized it really was a gathering of celebrities. She recognized Harold Lloyd, Tom Mix, Bebe Daniels, and Douglas Fairbanks. Then Charlie Chaplin leaned forward holding a spoonful of ice cream temptingly to her lips.

"Have some nectar, little fairy queen," he said laughingly. But Miss Pickford intervened. "Shame on you, Charlie. She's had too many sweets already. Look at the poor darling's skin."

"Oh, honest," June burst out defensively, "these bumps on my face aren't from too many candies; I'm in the middle of having chicken pox."

After a brief but profound silence Mary Pickford lowered the child slowly to the floor. "Now run along to your mother, dear."

The evening had ended ignominiously, but Rose could take comfort in the reviews. The Los Angeles *Tribune* said, "Words positively fail one in a description of this dainty, delightful, feylike elf — this dream baby doll, the youngest toe dancer in the world."

Well, vaudeville was out there, hundreds of theaters were waiting for a talent Hollywood was not yet ready for — Baby June, the Pocket Size Pavlova. Mama Rose was relentless.

*

The Flying Johnsons were, as their name implied, a husband-and-wife aerialist team. They were touring with the Sels Floto Circus in 1917, when their only son, Frank, was born in Chicago. The elder Johnson conscientiously started training Frankie for the family act as soon as he could toddle, but was dismayed to find he exhibited an unforgivable fear of heights. Despite his mother's pleas that they wait until the baby was older to break him in, the terrified little boy was drilled every day between performances by his father, who was determined to vanquish the forbidden phobia. First a tight wire was stretched between two posts, scarcely a foot above the ground. Frankie was placed upon it and forced to walk unsteadily the entire ten-foot length. Gradually the wire was raised, first to three feet, then to six, ten, and so on.

The fear did not go away, but Frankie forced it to retreat to a secret place inside himself where it could no longer be seen or its existence even sensed by his domineering father. Meanwhile Frankie added tumbling and acrobatics to his skills. Soon he knew his father would be inviting him to climb the tall ladder to the platform at the top of the tent from which his father, his mother, and a new Italian partner whirled through their sensational routines.

But that day never came. When the circus set up for its 1922 engagement in Long Beach, California, Frankie's diminutive Italian mother was unable to go on. She collapsed in a complete nervous breakdown. A few days later the circus moved on without the Flying Johnsons. The family was stranded.

With his wife prostrate and himself untrained at anything outside his own specialty, the elder Johnson looked to dark-eyed, muscular, five-year-old Frankie as a potential source of income. Somewhere in his travels Johnson had made the acquaintance of a man named Ralph Ince, who was now a movie producer in Hollywood. He took the boy out to his old friend's studio, where he was interviewed. Ince needed a five-year-old to appear in a movie called *Judgment of the Storm*, starring Wallace Beery. Changing the boy's name to Frankie Darro, he gave him the role.

The distaff side of "Jack and Virginia Lee, Sweet Southern Singers" sat in the pit of the darkened theater providing piano accompaniment to a Rudolph Valentino movie. Gazing up at Valentino's flaring nostrils on a profile big enough to fit on Mount Rushmore, she was glad she had learned to play the piano, even though she had paid twenty-five cents a lesson and dropped out of school in the fifth grade to do it. Her accomplishment had enabled her to be on her own, earning a living selling (and playing) sheet music in the local dime store. It had also introduced her to her husband, a handsome Irish tenor, who led the community singing at the Princess Theatre in Superior, Wisconsin, where she played piano in the summer of 1914. Now they had their own theater, the New Grand, in Grand Rapids, Minnesota, and in addition to managing it and providing the piano accompaniment to the films, the couple played and sang old favorites each evening during the break between screenings. Although their real names were Frank and Ethel Gumm, both felt Jack and Virginia Lee sounded more professional.

However they billed themselves, their act was uniformly bad. Frank opened it by having Ethel sit sideways on the piano stool, facing the audience, and hold up her small hands to impress upon them the marvel of music that would flow from those tiny fingers. His tenor voice was pleasant, but their presentation was mediocre and imitative. Still, Ethel loved what she regarded as show business, even though bookings off their own stage had been on the obscure Gus Sun circuit, a mere theatrical trace meandering through the central and southern states. It was known as "the death trail" to old pros.

Three girls, Jane, Virginia, and the baby, Frances, were born to the Gumms between 1916 and 1922. Ethel taught them all to sing and dance, first as a sister team and later as a trio, and introduced them to the low-key excitement of backstage life at the New Grand. But while it was certainly a far cry from the big time, the theater was the only sprig of parsley dressing up the Gumm family's plain meat-and-potatoes existence. Frank sang in the church choir, Ethel played for school functions, the girls were interchangeable with any other three children their age in Grand Rapids. Their interests were firmly rooted in home, church, school, family, and friends.

But, almost without realizing it, Ethel was being exposed nightly to another and far more exotic way of life — the movies. She saw the Jackie Coogan films, all of them, when they played. She watched Baby Peggy, the *Our Gang* kids, winsome Philippe de Lacy, and an increasingly youthful Mary Pickford, who was now nearing thirty, yet consistently remained under twelve on the screen. Ethel also recognized in her youngest child a certain indefinable spark — part pugnacity, part fey — that was lacking in her older sisters. Life was safe in Grand Rapids; the girls were growing up as American as homespun. But Ethel was restless. Some hidden, inner force was driving her to discontent. She drummed up more bookings for the trio, straying farther and farther from the narrow horizons of Grand Rapids.

At last, in the summer of 1926, when Frances was four, Ethel persuaded Frank to take a working vacation and drive the whole family out to California. Maybe they could find a movie house in Hollywood that they could buy. Booking themselves into small-town theaters along the route, all five Gumms harmonizing "California, Here I Come!" on the open highway with a genial Frank behind the wheel, it was an unforgettable trip. But years later, when bubbly Baby Frances had become star-crossed Judy Garland, she would recall that the family was never the same after that first taste of Hollywood.

Little Edith Fellows's mother left her when she was only two and her paternal grandmother took the child to her home in Atlanta, Georgia, and raised her as her own. Edith proved a sweet-natured and pretty little girl, but she was hopelessly pigeon-toed. When Mrs. Fellows consulted a physician, he recommended dancing lessons, the various ballet positions often proving very helpful in reforming pliable young bones. Mrs. Fellows enrolled Edith in the best school she could find.

Gray-eyed Edith did very well at dancing school, so well, in fact, that when she was four she was starred in a program, a kind of one-baby show, in which she exhibited her professional achievements. She did ballet, tap-danced, and sang, her voice giving promise of becoming operatic in quality. After the show, when classmates, teachers, and relatives were gathered around to congratulate the young star, a dignified, white-haired gentleman appeared and introduced himself. He was a talent scout from Hollywood, and he had seldom seen a more genuinely gifted child than Edith. Had her grandmother ever thought of taking her to Hollywood? Mrs. Fellows felt her hands grow cold. Hollywood? That's right, the gentleman said, virtually guaranteeing Edith a screen test if her grandmother could bring her out. All he asked in exchange was a modest agent's fee of $50 for enlisting his aid, a sum that Mrs. Fellows was glad enough to pay. In return he gave her his business card and urged her to waste no time contacting him as soon as she reached Hollywood.

If Elizabeth Fellows had to dig deep for the agent's advance, where would she ever lay hands on enough cash to get herself and Edith to the Coast? Mrs. Fellows did not drive, and the train fare was quite beyond her means. Understanding her dilemma, the dancing school staff went into emergency session. How could they let this golden chance go by for darling, hard-working little Edith? Besides, it would be good publicity for the school if Edith became a famous child star and people were told where she had gotten her start. The next day the staff called on Mrs. Fellows in a body, brimming with excitement. As they handed her an envelope bulging with crisp green bills, they explained that they had all chipped in, not enough to hurt any one of them, of course, but enough at least to pay for the train fare out to Hollywood. Edith and Elizabeth Fellows responded with hugs and tears and heartfelt expressions of gratitude for southern generosity.

The train trip was a wonderful adventure for four-year-old Edith, nearly as exciting for her grandmother. Upon arrival they checked into a Hollywood Boulevard hotel, got a good night's rest, and the following morning, with Edith dressed in her best, set out for their first interview with their agent.

They were baffled by the manner in which Hollywood was laid out. The town seemed to have been thrown together without any purpose or plan. There was no downtown, uptown, or main street such as they were accustomed to. Hollywood seemed one big sprawl from the dusty-blue mountains, on whose barren slopes HOLLYWOODLAND was spelled out in giant electric-light-bulb letters, all the way to the distant surf at Santa Monica. On any given block one might find a pseudo-Spanish pink stucco mansion, a low string of white, two-story office buildings, sparkling like cake icing under the brilliant California sun, and a haphazard collection of studio stages. To make it all still more confusing, sprinkled in between these mismatched structures were vacant lots on which fennel, wild California poppies, and clouds of yellow mustard, as tall as summer corn, nodded in the gentle breeze.

It was extremely difficult for total strangers to find their way around in such bewildering surroundings, so Mrs. Fellows asked a policeman to help them out. Taking the agent's card, the officer looked long and hard at the address. "This is the number right here," he said, and then his voice trailed off. Edith would never forget the look on her grandmother's face as she said, "But officer, *right here* is — *a vacant lot!*"

Not all Hollywood mothers set out to be such. Hollywood was infamous for being a kind of wrecking yard for bad marriages and a burial ground for ailing husbands. Tuberculosis, in those days often fatal, drew many heads of families west to the sanitariums for which California was renowned. The permanent incapacity or eventual death of these husbands and fathers left countless wives and mothers stranded in the area. If one had no job skills — and the vast majority did not — one might find employment as a switchboard operator, a waitress, or as a drive-in carhop. If one had youth and a good face and figure, there was always the burlesque on Main Street. And, of course, if one had given birth to anything short of a monster, one could always try to put the kid in pictures.

In 1927, when Ray Sperry, his brother, and his parents came to Hollywood by Greyhound bus from Cincinnati, they believed they were coming to a land of plenty. Mr. Sperry had been a theater stagehand, but he was never able to crack the Hollywood studio unions. Mrs. Sperry, a former chorus girl, could not get a movie break. "You know how it is when everyone's broke," Ray recently told me as though it were an ordinary fact of life, "they start looking around to see what the kids can do."

As it turned out, Ray got on as a stand-in for child actor Freddie Bartholomew. After three years, Ray suddenly shot up several inches over Freddie's height, and his own younger brother then stepped into his shoes, serving as the young star's stand-in to the end of his career. As in so many cases in Hollywood, the kids became the breadwinners, bringing home the bacon when their parents could not.

8
Pilgrims and Strangers

Welcome to the Hotel California,
Such a lovely place (such a lovely face)
Plenty of room at the Hotel California,
Any time of year, you can find it here.

Mirrors on the ceiling,
The pink champagne on ice
And she said "We are all just prisoners here,
Of our own device."

       .   .   .

Last thing I remember I was
Running for the door,
I had to find the passage back
To the place I was before.
"Relax," said the night man,
"We are programmed to receive.
You can check out any time you like,
But you can never leave."
           — *"The Hotel California,"* 1976

HOLLYWOOD, IT WAS PRESUMED, could be as many different dream-come-true towns as there were starry-eyed newcomers with dreams — solid booking on a transfixed big time for
travel-weary hoofers like Nell Carter and the Coogans, a back-lot
replica of the vanished real West for cowboys like my father, a
better fish market for Charlotte Pickford, and the land of promise
at last for those Jewish entrepreneurs who were now migrating
there for the second time in their lives.

The town proved to be none of these things, despite the fact
that succeeding waves of invaders continued to invest it with

virtues it never possessed. A stubborn few, like my mother, refused to the bitter end to admit that Hollywood was among the least tolerant communities in America. What on the surface gave every appearance of being a benign, live-and-let-live society was in fact interwoven with a tough-fibered web of prejudice and bigotry. Paradoxically, however, it proved to be a highly impartial intolerance and sooner or later caught everyone in the motion picture industry in its invisible mesh of moral, social, religious, and racial illiberality.

The founding fathers had set the tone around the turn of the century. They were the same narrow fundamentalists who "back home" had relegated their seediest hotels to show people and, in most towns, none at all to wayfarers of color. (Two or three neighboring hamlets in Southern California's Orange Empire went so far as to post signs just inside their city limits reading: "Nigger, Don't Let the Sun Set on You Here.") They were the same crusading Christians who had contrived to shutter the nation's thriving distilleries, breweries, wineries, and saloons. Because Prohibition marked the rural Protestant's moral triumph over his urban Catholic rival, it was no secret what kind of town Hollywood's founders had in mind. Carrie Nation and Billy Sunday may not have been household gods exactly, but honored they were. And lest they be accused of singling out liquor to the neglect of other vices, throughout the 1920s local zealots preached just as strongly against dancing, swearing, acting, gambling, playing cards, and even attending movies and the theater.

Those among them who had been "sooners" in the California land rush of the 1880s had been no easier on the local Mexicans. Buying them out for a song or marrying into the already pauperized Californio aristocracy, they had conquered an important Catholic province for Yankee thrift and ingenuity. Against the local Chinese, Japanese, Filipinos, Indians, Negroes, and those few settlers quaintly referred to as "being of the Jewish persuasion," these newly minted Californians took an equally firm stand. By virtue of self-endowed membership in their own club, the first California-born "Native Sons of the Golden West" demanded preferential treatment, first rights to agriculture, real estate, jobs, and to any other prime benefits around. Obviously the master plan was to keep the barbarians out. But in every time and place there never lacks the needy farmer, householder, or widow to whom one man's dollar is as sound as the next. Betrayed by their own, the founders soon saw resort hotels, theaters, studios, stucco palaces, and other pleasure domes arise where honest barns and sober homes once stood.

Those closest to the bottom of Hollywood's complex social pyramid were the Orientals. The general attitude toward them was summed up in the working title for a D. W. Griffith classic about a rare Chinese hero who befriends a white child beaten by a cruel father: *The Chink and the Child*. Its change to *Broken Blossoms* reflected no deference to Chinese protest or pressure. Griffith merely felt audiences might not attend a movie with a "Chink" as the star, even though Caucasian Richard Barthelmess played the role with alabaster-white Lillian Gish playing the child.

The Chinese fortified themselves culturally in their own Chinatown. The Japanese had a tougher time of it. Entire families grew to old age engaged in backbreaking labor, hand-tilling thousands of as yet undesirable acres in the sweltering San Fernando Valley and the fog-ridden area around San Pedro and Wilmington. A few became prosperous produce grocers, but the vast majority were employed as gardeners. When I was growing up in Beverly Hills, Japanese was synonymous with gardener. Their little pickup trucks, the back end loaded with neatly stacked bamboo rakes and other tools, were never off the quiet streets. A few Japanese and Filipinos occupied lucrative posts as servants in the great homes of film moguls and stars,* while Negroes with impeccable references staffed most Beverly Hills mansions, including our own.

The Hollywood of the 1920s fit perfectly Saint Paul's definition of a land of itching ears. In a town whose main business was pleasure, religion was easily relegated to just another form of entertainment. Most people went to tent shows, fortunetellers, and the Angelus Temple for the same reason they frequented the faddish Hula Hut restaurant, where three times nightly the man-

---

* A small but distinguished colony of Japanese actors included Sessue Hayakawa, Yukio Aoyama, and Aoyama's small son, Arthur, a popular child actor appearing often in *The Us Bunch* comedy series.

agement titillated patrons by bombarding the palm-thatched roof with a rain of pebbles simulating a tropical monsoon — simply to be amused.

Every Saturday, visiting preachers, swamis, and spiritualists took out impressive half-page display ads in the religious section of the local newspapers, a section aptly dubbed "the racket sheet." There these sawdust-trail messiahs accorded themselves the same name-above-the-sermon star billing that movie studios reserved for the biggest names in films. Where everyone was in effect from someplace else, there were few maiden aunts, priest uncles, or Jewish mothers around to preach, scold, threaten, cajole, or shame one into keeping the traditional faith.

Torn from familiar religious moorings, these various Robinson Crusoes tried to improvise doctrinal shelters with what little cultural baggage they had salvaged from their shipwreck on California's exotic shore. Not surprisingly, the vast majority of rootless picture people eventually drifted into what some regarded as undemanding do-it-yourself sects that provided a "daily word" or "good thought" in monthly magazine form. More than one Hollywood mother of my acquaintance, having stumbled upon such a magazine just as her child's career was beginning to make progress, became a lifelong adherent to Unity or Religious Science, convinced her conversion had brought about the long-delayed success. Such earn-extra-grace-in-your-spare-time-at-home beliefs were perfect for on-the-go picture people, whose only true temple of worship was, after all, the studio.

Former vaudevillians comprised a distinct colony in early Hollywood. From 1912 until the final demise of vaudeville and big-time radio in the late 1930s, the movie town was the favored jumping-off place for acts quitting the circuits and hoping either to launch a film career or to retire in the sun. Roscoe "Fatty" Arbuckle, Marie Dressler, Stan Laurel, and a host of other former troupers were gathered at Mack Sennett's Keystone and formed the nucleus of the group. After Jackie's discovery, the Coogans joined their ranks.

Another tightly knit social unit that took root in Hollywood were the cowboys. Having established close bonds earlier in a different but common culture, they remained pretty much a closed club. Stars like Tim McCoy, Hoot Gibson and Neal Hart, who had struck it rich in Westerns, were lavish in personal gifts and loans to temporarily "gimpy" and permanently "busted up" riders who were out of work. Father's own daily handouts to such needy cowboy friends, averaging $25 to $50 a day, triggered the first quarrels that soon evolved into constant bickering between my parents.

Like the vaudevillians, the cowboys carried with them their own set of rules and values. Known and respected on the old open range as the Code of the West, it still worked well for them. But turned inside out it bristled with its own intolerances. Steeped as they were in the cavalier mentality that he who goes a-horseback into life is, by that very fact, the better man, their code gave short shrift to men on foot. Even such impressive Old West figures as Wyatt Earp and Wild Bill Hickok were looked down upon as mere "carpet knights" — dance-hall dandies and dealers for the house.

Considering that they had to work with Jewish filmmakers for the rest of their lives, it was unfortunate that the cowboys' attitude toward Jews had crystallized long before they rode into Hollywood. The only Jewish people Father and his friends had ever known in cow country either ran the local pawn shop or were peddlers. The more prosperous of the latter sold their goods off the tailgate of a mule-drawn wagon parked in the center of town. Others worked out of small pushcarts that, incredibly enough, they had propelled by hand all the way from some distant city far beyond the eastern plains. In a country where the horseman was king, these peddlers not only went on foot, they did mule's work as well.

Even as he viewed them through this clouded glass of memory, Father was intimidated by Hollywood's Jewish contingent. They were born wizards at buying, selling, and bargaining, and the property over which they were now haggling was his own three-and-a-half-year-old daughter. Her current price tag was about $300 a week. On each Baby Peggy comedy the Stern brothers expended no more than $5000, including salaries. It was then sold to Uncle Carl for $50,000, who distributed it worldwide for a gross return of between $300,000 and $500,000. Simply working backward from Universal's ledger, Father reasoned that it was criminally exploitative for anyone to reap 1000 per cent profit on someone else's services. Even $75 a week had looked rosy back when I was still young, but now that I was pushing four the full import of what six more years could mean in lost potential came home to him. Time was the crucial factor. But his prejudice prevented him from seeking or accepting the services of the men best qualified to help him — Jewish agents and financial advisers. And so Poverty Row remained the false-fronted western street where the boys in the front office always got theirs, while Father — horseman or not — was forever without the proper badge or .45 that got things done in Hollywood.

The Jewish community in Hollywood represented management in an industry that was still operating at the very lowest level of employee motivation and reward. For years actors went uncompensated for nightwork, overtime, weekends, or holidays. Anything short of heroic dedication to the needs of the studio bosses was met with threats and reprisals. Men like Carl Laemmle, the Stern brothers, and Louis B. Mayer had never been strangers to hard work — in Mayer's case, even heavy physical labor in the family junk business. Not a few possessed a firsthand acquaintance with sweatshop conditions or had done piecework in New York's steaming East Side ghetto tenements, parents and children slaving side by side in dimly lit rooms for fourteen and fifteen hours a day. While most studio heads were strongly paternalistic and even sentimental, their background tended to make them manipulative and dictatorial. They were slow to sympathize with any adult or child performer who complained of hard work, long hours, or low pay in what they saw as the comparatively sumptuous surroundings of a motion picture studio.

Management, however, was clear-eyed and coldly objective about what sold at the box office. In the 1920s the American ideal of beauty, and consequently the current fashion in film stars, was definitely not based on eastern European or Semitic standards of comeliness, male or female. Aside from Mexican spitfires, foreign heavies, and traitorous gypsies (Valentino and one or two others excepted), the preference for film stars was strictly Anglo-Saxon. Not only had the day of a Barbra Streisand not yet dawned, it was, even for Jewish producers themselves, unthinkable.

Those representing labor in the film industry had their own peculiar problems and preferences. Most stars and supporting players were motivated by a single-minded drive toward money and fame that made it possible for them to bear up under the harsh demands of management. As Hortense Powdermaker shrewdly observed, in Hollywood, property was considered far more important than men, and human values had to struggle to exist at all. Not only objects but people were evaluated in terms of how much they cost.

> In one sense the psychological situation is worse than that of slavery. In that situation, owners regarded their slaves as property, but the slaves themselves did not necessarily share this attitude. They were in bondage but they did not sell themselves to the highest bidder. In Hollywood, no master forces men to sell themselves for the duration of a contract. No one even forces people to come to Hollywood. They come of their own will and voluntarily sell their freedom to the highest buyer. Yet men who have known freedom cannot give it up without resentment and bitterness. The fact that they give it up of their own will adds ambivalence and guilt to an already difficult situation.*

When these attractive and sometimes talented young players who believed themselves chattel looked about for amusement, they discovered they had become too jaded for their former small-town pastimes. If the Hollywood social whirl of 1920 could be said to have a character of its own, it was one closely modeled after shipboard society, where so many silent film stars had found a highly flattering acceptance from a group they traditionally regarded as far above their own station in life.

Both during and after the Great War, when the Gish girls, the Janises, and the Pickford clan were shuttling back and forth between New York and Europe, transatlantic steamers were literally palaces afloat. In terms of food, comfort, furnishings, and

* Hortense Powdermaker, *Hollywood: The Dream Factory* (Boston: Little, Brown, 1950), p. 305.

personal service, first-class travel would never be so first-class again. And since getting there was half the fun, acceptance into this elegant company was indeed a social coup.

Mere entertainers and movie stars, who would have been ushered in through the back door of most upper-class mansions, now found themselves much sought after at the captain's table. Here snobbish socialites could afford to be more indulgent and democratic than at home. The idle rich placed a high premium on entertainment, and picture people entertained them — both on and off the screen. If it wasn't opening night for Elsie Janis or Irene Castle in London, it was bon voyage for Lillian and Dorothy Gish in Paris. This was the world of champagne, cablegrams, roses, and glazed fruits wherein Mary Pickford and Douglas Fairbanks found such a gratifying welcome on their headlined European honeymoon in June of 1920. Mary, who had always felt a strong distaste for vulgar things, now set about making Pickfair the land-based equivalent of these celebrity-studded, democratic shipboard soirées. Entranced at the prospect of being able to play hostess to Europe's minor nobility, the new Mrs. Fairbanks now withdrew almost entirely from the sordid details of the bargaining table, leaving it to Charlotte. Her mother still relished the fight, even though money had long since ceased to constitute the coveted prize.

Climbers like Charlotte believed in the status quo, now that they were home free. Charlotte was not about to let anyone forget that, even with her Irish brogue, her Canadian birth certificate, and her near-treasonable loyalty to the Pope, she was three times more acceptable to Hollywood's new society than any "foreign born" producer from whom she had wrung the Pickford millions. She and other factory employees were only too happy to support the Native Sons' tradition of restricting membership in hotels, country clubs, and expensive resorts. After all, what was the point of making it to the top if the top was not exclusive? At work they might be slaves. At play they were free.

As a consequence, some of the richest and most powerful men in Hollywood found themselves locked out of many spas where their pampered and highly paid employees chose to frolic. The town was invisibly divided into two distinct camps: the studio, or world of work, where management tyrannized labor, and the social world, from which management (or at least Jewish management) was arbitrarily barred. But reprisals worked both ways, and producers were not without their own lethal weapon, which they were careful to keep suspended over the heads of their workers. Driven far enough by an incalcitrant actor, or even by an intractable child star's parent, a studio boss could, by means of a few carefully placed "family phone calls," shutter every studio door in town to "that gentile" forever. It was called being blackballed from the industry, and it was one of the two worst things that could happen to an actor. The other was to be blackballed at the box office by the moviegoing public. In 1921, the latter unexpectedly forced both camps to shelve their petty differences for the sake of the industry's very survival, for scandal nearly closed down the shop.

That year Roscoe "Fatty" Arbuckle was the second highest paid comedian in films. Having just finished a new picture, he and his close friend Fred Fishback drove up to San Francisco to spend the long Labor Day weekend relaxing at the St. Francis Hotel. While Fishback drove out to the seacoast to look at some seals for a proposed location shot, Arbuckle played host to a few friends and strangers at what developed into an unplanned party in his suite. One former extra girl he had known from Hollywood got very drunk and very sick. He finally called the hotel doctor and had her moved to another room, where she could sleep it off under the care of a woman friend. The next day he took ship for the leisurely voyage back to San Pedro Harbor and Hollywood.

The following Friday night, while he was at home studying the script for his next film, his butler admitted two Los Angeles detectives. They informed him that Virginia Rappé, the girl who had become ill in his San Francisco suite, was dead and he was charged with rape and manslaughter. During Arbuckle's three trials, a loyal Fred Fishback appeared as star witness for the defense, while the Jack Coogans rallied to their old friend's support. But although Roscoe was finally acquitted, his career was sentenced to death by the moviegoing public.*

---

* For a fascinating study of the Arbuckle scandal, see David Yallop, *The Day the Laughter Stopped* (New York: St. Martin's Press, 1976).

Little Cordelia Howard, age five, as Little Eva in *Uncle Tom's Cabin*, 1853. (Lithograph after a daguerreotype by Matthew Brady.)

Lotta Crabtree as a child in the 1850s—the "fairy star" of the California mining camps.

The indomitable Mary Ann Crabtree with her son John Ashworth and Lotta, about 1879, when Lotta was the toast of two continents.

Mary Ann in her last years, around 1900.

Jenny Bierbower Janis and Little Elsie in Buffalo, New York, 1897.

The Smith family in front of their Toronto home in 1898. Mother Charlotte is at center, with Lottie on the right and Jack seated on the steps. At far left is Baby Gladys, later Mary Pickford. The two young women are unidentified relatives.

Mary Pickford and Charlotte at the height of Mary's fame as "America's Sweetheart."

Eight-year-old Baby Gladys trouping on the "kerosene circuit," around 1900.

Looking east on Sunset Boulevard, this 1921 photograph shows the studios and film laboratories that comprised Hollywood's original "Poverty Row," where Century Studio was also located.

Four-year-old Jackie Coogan with Charlie Chaplin in *The Kid* (1919), in the scene in which he cries real tears when officials threaten to take him away from the Little Tramp.

AT LEFT: Baby Peggy, age twenty months, with Brownie the Wonder Dog in *Playmates*, her first two-reel comedy for Century, in April 1920. AT RIGHT: With director Fred Fishback on the set of *The Kid Reporter*, a 1921 two-reeler.

On location at Camp Curry, Yosemite National Park, 1921. Surrounded by curious vacationers are, center, Baby Peggy and sister Louise with their father, Jack Montgomery. Seated in the right foreground is Marian Montgomery; at far right, in shirt and tie, is Century director Alf Goulding.

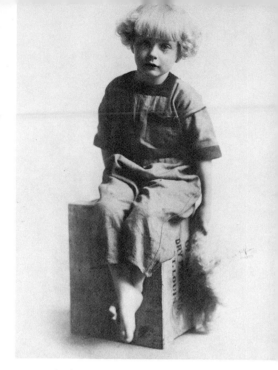

Franklin Delano Roosevelt, far left, and convention mascot Baby Peggy, holding flag and megaphone at the 1924 Democratic National Convention in Madison Square Garden — where Roosevelt's "Happy Warrior" speech won the presidential nomination for Governor Alfred E. Smith.

Two-and-a-half-year-old Baby June Hovick (later June Havoc) in a tearful scene during her Hollywood movie career in the early 1920s.

Century head Julius Stern, Baby Peggy, and censorship czar Will Hays on the set of *Hansel and Gretel*, 1922.

Mickey Rooney in an early Mickey McGuire two-reel comedy, around the mid-1920s.

Hal Roach, creator and producer of the durable *Our Gang* comedies, photographed in 1929 surrounded by Gang regulars. Left to right: Pete the Pup, Joe Cobb, "Farina" Hoskins, Harry Speer, Mary Ann Jackson, Jean Darling, and "Wheezer" Hutchins. (Photo courtesy of Richard W. Bann, reprinted from *Our Gang: The Life and Times of the Little Rascals.*)

The Parrish children—Baby Helen, Beverly, Robert, and Gordon—in a 1928 issue of the *Casting Director's Album of Screen Children*.

Twelve-year-old Dainty June (June Havoc) and her older sister Louise (Gypsy Rose Lee) during their days as vaudeville headliners in the family act in the late 1920s.

The Johnson clan, advertised as "Experienced Troupers" beneath this casting directory photo. Left to right: Seesal Anne, Payne, Dick Winslow, Cammilla, and Carmencita, with the various musical instruments they could play.

A typical full-stage (one hundred and one strong) Famous Meglin Kiddies production in the early
1930s.

Jackie Cooper starts to cry as co-star Wallace
Beery looks on apprehensively in this scene from
their 1931 screen triumph, *The Champ*.

Off-screen friends Dick Winslow and Jackie
Coogan slug it out on screen as the dude and
the country boy in MGM's 1932 production of
Tom Sawyer.

Shirley Temple and her youthful escort in *Glad Rags to Riches* (1932), an early *Baby Burlesk* two-reeler.

Shirley with James Dunn in her famed song and dance number, "Baby Take a Bow," in *Stand Up and Cheer*, 1934. In that same year, she made a grand total of nine films.

Shirley and her parents caught by a roving photographer at a Hollywood première when Shirley was the number one box office star.

Eleven-year-old Frances Gumm — soon to be Judy Garland — as she appeared when she sang for her schoolmates at Lawlor's Professional School in the spring of 1934.

Schooltime at Universal Studios in the early 1930s. FROM TOP LEFT: Helen Parrish, Dawn O'Day (Anne Shirley), studio teacher Mrs. West holding Dickie Moore and flanked by Dick Winslow. Seated in center foreground are David Durand and three unidentified child actors.

Freddie Bartholomew kisses his Aunt Cissie as they celebrate her birthday in his dressing room during the filming of *Captains Courageous* in 1936.

ABOVE: Youthful songbird Deanna Durbin in 1935 at the start of her remarkable career and Darla Hood with her mother around 1936, shortly after Darla's debut as the leading lady in *Our Gang.* BELOW: Bouncy Jane Withers in a typical buoyant pose and soulful Edith Fellows in the 1934 Paramount production of *Mrs. Wiggs of the Cabbage Patch.* (Darla Hood photo courtesy of Richard W. Bann, reprinted from *Our Gang: The Life and Times of the Little Rascals.*)

An anguished Arthur Bernstein, business manager for the Jackie Coogan Corporation, and Jackie support a grief-stricken Lillian Coogan at the funeral of her husband, killed in an auto accident in May 1935.

An exuberant Mickey Rooney, under contract to MGM, playing himself in an Andy Hardy film, 1938.

Robert Young, as the responsible and worried adult, with five-year-old Margaret O'Brien as the war orphan in MGM's 1942 hit *Journey for Margaret*. Little Margaret symbolized the child of a new time, helpless and vulnerable in a world threatened by wholesale devastation as World War II and its aftermath marked the end of the child star era.

Soon afterward, director Desmond Taylor was found mysteriously shot in his Los Angeles home. Two close friends of the dead man, film stars Mabel Normand and Mary Miles Minter, were already suspected of being drug users, and when it was revealed that Taylor dealt in morphine and cocaine, both women became poison at the box office. Next, matinee idol Walter Reid, the epitome of clean-living American manhood, was discovered to be hopelessly addicted to morphine. Six months after being committed to a sanitarium, he died in a padded cell.

Twenty-year-old Olive Thomas, the beauteous wife of Mary Pickford's brother, Jack, drank a vial of lethal liquid mercury in Paris after a night on the town. Rumors strongly linked her suicide to her own and her husband's mounting drug needs. Mary and Charlotte were numbed by the depth of these implications. Jack had liked his liquor, of course, but drugs — never!

Then the Chaplin scandal broke. Chaplin's earlier interest in twelve-year-old Lilita McMurray had suffered a brief setback after the filming of *The Kid,* when Mrs. McMurray angrily accused him of trying to seduce the girl. But after Charlie returned from his triumphant European tour their paths crossed again, and this time Chaplin seemed obsessed with her. While it was whispered that they were carrying on a clandestine affair, few in Hollywood believed the famous comedian would risk involvement with a mere child, or "San Quentin quail," as the less cultured referred to girls under eighteen. But Chaplin appeared determined to make her a star. He changed her name to Lita Grey and announced to the press that his "discovery" would play his leading lady in *The Gold Rush.* Halfway through the film Lita collapsed on the set, and another actress was rushed in to replace her. Three days later a haggard Charlie and Lita turned up mysteriously in remote Empalme, Mexico, where they were married by a local magistrate. It soon became an open secret that the child bride, who had just turned fifteen, was soon to become a mother, with Chaplin the less than happy father. This Mexican shotgun wedding did not sit at all well with the Little Tramp's fans.

Last of all, millionaire journalist William Randolph Hearst, whose newspapers had helped crucify the hapless Arbuckle during his ordeal, found himself embroiled in yet another Hollywood scandal, with murder itself the charge. On November 19, 1924, popular director Thomas Ince died mysteriously during a shipboard party on the Hearst yacht, *Oneida,* off the coast of Del Mar, California. It was well known that actress Marion Davies was the newspaper magnate's mistress, while both Charlie Chaplin and Thomas Ince had been rumored to be his rivals for her affections. Both men had been on board the *Oneida.* Soon word got around Hollywood that every member of Hearst's yacht party had received a gift of a million dollars just to keep mum about how Ince had died. When Louella Parsons, who had been among the guests on the *Oneida,* was named to a lifetime post as movie columnist for the Hearst newspapers, still more eyebrows were raised.

I can still see Mother and Father in our sun-dappled Laurel Canyon breakfast room discussing the details of the so-called Ince murder case.

"I just don't believe it was murder," Mother insisted with typical loyalty to the industry. "Hollywood is as decent as any other small town. Everyone is envious of picture people, that's all." What she said was truer than she knew.

For almost two decades the American public had been fascinated with movies and movie stars. Rivers of adulation had flowed into Hollywood's vast reservoir of popularity and good will. But also present at dangerously high levels, and unnoticed by both producers and stars, was a growing element of censure and envy. For years religious, educational, and prohibitionist groups had felt that films and the scandalous private lives of many film stars were leading American youth down the primrose path to eternal damnation. Now, as scandal crowned scandal, the national mood toward Hollywood stars turned alarmingly mean. Even Goody Two-shoes Mary Pickford had her divorce from Owen Moore and her second marriage to Fairbanks held up to the cruel light of the gospel.

At last the pressure of public indignation burst and sent a torrential flood of damning letters, sermons, and massive box-office boycotts down upon the unsuspecting industry. Outraged members of women's clubs and church groups and other crusading moralists rose up as one. The motion picture business was the woman taken in adultery, and everyone wanted to cast the first stone. Studio heads, producers, directors, stars, their bankers and lawyers, were locked in emergency sessions behind closed doors. How could they save the industry from the wrath of the public? How could they whitewash each other and their town?

If virtue had come in spray cans, Hollywood would have cornered the market during those black, scandal-ridden days. Lacking such a moral deodorant, the next best thing was to brandish some well-known and well-loved child star whose presence might be capable of purifying the air. As soon as he was delivered from the dock, Roscoe Arbuckle was photographed with Jackie Coogan, shown hugging him like the good friend — and good man — he undoubtedly was. Immediately after the desperate industry named Will Hays as its own self-appointed censorship czar, he, too, was duly photographed with Jackie. Next, Hays paid a highly publicized visit to my set at Century, where the still man was careful to snap us together with Julius Stern, the three of us holding hands.

To launder its image further, the Hollywood Chamber of Commerce judiciously rushed me aboard their flower-decked entry in Pasadena's annual Rose Parade. On the float I shared honors with the irreproachable Roman Catholic actress May McAvoy (just back from an audience with the Pope) and a recent Better Babies contest winner, four-year-old Billy Lord, whose private life was also above suspicion. But, as cowboy star Tim McCoy recounted it to me many years later, the Rose Parade was really a second choice. "Originally the Chamber of Commerce had planned to stage an impressive parade of virgins down Hollywood Boulevard, as a show of moral strength," so the classic story went, "but it had to be called off at the last minute because May McAvoy came down with the flu and Baby Peggy refused to march alone!"

While nearly everyone in Hollywood had come from someplace else and the various groups dealt with each other from widely divergent backgrounds and viewpoints, the scandals of the 1920s welded them into a mutually protective body. For decades thereafter studio heads felt justified in dictating to their major stars who and when they might date or marry. As much pressure as possible was later brought to bear on such youthful stars as

Mickey Rooney, Judy Garland, and Elizabeth Taylor to steer clear of romantic entanglements that could catapult them from childhood to maturity. The saving innocence of children remained morally essential to the industry as long as the star system prevailed.

9
The Child's-Eye View

Happy families are all alike: every unhappy family is unhappy in its own way.

> — Leo Tolstoy,
> *Anna Karenina*, 1873

WHILE SERVING AS A SYMBOL of purity for the motion picture industry and a pharos of hope for aspiring movie mothers everywhere, Baby Peggy was having serious problems keeping her own beacon lit. Fortunately I was healthy and endowed with a seemingly bottomless supply of energy, but (Mother's published protestations to the contrary) the work I did *was* demanding and the hours were long. As I was not yet of school age, the four hours usually set aside by law for movie children to study on the set did not apply to me. Except for periodic visits to the downtown Office of Child Welfare to keep my work permit current by checking my eyesight, my hearing, and being declared free of tuberculosis, I never saw a health or welfare worker. I existed in a state of perpetual motion.

A typical day would start out with the gag man dreaming up a comic bit of business built around a manhole at Sunset and Vine, where a top-hatted embodiment of pomposity and authority was deflated by a combination of nature and a calculating child. From there the gag man's fertile wit would lead us to another sequence, perhaps over at Westlake Park, where the turtledoves cooed in the palms and passersby maneuvered themselves into the background so they could wave at the folks back home from the screen. Later we might drift to Hollywood Boulevard, where decorous retirees and marveling tourists crowded the veranda of the Hollywood Hotel to watch us shoot our scenes. At the end of a long day we would troop back to the first manhole for a wrap-up shot and then home to Century, lugging our cameras and a million dollars' worth of laughs in a couple of tins of film. In one sense I loved it; in another I was unbelievably overextended.

I was purposely surrounded by actors, animals, and sets that would accentuate my smallness. Nineteen-year-old Jack Earle, who later became a famous circus giant, was already close to his record eight feet six inches when he worked with me in some forty Baby Peggy comedies. Blanche Payson, a strapping six-foot-four, two-hundred-and-fifty-pound titaness, was a former Los Angeles policewoman whom Mack Sennett had hired to chaperone his bevy of luscious but empty-headed bathing beauties. Despairing of her assignment to keep the Keystone harem virgin, Blanche heeded an offer from Julius to lend her Amazonian presence to my films. Locations were also selected that would dwarf me further still.

In addition to work, there were constant product endorsements, publicity stills, home layouts for fan magazines and interviews, some of which were bewildering to a four-year-old.

> Baby Peggy received me with gravity: a gravity that could be no more impressively shown by my future pallbearers . . . she is the queen complete.
>   . . . "And now," I begged, "just answer me one question. What do you want to be when you grow up — an actress?"
>   She shook her head solemnly.
>   "No," she said gravely, "I want to be a lady."
>   "Hmmm," I said thoughtfully, glancing edgewise at her mother who seemed to be a little alarmed, "and can't you be both?"
>   "I'm afraid," said Peggy, twisting the corner of her jacket, "I'm afraid I'm not big enough." *

Most distressing of all, there was trouble at home. My youthful parents had begun quarreling almost nightly. I loved them both, but in quite different ways. Toward Mother I was protective,

* Willis Goldbeck, "Seen But Not Heard," *Motion Picture Classic*, October 1922.

almost as if she were the child and I the parent. Still, I was proud of her beauty and style, and pleased that people unfailingly marveled that such a "slip of a girl" could be the mother of two children. Father was the almighty in my otherwise godless world. His word was law, his judgments always fair. For all I knew he could have created the universe. Our working relationship was based on male camaraderie and restraint, both highly prized values on the range. Praise was needless and approval conveyed more by gesture and glance than words, a fact that caused casual observers on my set to think him too severe. I would have been embarrassed by a public display of emotion. At home both Louise and I kissed our parents good morning and good night; otherwise we were not a kissing family. Consequently, I was a warm and affectionate child, but decidedly undemonstrative.

Hearing them quarrel worried me, because at the studio I was accustomed to doing things to solve problems, and in this situation there seemed nothing I could do. What made it still more confusing was that their quarrels were most often about me — or, to be more specific, about my money: how Father was spending it, how he should have seen that I earned more, what he did and did not do properly at the outset of my career. On his part, he was insanely jealous. He accused Mother of being flirtatious at parties and drinking too much.

My distress took the form of a vivid and frightening dream: our house was on fire, and Mother, Father, and Louise were all trapped inside. Suddenly my helplessness vanished, for a tiny toy fire engine miraculously appeared, and when I pressed the button it poured out torrents of water and extinguished the flames. Then, one by one, with tremendous effort, I carried them all out to safety. It was so real that I was still shaking when I awoke. When I told my parents what I had dreamed, they just laughed and said it was really a very funny dream about a toy fire engine, and would I like them to buy me one? (At that time no average parent, least of all my own, would have believed that a child of four could possibly be suffering psychological or emotional frustrations. How-to books on child rearing were still far in the future, and I doubt if either of my parents had even heard of Dr. Freud.)

Louise was a sensitive child. Two and a half years older than I, she had been Father's admitted favorite, even after I was born. But once I started in movies, he and I were inseparable, and there was no way she could compete or win back his full attention. Still, she tried; she labored over piano and took ballet. Mother was careful to plan big parties for her every birthday. But the wounds went deep and these were only surface remedies. Once or twice, when people were visiting and the talk turned to what really made a child star tick, Father brought Louise into the living room in an effort to prove that she was just as talented as I and that obedience was the real secret. But poor Louise was born with stage fright. Being the center of attention sent her into a panic, and she usually fled the room in tears before Father could demonstrate his point. After a few such tries he gave up on her, and she felt even more rejected than before.

While Louise sat by the fire, I toured the realm. Virtually every night I was out on some fund-raising promotion, selling dolls for crippled children, appearing on behalf of the Motion Picture Relief Fund, attending parties, premières, previews, rodeos, and horse shows. And as these duties proliferated I automatically developed an almost queenly sense of duty toward the public. One did not just romp through such obligatory state occasions, however tedious they might be. One presided. Realizing that Louise felt left out (even though I often envied her being able to stay at home and play), I was careful to ask for a second balloon or party favor to bring back to her. While she knew the gesture was sincere, she nevertheless felt patronized. Reporters rarely referred to her as anything except "Baby Peggy's little sister," which galled her on two counts.

By 1922 Mother was no longer the shy young bride from Lancaster, Wisconsin. Her long hair was permanented and bobbed, she wore lip rouge and powder, her heels were high and her silk hose sheer. Her almost bosomless, pencil-thin figure was perfect for the shapeless styles of the day. She bought the most expensive French perfume, carried a chic "swagger stick" when she shopped along fashionable Hollywood Boulevard, and owned a closet full of lovely gowns, fur pieces, and evening wraps. She lived in a palatial home, appropriately decorated with Chinese rugs, Spanish shawls, and Maxfield Parrish prints. Her staff of servants included a cook, two maids, a Japanese gardener, a chauffeur, her own Pierce-Arrow, a family dressmaker, a live-in governess for the children, and a piano teacher for Louise. Although she declined cigarettes, she took to drinking, dancing, and partying as if born for good times, much to Father's alarm.

Father, now thirty-one, owned several expensive saddle horses. He sported the best set of golf clubs money could buy and held expensive memberships in the swankest country clubs. His wardrobe included golf togs and tuxedos and a dozen pure silk monogrammed shirts. He prided himself on importing the finest liquor that could be bootlegged out of Tijuana and was a charming, earthy host who made every evening memorable with his colorfully told Western tales. He invested heavily in insurance policies on his own life because he felt it was an absolutely sound investment. He feared he would die young, plagued as he was with malaria, which he had picked up while riding California's boggy San Joaquin River bottoms. He also suffered from chronic stomach trouble (which a modern physician might diagnose as psychosomatic, from deep-seated anxiety and insecurity). From time to time he went on the wagon until he convinced himself that White Rock water was no kinder to his ulcer than good Scotch.

His bookcase was lined with the novels of Zane Grey and James Oliver Curwood, and his smoking table held a red leatherbound set of the *Complete Works* of Robert W. Service. Framed and hanging in a prominent place in the entry hall, as though he wished to make a statement about himself to all who entered his home, were two poems that embodied what he regarded quite simply as his credo. One was Joaquin Miller's "Out Where the West Begins"; the other, Rudyard Kipling's advice to his son on what makes a man, "If."

Surprisingly, considering the disparity of their backgrounds, the Coogans and the Montgomerys struck up an off-screen friendship. Possibly they felt they had as much in common as most people in Hollywood. Whatever prompted it, the friendship was amiable, enduring, but never very deep.

Vaudeville had provided Jack Coogan with a recognized historical model for child star and parent sharing the limelight. (Father, of course, had no such precedent to justify his psychologically distressing relationship with me.) Jack Coogan's friends were veteran troupers who daily reinforced the former hoofer's jaunty illusion that it was still his act and Jackie was merely doing his usual small turn.

One for whom this fantasy was more difficult to support was Lillian Coogan. While she dressed in furs and jewels and lived in the house that Jackie's millions built, most of the time she felt like someone out of a job. Jackie and his father were away at the studio every day; her husband wrote many of Jackie's scripts; he handled the money, arranged the contracts, and in general ran the show. The one-time Baby Lillian, who had grown up in the spotlight, nurtured by recognition and applause, had been retired to the wings. Her primary function was to appear, as fashionably gowned as her increasingly stout figure would permit, at public events that focused on Jackie. She had ceased to be someone in her own right, was no longer considered the other half of the act, and was only rarely referred to as her husband's wife. She had become strictly Jackie Coogan's mother.

Father was being threatened with an even more critical loss of identity. His friends were not show people but cowboys, individualists who measured a man according to his independence, courage, and self-respect. In order to create an image he could live with, Father gradually evolved a viewpoint that sought to explain his conflicts to himself and his critics. This philosophy took the form of a seemingly impromptu speech, delivered in private conversation or more often from a platform or stage. Its burden was that Baby Peggy was *not* a genius, not even an exceptionally talented child. No, all that really set her apart was her ability to take direction and do exactly what she was told. He himself had trained her from babyhood, he directed her in her films, and he knew that any ordinary child could do the same with similar direction.

This thesis not only justified his otherwise unacceptable position of dependence upon me, but it made both my talent and my performance contingent upon his indispensable dominance over my career. It was also a rather flattering reflection upon his strong will and ability to inspire and command. It was all he had to bolster his ego and help it withstand what proved to be a lifelong siege.

While reporters never referred unkindly to the Coogans' start as hoofers or Father's cowpunching days, it was a point of interest to all that two such remarkable children had sprung from such truly humble stock. Being the parents of child stars had transformed these two simplehearted, sketchily educated couples into elegantly dressed celebrities who were always in the public eye. But even more was asked of them. As regents of filmdom's crown prince and princess, they were expected to understand and expound the fine points of child rearing and child psychology. At interviews they must display as much composure and diplomacy as monarchs holding court while retaining the unspoiled simplicity of peasants and the humility of saints. Unfortunately, all of their finest qualities, which in another circumstance might have set them apart as attractive, exceptional individuals, were viewed only through the reducing glass of their relationship to a performing child, a glass that cruelly sharpened their hard edges even as it diminished their stature.

Jack Coogan and Father were equally jealous and fearful of letting outsiders manage their wealth. They also were of one mind that Jackie and Peggy were unique: they must not be photographed together, much less appear in the same movie. While our forerunners, Baby Marie Osborne, Wesley Barry, the Fox Kiddies and others were packaged and marketed as the kids next door, we, like Pickford, Garbo, and Gilbert, were "personality stars." Granted, it had taken some dramatic and comic talent to get us where we were, but what kept us there was that special ingredient — star quality. Jackie's glorious eyes and his spiritual qualities Jackie Cooganized every waif he ever played. Whether I was playing Little Red Riding Hood or the Sheik, I, too, was never anyone else but Baby Peggy. The suggeston that Jackie and I costar in a juvenile version of *Romeo and Juliet* brought cold stares from both fathers, although when reporters implied that we were secretly betrothed, as in some old-world alliance between powerful families, both Jacks beamed. But lying just beneath the surface friendship was an unspoken sense of competition between the two families that manifested itself in a surprising way.

One afternoon Jackie and I and our parents attended a première at Grauman's Egyptian Theater. We signed autographs and performed our usual public function of modestly murmuring thanks to gushing fans who found us darling, cute, adorable, and sweet.

Afterward, both families retired across the street to the film colony's fashionable Montmartre Café on Hollywood Boulevard to enjoy a belated lunch. As usual, the popular place was crowded, and as there was no table large enough to accommodate us together, the Coogans were seated inside while Father, Mother, and I were shown to a second table outside on the bright blue balcony. A few moments later, as we were waiting to be served, I glanced up and saw a very troubled-looking Jackie striding toward us. He was eight and dressed in a sailor suit. I was almost four. I had always considered us friends, but something in his manner put me off. He walked right up to me and, looking me straight in the eye, he banged his small fist on the white tablecloth and said in his clear, precise diction: *"I am too, younger than you!"* Having delivered this ultimatum, he turned and marched back inside.

I blinked in surprise, unable to grasp the import of what he had said. My parents were nonplussed. But as I grew older I realized that being the *youngest* child star might be as important as being the *first* and the *richest*. It was a precarious pedestal to occupy at best. Overhearing from adults that Baby Peggy was younger and nearly as rich had no doubt made him feel threatened. My parents later laughed off the incident, but Jackie and I were never really close again.

One of Century's most gifted and innovative directors was Australian-born Alf Goulding. Alf had grown up as a kid performer himself, touring the outback first with his own family's act and later with the Pollard clan. Snub Pollard, who became one of Hal Roach's comedy stars, teamed up with Alf and together they came to America. Now a widower with a handsome six-year-old son, Alf had problems trying to care for the boy and work too. He solved this dilemma by bringing little Alfie to the studio and putting him to work as my leading man.

Thanks to his own professional childhood, Goulding had a

keen sense of comedy potential in children. He taught me how to hold a beribboned monocle in one eye and keep it in place even while being held upside down and soundly shaken by towering Blanche Payson. It was he who created some of my finest parodies of classic films, and one day he came up with the idea of satirizing *The Girl of the Golden West* and *The Squaw Man* in a single two-reeler. I was to play a Canadian mounted police officer as well as the bedraggled half-breed woman trying to scrounge an existence alone in a shack in the Sierra. Even Julius agreed that this story deserved a better location than Griffith Park. Nothing would do but that we shoot it in Yosemite, against the towering granite walls and waterfalls of my infancy.

Less than three years earlier, Father had served as a lowly ranger in Yosemite, living in a tent with his wife and two babies. Still earlier, he had worked as a stage driver for old Dave Curry, who ran Camp Curry. Father and Curry had disagreed violently over tourist pickup and delivery procedures, and the two men had parted in anger. Now, however, the one-time fractious driver and humble ranger was returning in triumph, a near-millionaire, father of a world-famous child star and self-styled guide behind her "genius." Curry, elated over the fat rental fees Century would be paying him for putting the company up in his log cabins, proved only too eager to bury the hatchet, and Father was quick to agree. After all, it was easy for Father to be magnanimous under such deeply gratifying circumstances, even though difficult not to gloat over his former adversaries.

The film went well. Jack Earle played some sort of mountain giant; Louise and Mother came along, and so did little Alfie, whose doting father had given him his own play camera, a perfect replica of the real one. Throughout our stay he continued to grind away at the toy crank, convinced he was really filming every scene for his dad. Then, late one afternoon, Dave Curry asked Father if I would appear at the entertainment he staged each evening for the campground guests.

I was an old hand at personal appearances. I had made several on the stage of the Million Dollar Theater in Los Angeles and had never known stage fright. But something about this night was different. Above everything else, my head hurt from having my hair, which was normally worn straight, tightly screwed into kid curlers and tied in calico rags for my part as the hapless squaw. There wasn't time after work and dinner to change before the appearance, so I went on in costume. Father and I strode out together onto the small stage, which faced a natural amphitheater seating perhaps three hundred people. The air was tangy with the scent of pine and the night hummed with the high, sweet ring of silence.

Father launched into his short preamble, the speech about Peggy not being a genius but an ordinary little girl whose only difference from your own or any other child is that she is obedient and does exactly what she is told. To demonstrate his point, he would now put me through some of the usual pantomime required in an average day at the studio. Delight, surprise, anger, laughter, tears — each expression a Baby Peggy trademark. At last came the final command: "Cry!"

Tears were always on tap inside of me. I never used glycerine on the set, as some grown-up actors had to do, and I realized this was an accomplishment in which one could take a justifiable professional pride. I never had to be tricked into producing tears, as Jackie was on the set of *The Kid* or other children I had seen, whose parents deliberately lied to them, saying their pet dog had been run over and killed. I did not even have to think of anything sad. But tears did take more concentration and effort than any of the other emotions. And tonight my head really hurt, and somehow I simply didn't feel up to the effort it would take to prime that mysterious inner pump.

Once again came the familiar command: "Cry!" As though I were seeing Father for the very first time in my life, I looked all the way up from my two feet four inches to his six-foot-two. For some reason, there in Yosemite, he didn't seem as tall as he did back in Hollywood.

"I won't!" came the bell-like reply.

At first I thought someone else had said it, and then I realized it must have been me. *"I won't!"* seemed to ricochet in everwidening echoes from every granite cliff and wall in the valley. Father turned ashen. If I had planned it, I could not have chosen a time and a place where his pride was more vulnerable or his humiliation more complete.

"What did you say?" he asked in a voice husky with hurt and disbelief.

Never had anything given me such a sense of satisfaction and power as those two words. As if to savor their sweetness again, I repeated, loud and clear, "I won't!"

In a single gesture, Father picked me up, turned me over his knee, and paddled me soundly with his open palm while three hundred spectators looked on in shocked silence. Setting me back down on my feet, he leaned over and in a whisper warned me not to shed a tear or I would get more of the same.

"Laugh!" came the next command.

Fighting back the tears, I laughed.

10
The Merchants of Childhood

Public adoration is the greatest thing in the world.
— Jackie Coogan, in the New York
Herald Tribune, January 30, 1958

WHILE ADULT PERFORMERS could voluntarily place themselves on the movie capital's slave block, Hollywood's children were given no such option. Too young to vend the product, which they soon discovered was themselves, they constituted a commodity in which only grownups dealt. Marketed by agents, sold by their parents, and purchased by studios, they were often repriced and repackaged before being retailed to the public at large. Then, in the front office, the real bartering began. Studios excelled at such sophisticated merchandising techniques as publicity handouts, studio portraits, personal appearance tours, star interviews, and negotiation of rights and royalties for the endorsement of selected products. Producers also loaned their contract child stars out to other studios for as much as three times what they were receiving on the home lot. (Not a penny of such loan-out profits was passed on to either parent or child.)

Although the child star business was a very new line to be in, it opened up a wide choice of jobs for many otherwise unskilled workers, and it grew with remarkable speed. Speed was, in fact, the name of the game. Parents, agents, producers, business managers, and a host of lesser hangers-on were all engaged in a desperate race to keep ahead of their meal ticket's inexorable march from cuddly infant to graceless adolescent. These parasitic hucksters proved resourceful in devising clever ways to thwart the growth of their host plant even while forcing it to flower prematurely. Birth dates were quietly set forward a year or two and earlier biographies quashed. The tyke was further stunted by the adult imposition of perennially childish mannerisms, hair styles, dress, and, of course, screen roles.

Still, despite every delaying tactic, the inevitable day arrived when all concerned must reluctantly celebrate the rites of puberty and be forced off the gravy train at last. At this point, however, the more resourceful child merchants merely turned to another gifted tot. Tying themselves to a rising new skyrocket enabled them to make the entire child star trip a second or even a third time. Hal Roach was a master at the game. So, too, were Sol Lesser and Arthur Bernstein.

Hal Roach, it was said, loved children. He also admired their independence, inventiveness, and collective spunk in the face of parental attempts to restrain or frustrate their spontaneous creativity. The idea for *Our Gang* was born one day when Roach accidentally eavesdropped on a band of typical neighborhood kids playing around a lumber pile near the studio. Struck by their refreshing naturalness, as opposed to the primped and powdered prettiness of most movie children, he set out to capture the essence of American childhood on film and sell it back to millions of moviegoing parents and children.

Because of the indwelling presence of *Our Gang*, the ivy-covered Hal Roach Studio in Culver City became a national shrine, to which thousands of mothers came on pilgrimage every year. But it was a family fiefdom as well. Hal Roach owned the studio and produced his own films, having launched such resoundingly successful talents as Harold Lloyd, Snub Pollard, Charlie Chase, and Laurel and Hardy. His brother Jack worked as cameraman and doubled as talent and location scout. Jack's two little daughters worked extra in *Our Gang* and enjoyed the run of their uncle's studio. When Hal and Jack brought their mother out from the East and offered to build her a house in Hollywood, the matriarch said she wanted to live in the thick of things. By that she meant right on the Hal Roach lot, and so it was done. Mother Roach had her meals sent in from the studio commissary, she amused herself watching movies being made and rushes being run, and she was so content with the good life she delayed departing it until her ninetieth year.

In typical Roach fashion, the original members of the Gang were children picked up within the studio family. Blond, brown-eyed Mary Kornman was the still photographer's daughter, while Mickey Daniels was her childhood friend and neighbor. Sunshine Sammy was already working on the lot, and Johnny Downs had only to be pulled out of another Roach series starring Charlie Chase. Such outsiders as Jean Darling and Mary Ann Jackson lived no farther away than Glendale and Santa Monica. But once the Gang's success was established, applicants came from every state in the union hoping to win membership and fame.

Over the seventeen years that Roach kept such records, no less than 140,000 children were interviewed by his assistants. Of these, a mere 176 appeared in an *Our Gang* comedy, and only 41 were placed under contract at salaries ranging from $37.50 to $75.00 a week. Impossible as it seems, the hard-to-miss comic talents of Mickey Rooney were passed over in the winnowing process, while the richly gifted and persistent Shirley Temple was turned away several times by an equally blind recruiter. Still, Roach did provide a valuable proving ground for such indefatigable child professionals as Edith Fellows, Marcia Mae Jones, Helen Parrish and Darryl Hickman.

Though surfeited with applicants, Roach kept his brother Jack busy on the road setting up Saturday matinee talent contests in theaters across the country. He also continued to run his printed appeals for talented children in city and small-town papers, more as a means of keeping *Our Gang* before the public eye than for enlisting new members. As one set of youngsters outgrew their roles, they were replaced by others, who were literally waiting just outside the front office to step into their shoes and pick up their paychecks.

Roach's biggest loan-out bonanza was durable Spanky McFarland. In a single year in the 1930s, when little Spanky was at the peak of his fame, he appeared in only six *Gang* comedies instead of the usual twelve because Roach had him out on loan to RKO, Paramount, and Warner Brothers for major films. With the fat fees he was receiving for Spanky's services, Roach could hardly afford to use him at home.

Jackie Cooper was another Hal Roach find who proved a windfall to his discoverer. Jackie's parents were vaudevillians, but when the boy was two his father disappeared. (After seven years Mrs. Cooper had him legally declared dead.) Left in the care of his grandmother while his mother toured, three-year-old Jackie was soon making the rounds of casting offices and landing occasional extra jobs to augment his grandmother's earnings from the same source. When he was seven, an alert Hal Roach scout spotted and hired him for a 1929 *Our Gang* comedy. A year later Paramount Pictures selected him to play the lead in *Skippy*, a movie version of Percy Crosby's famous comic-strip character. Roach, who had Jackie under contract, was happy to oblige Paramount with the loan of his fifty-dollar-a-week player. In 1931, following the enormous success of *Skippy*, Jackie's contract was purchased by MGM for a flat $150,000. Jackie's salary rose to $1100 a week, and by the time he was terminated by Louis B. Mayer in 1937, his movie earnings totaled $600,000. But of course he had worked hard for it over six long years, while Roach had collected his Jackie Cooper income quite effortlessly.

Even while they slept, the children of *Our Gang* enriched their creator, earning royalties from those products on which their names, faces, and endorsements appeared. Scores of items bore the members' million-dollar stamp of approval: lunch boxes, coloring books, clothes, shoes, balloons, roller skates, and gum, to name only a few. The Kellogg Corporation and Hal Roach entered into a mutually profitable agreement whereby Kellogg blanketed the country with five thousand copies of a twenty-four-sheet poster for billboards and for the ends and sides of trolleys, subways, and elevated trains. The add — "*Our Gang* peps up with Pep, the peppy cereal food" — also appeared in such diverse magazines as *Photoplay*, *Liberty*, *Boy's Life*, and *Cosmopolitan*. As *Film Daily* pointed out to exhibitors, all a theater owner had to do to turn this nationwide campaign into a free ride was to arrange with his local newspaper to add the words: "See the *Our Gang* kids now at the ——— Theater in their latest comedy." Cash registers in both grocery stores and box offices played an equally merry tune. None of the Gang, however, received a share of the take.*

Such regulars of the series as Mary Kornman, Jean Darling, Peggy Eames, Mickey Daniels, and Johnny Downs also took to the road in vaudeville, playing "in person" those same towns and cities already saturated with Kellogg advertisements. Look-alike contests at Saturday matinees provided local youngsters and their parents with still another irresistible *Our Gang* theater attraction.

However, the same four dozen or so hard-working children who became a cherished part of everyone else's normal childhood sacrificed a great part of their own in the process. And the man for whom they made a fortune seemed oddly unaware of the price the real Gang kids had paid for his twenty-odd-year festival of fun.

But Roach was not alone in merchandising childhood. Jack Coogan, who bragged in print that his seven-year-old son's investments in real estate and oil wells totaled $1,200,000, was quick to point out the additional value of endorsements. Jackie earned fifty cents on each Jackie Coogan coaster sold and seven cents on every Jackie Coogan cap. In addition there were Jackie Coogan dolls, statuettes, books, and clothing of every sort.

"But we seldom refer to money before him," the little star's father was quick to explain to every curious reporter. "He has almost no appreciation of the fortune he has earned." Shortly after signing his first million-dollar contract, a family friend teasingly asked Jackie what he would take for it, whereupon Jackie replied in all earnestness, "Will you give me a dollar and a quarter in cash? I need that to get a new pair of roller skates."

Jackie's first picture following *The Kid* was *Peck's Bad Boy*, produced by a small, independent filmmaker. When the film was half-completed, Jackie, his father, and a script girl were involved in a serious auto collision on the way to the studio. Coogan and the girl received minor injuries, but Jackie suffered a double basal fracture, his head split in five places. Rushed to the nearest hospital, he was pronounced dead on arrival. Like Mark Twain's death, his obituary proved to be considerably exaggerated, but

* Leonard Maltin and Richard W. Bann, *Our Gang, The Life and Times of the Little Rascals* (New York: Crown, 1977).

while he recovered the independent producer went broke, forcing Coogan to seriously rethink Jackie's silver-lined future. The former druggist's son from Syracuse now began talking about "owning the store." His lawyers assured him it was the only smart thing to do. Pooling the $5000 bonus that Chaplin had given him for *The Kid* with the $5000 weekly salary Jackie had been paid for *Peck's Bad Boy,* Coogan set up Jackie Coogan Productions, incorporating it for $60,000. When Jackie was again well enough to work, they scrapped the earlier footage and began the film again, this time with Sol Lesser in charge of production.

Sol Lesser was something of an anomaly among Hollywood moguls. Although he sprang from Jewish stock, he was that rarity in their ranks, a native American and a Westerner, born in Spokane, Washington, and raised in San Francisco, where he owned his own theater by the time he was fifteen. In 1919, already versed in the intricacies of film distribution and the Byzantine politics of exhibitors, he moved to Hollywood, where at thirty he established himself as an independent producer. Lesser was one of the first men in the industry to recognize that, even though a child star's career was necessarily brief, a great deal more money could be extracted from those few years than might be surmised. In Jack Coogan he found a man as eager as he to make hay while the sun shone.

Released in 1921, *Peck's Bad Boy* established Jackie as a major star in his own right. A year later, Lesser presented him in *Oliver Twist* as "the greatest boy actor in the world." That same year he was rushed through two more features, *My Boy* and *Trouble,* both original screenplays from the pen of Jack Coogan, Sr. In 1923 *Daddy* and *Circus Days,* two more saccharine films, were ground out by Lesser for First National, but weak and repetitious stories were beginning to undermine Jackie's popularity. Even Chaplin was sharply critical of these later films. "I don't like to see a child in scenes of emotion, weeping over deathbeds and such," sniffed the architect of the workhouse scene in *The Kid.* "A child should be joyous . . . joyous, sunny and natural."

Jackie's career was at a dangerous impasse; so was mine. Earlier in 1922 Father had finally laid his conflict with the Stern brothers squarely before Uncle Carl. It was a tradition at Universal that anyone who had a complaint could go over the head of even a close Laemmle relative and be assured a fair and unbiased hearing. Uncle Carl studied the Baby Peggy problem. He felt the day of the two-reeler featuring a single comic was over. He would prefer to bring "the baby" up from Poverty Row comedies to full-length features. He had been watching Coogan score at the box office as a woeful waif and believed Baby Peggy was every bit as good at looking lost. "To be taken seriously," he said, "a child star should make you cry."

I was never told the full details of the judgment handed down by Uncle Carl, but it satisfied everyone concerned. My salary soared to $10,000 a week, one of the highest ever paid a child star up to that time (although for a brief period Jackie earned $22,500). Overnight our whole world changed.

"Look Daddy, a window!" I exclaimed, clapping my hands in delight as we were shown my spacious Universal dressing room. Besides the miraculous window, there was scaled-down furniture and a soft bed on which to take my naps. A small dressing room on wheels and my own quartet of musicians, to play such "cry music" as "Roses of Picardy" and "My Buddy," were also provided for me on the set.

Uncle Carl starred me first in an all-American melodrama, *The Darling of New York*. Directed by King Baggott, it focused on the trials and triumphs of an Italian immigrant child and won me a host of new fans, both among those who had already passed through Ellis Island and those abroad who planned to do so. To Uncle Carl's immense satisfaction, I made him cry. Two more major films followed this first Universal success.

Every afternoon I viewed the uncut rushes with the director and sometimes with Uncle Carl himself. During these sessions I began to study my screen performances and listen closely to the comments and suggestions of my coworkers. I was no longer working with chickens and dogs and chimps, but with veterans of the legitimate stage — Sheldon Lewis, Gladys Brockwell, Lionel Belmore and Theodore Roberts, the latter playing Moses in Cecil B. De Mille's *Ten Commandments* the same year he worked with me.

Now, too, Baby Peggy products flooded the market, and royalties were pouring in. Two bisque-headed Baby Peggy dolls with real hair and eyes that closed were produced by Amberg of Germany, both a serious and a smiling version. There were also endorsements for American Caramel, Orange Crush, and other sweet products forbidden to me. Prospering, Father grew increasingly concerned over his inability to control the gusher. My salary, after all, was a drop in the bucket compared to what Universal was making off of me. He talked with Jack Coogan and Coogan's friend Arthur Bernstein about setting up a Baby Peggy Corporation. He hired two or three business managers. One persuaded him to invest $50,000 in a beanfield south of Santa Monica Boulevard called the Miracle Mile. Shortly after, another advised him to get his money out and sink it instead in a gold mine in the Mojave Desert. He prudently withdrew his share from what would become the Wilshire district; two years later, the man who took his place made $2 million on the deal. The gold mine proved rich in worthless mica.

In an era when only the deserving rich were entitled to drive a rich man's car, the difference between a Cadillac and a Ford was painfully visible to the naked eye. Hollywood royalty was not expected to tool around town in a farmboy's car any more than actresses were expected to attend a world première in housedress and tennis shoes. Studio heads as well as fans demanded that stars live up to their station, and one way of measuring status was by the distance between the ornamental nickel-plated radiator cap and the wire-wheeled spare tire on the rear trunk of one's limousine.

As a consequence, we went through several Packards and Pierce-Arrows before Father finally became the proud owner of the 1920s' equivalent of what his grandfather back in Tipperary had called "a smart rig." It was a fire engine red, custom-made Dusenberg, with black wire wheels, whitewall tires, tonneau, black leather upholstery, and just about every other deluxe extra the jubilant salesman could get the plant to tack on. The final price tag was in the neighborhood of $30,000. But there was nothing so special about that in Hollywood. Tom Mix sported a Rolls. The Coogans had two, and they even owned the Rolls-Royce dealership in town. The Dusenberg simply reinforced Father's battered ego and gave him an identity. He was sick of being introduced as Baby Peggy's father or, even more galling, Mr. Baby Peggy.

Still, he considered himself anything but self-indulgent. Even Marian said he was generous to a fault, especially to the cowboy friends she labeled rodeo bums.

"Dammit, I've ridden through blizzards with these men in my time," was his standard defense. "I'm no saddlebag banker. If a man can pay me back he will, without me passing out I.O.U.'s. If he can't, what am I supposed to do — take his horse and his saddle and put the poor bastard afoot?"

In retaliation, he could always point to the comforts she enjoyed, taken out of the same kitty. "You've got a nice house, clothes, servants, everything you ever wanted."

"Everything except being able to run my own home," she shot back. "You know all I ever wanted was to have enough to pay our bills and call my soul my own. But your high and mighty stepfather runs everything now that you've made him head of the corporation. He even tells the cook what menus to serve!"

Mother felt herself surrounded by Montgomerys. "J.G.," as he was known, was the very same portly and pompous stepfather who had prompted Father to run away from home as a boy. But he was a banker, he understood finances, and he had been willing to leave a fine position in a Chicago bank to come west and serve as vice president of the newly formed Baby Peggy Corporation at a salary commensurate with his responsibility and skills. Like the Chaplins and the Pickfords, Father was by now afraid to trust anyone but kinfolk with the vast sums rolling in. With J.G. came Father's mother and a twenty-three-year-old half-brother who had an abiding weakness for marrying, siring children, and remarrying without attending to the legal trivia of obtaining a divorce. Between bigamist arrests he worked extra in my pictures, but it seemed to Mother that all we did was bail him out of jail at $100 a throw. Why was there never any money to buy a member of the Baxter clan a ticket west, Mother wanted to know.

Almost as a public acknowledgment of my new stature as a full-fledged dramatic actress, I received a formal invitation to lunch at Pickfair. Mother and Father were awed and responded to the summons as to a royal command. We spent an entire afternoon in the rarefied atmosphere at Hollywood's social peak. While Mother sipped iced tea and chatted with Mary Pickford on the wide terrace, Douglas Fairbanks treated Father and me to a guided tour of the grounds. I felt more comfortable with the handsome, bronze-skinned Doug than with the seemingly withdrawn Miss Pickford, perhaps because he was a man.

I thought Father had liked him, too, as indeed he did, which was why I was so puzzled when a few days later I heard him discussing Fairbanks with Jack Coogan over lunch. Yes, the two men agreed, Doug's dark complexion was not merely due to his fetish for the sun. It was rumoured that he was Jewish on his father's side. Charlie and Syd Chaplin were also half-Jewish, Coogan said, although Charlie claimed "gypsy blood" from his maternal grandmother. So, of course, that explained why Doug and Charlie got along so well, and why Chaplin was always welcome at Pickfair when other acknowledged members of the Jewish community were not. It was my first introduction to Hollywood's complicated maze of racial attitudes, and I was still more bewildered when both men seemingly reversed their position by agreeing again that some of their own best friends were Jews, among them Fred Fishback and Arthur Bernstein.

One evening Jackie's parents came to our Laurel Canyon home for clandestine cocktails before going on to an evening of dancing under the make-believe palms of the Cocoanut Grove. Although Louise and I had already dined with our governess, we were permitted down stairs in our Doctor Dentons to see the guests. I remember how pretty the two ladies looked — Mother in her salmon-pink brocaded dress bordered in soft brown mink, Mrs. Coogan looking almost slim in black velvet and lustrous pearls.

Mother was regaling the Coogans with amusing tales of her days as a poor ranger's wife in the wilds of Arizona. The two stage-door veterans marveled that anyone could survive such harrowing adventures. Jack Coogan was a great storyteller, too, and I always enjoyed watching him tell them, complete with gestures and foreign dialects.

"By the way, Jack," Coogan remarked while Father was pouring illicit gin cocktails all around, "Arthur Bernstein told me another

wonderful Jewish story today." Leaning against our white mantelpiece, Coogan launched into his tale while I, sitting on the stairs,
waited expectantly. I felt happier than I had since my fire engine
dream. I always breathed easier when grownups were laughing
and telling jokes.

"There's this Jewish merchant, see, and his little kid named
Abie. 'Abie,' he tells the four-year-old kid, 'I want you should be a
businessman when you grow up. So for your first lesson stand up
here on the mantel and jump into my arms.' 'But Papa,' says
Abie, getting scared, 'I'm scared I'll fall!' " At this point Coogan
picked up an invisible child and lifted him carefully onto the
mantelpiece. " 'You won't fall, Abie. Trust me, I'm your father;
I'll catch you!' "

Dramatically Coogan held out his arms for the catch, crying,
" 'Jump Abie!' " at which point Coogan stepped back abruptly.
"So the kid jumps and smashes on the floor, screaming and crying.
'But Papa,' little Abie wails, 'you promised to catch me!' 'A-ha!'
says his old man, *That's the first lesson! In business don't even
trust your own father!' "

They all rocked with laughter while Father refilled everyone's
glass. But I was disappointed. Far from being a funny story, I
found it downright frightening. After all the times Father had
rescued me on the set and on locations, how could people even
think it was funny for a father to allow his child to be hurt?

Later, at the Cocoanut Grove, the Coogans and Montgomerys
were joined by Arthur Bernstein and his wife. After dinner Arthur
asked Mother for a dance. Once on the dance floor, he confided
to her that he really wanted to draw her away from the others so
they could talk alone.

In 1923 Arthur Bernstein was thirty-six, a slim, intelligent man
with a high, narrow forehead, a thin arched nose, and a firm mouth.
Severely handsome in his gold-rimmed glasses, he was always im-
peccably dressed. People said it was because he had come from
New York's garment district, where he had loaned money to clothing stores, carrying merchants through their off seasons until fall
and Christmas sales. Apparently he had come to California in the
same capacity. Now, however, he was a trusted adviser to Jack

Coogan and others and was considered a shrewd investor by the most knowledgeable men in the industry.

Arthur explained that he had approached Father on several occasions, trying to persuade him to allow him, Arthur, to manage my career, but Father seemed unwilling to trust him. Now Arthur told Mother that he had met with officials at Metro that very afternoon and they were ready to talk contract with him. He had convinced them that Baby Peggy was worth $50,000 a picture and a long-term contract, and they were the proper studio to shepherd her career. They had further agreed to a gradual transition to adult roles as I grew out of my baby image. Arthur was hoping that by approaching Jack through Marian he would stand a better chance of being accepted as manager of the Montgomerys' financial affairs.

Mother was convinced. Later that night, as she and Father drove home in the silvery moonlight, Father angrily accused her of being in love with Arthur Bernstein. Mother was indignant and told him the real reason she and Arthur had been engaged in such deep conversation on the dance floor. Father refused to believe that a businessman of Arthur's stature would even bother to discuss serious matters with an empty-headed woman. The more Mother pleaded with him, the more adamant Father was "against any man who tries to get at me through my wife," as he put it.

A week later headlines announced that Jack Coogan, who had grown increasingly restive under his arrangement with Sol Lesser, was moving to Metro, where Jackie had been awarded a "million-dollar contract" and a $50,000 advance for his first picture. The man who had negotiated the deal was Arthur L. Bernstein, newly appointed business manager of Jackie Coogan Productions.

Mother was sick with disappointment and Father kept pretty much to himself for the next few days. Then, toward the end of the week, while we sat at breakfast in the sun-drenched dining room, he solemnly unfolded the morning paper, turned it to the movie section, and read aloud:

> Baby's film salary $1,500,000 a year! One and a half million dollars a year for baby to spend, in addition to a little romper money

just for dolls, scoops and lollipops! Such is to be the good fortune
of Baby Peggy according to an announcement made here today by
Mr. Sol Lesser, motion picture magnate. Mr. Lesser said that he
had contracted for the services of Baby Peggy for three years, and
that a $500,000 bonus was just to "give the contract a good start!"

Tossing the paper to the floor like a pony express rider delivering the mail, Father fairly glowed in triumph. "Well, now doesn't
that beat hell out of the Metro offer? And we didn't need Arthur
Bernstein, either. I negotiated this one *myself!*"

In the restrictive arena where the child star's father moved,
there were no personal business triumphs, no million-dollar deals
of his own to be celebrated. Without even realizing it, men like
Father and Jack Coogan increasingly strove to keep the approval
and affection of their wives by the only means left to them —
furthering their child's career. Tragically, however, every financial victory for the child signified yet another moral defeat for
the father. No matter how they tried to rationalize it, only the
breadwinner earned the respect, and self-respect, proper to that
role.

Sol Lesser had learned a great deal about building a child star's
public image during his two and a half years with the Coogans.
If weak stories had hurt Jackie at First National, Lesser was determined not to repeat that mistake with me. Jointly with the
Baby Peggy Corporation he purchased the screen rights to three
children's classics: *Captain January, Helen's Babies,* and *Heidi.*
All enjoyed a wide readership and each offered a plum leading
role for a little girl.

Captain January was filmed on location at still-uninhabited
Laguna Beach in the summer of 1923. Even while it was being
edited, Lesser was mounting his most ambitious child star promotion yet to win support from theater owners and exhibitors. He
announced that for the next six months Baby Peggy would be
available to appear "in person" touring with *Captain January* in
first-run houses across the country.

A brand-new American-made Baby Peggy doll was being issued,
with the sales kickoff scheduled for Gimbel's Department Store
in New York, where I would be available all one day for auto-

graphs. Manufacturers had been signed up to turn out an entirely new assortment of Baby Peggy dresses, sweaters, handbags, toys, fairy-tale books, and what today would be called a movie tie-in edition of *Captain January*, illustrated with scenes from the film. A leading New York jewelry firm photographed me wearing their entire inventory of gems. Draped in gauze, my arms, shoulders, neck, and chest were literally paved with diamonds, emeralds, rubies, opals, and pearls set in bracelets, brooches, necklaces, and rings. The message was that America's million-dollar baby was wearing a million dollars' worth of jewels.

"Baby Peggy has reached the mature age of five," remarked a reporter for New York's *Sun Globe*, noting that I had come to New York for my very first visit and to celebrate this crucial birthday. "But her mother holds a contract by which the baby makes as much in the next five years as all the Presidents since Lincoln have drawn from the Treasury of the United States."

On a warm October afternoon in 1923, the white and gold banquet room of New York's Biltmore Hotel was crowded with more than five hundred elegantly dressed guests of the National Press Association, which was hosting the party for Baby Peggy. Celebrities were quickly recognized and cornered by newsmen and photographers. Great swags of ocher-colored smoke lazed in the upper reaches of the high-ceilinged room, and each T-shaped flash that ignited its sulfurous powder in a blinding burst of light only added to the thick, opaque clouds.

At the head of an enormous banquet table stood a towering four-tiered birthday cake with five tall candles. The only way I could see or be seen by the guests and the photographers was to stand on the seat of my rose throne chair. I made a brief speech of thanks to my hosts and to the assembled guests. Then George T. Bye, a renowned New York publicist and author, announced that he had just completed my official biography, all five years of it. Father acknowledged a wave of applause and spoke for less than a minute on the always fascinating theme of genius and obedience. Producer Joseph Schenck said he was glad to be there. Then the master of ceremonies introduced Mrs. Jack Coogan.

In a preamble he explained that Mrs. Coogan was there to represent her son, to whom it was rumored that the guest of honor was secretly engaged. Jackie was busy out in Hollywood making a new film, so his mother had brought his gift to his future bride. Would she please stand up and say a few words?

It had been a long time since Lillian Dolliver Coogan had been the center of so much attention. She was flattered, flustered, and unprepared. Rising to her feet, she began hesitantly, "Ladies and gentlemen," and then after a long pause she threw off her restraint and blurted out impulsively, "Well, why be formal? You all know who I am — I'm the goose that laid the *other* Golden Egg!"

As an embarrassed hush settled over the stunned guests, the master of ceremonies sprang gallantly to Mrs. Coogan's rescue by announcing that Peggy would like to be excused so that she could open all those exciting-looking birthday presents waiting for her at the other end of the room.

Among the gifts that I opened that day were three costly wristwatches, one valued at $1250 from the grateful jeweler whose fiery gems I had modeled. There were at least a dozen dolls, one of which I accidentally dropped and broke, while the rest, along with all the other toys, were left in our suite to be handed on to the children of the hotel chambermaids. As I did not care for dolls anyway, this was not quite the act of heroic renunciation it may have seemed. The only birthday present I fixed upon and cherished was a large white teddy bear that came in his own basket; it was the gift of Rose Smith Olson, self-styled president of the Baby Peggy Fan Club, who lived in New York City. Jimbo's chief fascination was that, like me, he was completely unbreakable and portable. Over the next few years he was my constant companion, and I gradually added an entire family of small bears to keep him company, all of whom fit neatly into a gray "bear bag" that I carried in and out of every train station and hotel.

For a full two weeks after my birthday we spent every day crisscrossing the city of New York. Accompanied by a police motorcycle escort, sirens screaming, we moved through the busy downtown traffic at forty-five miles an hour, darting from Gimbel's to Wanamaker's to Marx's Toy Store. Then we visited institutions — virtually every civic, Protestant, Catholic, and Jewish orphanage and hospital that wasn't currently under quarantine. The orphans were herded into a large central auditorium or dining room where I distributed balloons, signed autographs, and cut still one more large birthday cake. The children seemed almost speechless with excitement and awe. In the stifling children's hospital wards I moved grimly from bed to bed, totally unprepared and inwardly shaken by this massive exposure to confinement, sickness, and pain. But I understood that these pallid children with their haunted eyes and twisted limbs expected me to smile. Consequently I beamed delightedly as I handed out the little toys and autographed pictures I had brought along.

Every night for a week I appeared at the enormous Hippodrome Theatre, where I was backed up by a major production. The stage was crowded with real elephants, whirling circus ponies, all one hundred of Mr. Singer's famous midgets, and scores of chorus boys and girls dressed as toy soldiers and painted dolls. While a full orchestra played the stirring march from Victor Herbert's *Toyland*, I stepped out of a huge golden egg in a dainty silver lamé dress trimmed with satin rosebuds.

At this same time, along New York's busy streets a spry, seventy-six-year-old lady from Boston spent an exhausting day, walking all the way from Twenty-ninth to Forty-fifth Street shopping for antiques. It was Lotta Crabtree's last visit to New York, but it is probable that she took note of the hoopla surrounding Baby Peggy's fifth birthday. Fans were still showering child stars with expensive watches and other valued gifts, even though film and screen had replaced the bartops and rough-hewn stages of her own childhood. It was the kind of item that would have caught Lotta's eye.

For the rest of 1923, travel, performance, and promotion became an unremitting way of life for me. Louise and Mother were often left behind while Father and I played lucrative one-night stands in nearly inaccessible hamlets in the hinterland. Leaving St. Louis at midnight in the dead of winter, we changed trains at 3 A.M., Father carrying me, bundled in blankets and half-asleep, from one warm Pullman car to the next across a frosted web of tracks. At five we stepped off the spur line special at remote Mountain View, Missouri, high in the Ozark hills. There, on the train station's wooden platform, the town's combined Boy and Girl Scout troops stood at attention while a welcoming town band played "Baby Face" and the frosted breath of some fifty other equally dedicated fans steamed upward in the sub-zero dawn.

In Washington State, we played remote lumbering towns where few live shows, let alone movie stars, had ever visited. Silver being the sole coin of the realm, theater managers were obliged to pay us our half of the day's box-office receipts in silver dollars. Our share usually being between $2000 and $3000, Father was forced to buy a stout leather bag to carry our hefty loot — a bag that sounded very much like the one Mary Ann's fellow troupers claimed "clanked like a plumber's kit."

It seemed there was no end to the uses one could make of a child star in the complex world of grownups. When the Democratic party held its 1924 National Convention in New York's Madison Square Garden, I was named their mascot and asked to lead the parade onto the stadium floor. When the call came to start the parade, Father put me on his shoulders, I grabbed him around the neck, and we headed for the main arena.

What met our eyes was a scene of complete pandemonium. The entire stadium was packed with people, most of whom seemed to be wildly drunk and in a mood either to celebrate or to fight. Flanked by four towering Irish policemen, two ahead of us and one on each side, Father started out. As we marched through the press of inebriated or curious conventioneers and spectators, the policemen swung their nightsticks right and left, rhythmically cracking heads and shouting, "Clear the way! Keep back!" in what resembled a steady infantry advance through resisting enemy ranks.

When we finally reached our destination, the crowded speaker's platform, a handsome middle-aged man called down, warning someone "not to bring the baby up" as the wooden stand was already overloaded and in danger of collapse. But in the melee I was snatched from Father's shoulders and I found myself on the platform standing beside the nice-looking man, who was about to deliver a speech. As he struggled to his feet, I saw that he was crippled and braced with crutches. At the end of his speech, hundreds of balloons were released and everyone went into a frenzy of joy. Later, I was told the man was Franklin D. Roosevelt and his "Happy Warrior" speech had won the presidential nomination for Governor Alfred E. Smith and a reentry into the political arena for himself after a near-fatal illness.

In that same summer of 1924, another headlined event that Lotta Crabtree may have followed with more than passing interest was Jackie Coogan's unprecedented cross-country, transatlantic Children's Crusade. On this triumphant tour Jackie personally raised over $1,000,000 in funds, food, and clothing for 70,000 Greek and Armenian war orphans. Brooklyn's Prospect Park was jammed with 100,000 fans eager to meet the world's most famous boy and buy an autographed "mercy bond." In London impressive crowds lined the streets all the way from Waterloo Station to the Savoy Hotel. There, flanked by Jack Coogan and Arthur Bernstein (Mrs. Coogan was at home expecting another child), Jackie appeared on the balcony of his suite every few minutes, like a newly crowned monarch, saluting the multitudes in the streets as they clamored for one more glimpse of their reigning hero.

In Paris thousands turned out in welcome, and only the French premier, sharp-tongued old Georges Clemenceau, declined to share his countrymen's delirium over their idol. The same barbed wit that had once observed, "The United States is the only nation in history to have passed from barbarism to decadence without the usual interval of civilization," now penned an acid note to Jack Coogan: "I do not screen well enough nor am I celebrity enough to meet your illustrious son."

As ten-year-old Jackie toured the capitals of Europe and headed for the Middle East, receiving the homage and gratitude of millions, Lotta Crabtree took to her bed in what proved to be her last illness. Only weeks before her death on September 23, 1924, Jackie Coogan received from the hands of the reigning pontiff the Golden Cross of the Order of Jerusalem, the Vatican's most highly prized decoration. If friends at the Brewster Hotel informed Lotta of this bizarre achievement, she must have smiled reflectively. After all, it only proved that nothing had really changed since a grateful miner in Rabbit Creek had tossed Lotta her first fifty-dollar gold piece.

II

Women and Children First

I used to wonder if there wasn't a special sub-human species of womankind that bred children for the sole purpose of dragging them to Hollywood.

— Hedda Hopper

UNIQUELY HEARTLESS though movie mothers seemed, exploitation of the helpless young by powerful adults was hardly an invention of either Hollywood or the twentieth century. Since antiquity, the children of rich and royal house alike were deployed as pawns by ruthlessly ambitious parents who betrothed them in infancy, dispatched them to distant wars, or consigned them to the cloister, whatever best advanced the family's financial or political ends. The progeny of Europe's poor faced an even crueler fate. For centuries it was common practice to abandon newly born females or other unwanted infants, while many of those who proved bothersome in later childhood were deliberately taken to forest and wood and left in the hope that they would die of hunger and exposure.

In eighteenth-century Paris, street urchins were periodically rounded up by city officials and sold to professional beggars for three sous each. To make these waifs still more pitiable (and profitable) objects of charity, their buyers then broke their arms and legs. Once the alms of the pious rich had been thus deceitfully gleaned, the maimed victims were once more cast out on the streets to starve. As at least one historian contends, "The history of childhood is a nightmare from which we have only recently begun to awaken." *

But however roughly past ages may have dealt with the young, it remained for our own time to raise the hitherto haphazard manipulation and marketing of children to a multimillion-dollar industry. Not entirely by accident did Hollywood win world recognition as the first trade center in history to traffic in the gifted child. That parents flocked to this bazaar for the sole purpose of vending their own flesh and blood does not lessen the magnitude of the motion picture industry's contribution to the long and troubled history of the child.

When the child star craze was at its height — roughly between 1925 and 1945 — an estimated one hundred children poured into the Hollywood marketplace every fifteen minutes. The ratio of those who in an entire year earned so much as a single week's expenses from movie work was reckoned at less than one in fifteen thousand.† It is probable that at least half of those who arrived with dazzling dreams of stardom for their child were starved out and forced to return home at the end of the first two or three months. A small percentage, perhaps grubstaked by a husband's salary or a relative's nest egg to launch a more determined siege, might hold on for a year before giving up the fight. That left a small, fanatical corps of iron-willed survivors, women who preferred starvation and death to abandoning their dearly won positions before the very gates of fame.

While Jackie Coogan and I and a mere handful of others started out at or near the top, most youngsters had their screen image hammered together over a comparatively long and painful period. Beginning as a nameless and nearly faceless extra, the child moved from bit to line to featured role along a slow-moving studio assembly line. Inevitably — or so their parents devoutly believed — one day Baby would roll off this celluloid conveyer belt a complete and perfect Golden Egg.

* Lloyd DeMause, ed., *The History of Childhood* (New York: Psychohistory Press, 1974).

† Norman J. Zierold, *The Child Stars* (New York: Coward-McCann, 1965), p. 58.

Finding the front door to the plant where the assembly line began was therefore the crucial test facing every new mother in town. Her problem was compounded by the fact that few newcomers realized Hollywood's dream factory had not one but many doors. The quickest way to the nearest entrance was to ask a movie mother who already knew her way around and was obliging enough (or fool enough!) to share her hard-won intelligence with yet another contender in her own darling's race for fame. Surprisingly, given the ruthless competition, there were a few such helpful souls in Hollywood's predominantly predatory pack, and Reesie Parrish was one of them.

A southern lady from Columbus, Georgia, Reesie was neither threatened by nor envious of mothers from other climes. After all, her people had survived "thieving Yankees and free nigras," and nothing brought you low if you knew who you were. Besides, her own four stalwarts — Gordon, Robert, Beverly, and Baby Helen, aged fourteen to three — were already working as child extras and proving reliable breadwinners. A drummer for the Coca-Cola Company, Mr. Parrish had been transferred from his Georgia route to the Southern California territory. He spent most of his time on the road and his spare change on five-cent cigars. At home in Hollywood with five mouths to feed, Reesie spent her time figuring how to keep food on the table and still have a few pennies left over to indulge her favorite recreation — movies — which meant either seeing them in theaters or helping to make them on the set.

When Mr. Parrish returned from his route and learned that his wife had turned all four children into "picture kids," he expressed shock and disapproval. A lot of good it did. Whether it hurt her husband's pride or not, Reesie stood her ground. Times were tough, his salary too small, and those $5-a-day checks the children earned literally kept the wolf at bay. Besides, she insisted, the children loved the life. She was careful not to mention that she loved it most of all.

Frieda Jones was another enterprising mother with a secret passion for films. Like Reesie, her husband's employment brought her to Hollywood, but what had converted her into a true believer was living in the apartment across the hall from the Montgomery family when Baby Peggy was first discovered. Having witnessed that miracle with her own eyes, she was determined to enter her entire brood in the child star sweepstakes — Margaret, Macon, Marvin, and little Marcia Mae, every one a winner, given half a chance. Mr. Jones was a telegrapher with the Los Angeles *Times* newspaper, which gave Frieda ample time to devote to "putting the kids in pictures."

Wynonah Johnson would probably never have seen Hollywood but for a golden farming scheme that had lured her husband from their native Louisiana rice plantation to far-off Mexico. He sank his substantial fortune into that foreign land bubble, only to have a Mexican revolution wipe him out. Desperate to provide for his wife and five children, he took a job as an auditor for a downtown newspaper. Stranded in Hollywood in 1918, the gently reared Wynonah felt totally out of her element until she learned her neighbor was a fellow Southerner and struck up what proved to be a lifelong friendship with Reesie Parrish. The resourceful Reesie was quick to point out that Wynonah possessed a veritable treasure in her fleet of five young 'uns, three girls and two boys. All of them could sing and dance, and the older two played musical instruments as well.

And so Wynonah and Frieda and countless other mothers heeded Reesie's advice and followed her directions to their very first door, located, appropriately enough, at 6605 Hollywood Boulevard. There a photographer named Evansmith made a comfortable living specializing in photographing children trying to make it in movies. He guaranteed to turn out "clear, sharp natural portraits of kiddies so essential for casting — $35 per 100, $20 per 50, $12.50 per 25. Plenty of proofs to choose from. There is no 'pull' like a good photograph."

Armed with the indispensable portraits, the mother tried her second door, where she bought space in a specialized quarterly publication, *The Casting Director's Album of Screen Children*. A foreword assured the armchair shopper consulting its pages that "every player listed in this book has had screen experience." Most were toddlers of three or four who may or may not have even seen a movie in their time. But Reesie's success story made the cost seem worthwhile. After she entered her children's pictures, a Hal Roach casting director had called them for their very first job.

The third door was located on the tenth floor of the Taft Building, also on Hollywood Boulevard. Here *The Standard Casting Directory* was published every month. It listed players of all ages and types and was affiliated with the Film Test Laboratory, where screen tests were kept on file for studio reference, a highly valued plus for advertisers.

By 1926 *The Standard Casting Directory* had grown to a fat two hundred and sixty pages and resembled a small-town telephone book, except that it ran portraits of its subscribers as well as their telephone numbers. In Hollywood's professional hierarchy, performers were listed according to status and prestige. The first section featured those high priests of the industry, Directors and Managers. Next, in their proper order, came Leading Men, Juveniles (also all males), Heavy Men (villains), Character Men (odd, crochety, old), and Feature Comedians. They were followed by Feature Women, Leading Women, Ingénues, Second Women (vamps, paramours, soubrettes), and Character Women (gossips, skinny, fat, old). The following eight pages were given over to some two hundred assorted Hollywood children under fourteen, and the book closed with a final page devoted to the lowliest caste of all, studio dogs and their trainers.

Besides a good photo, mothers had to pack a great deal of information into a very few lines. The average ad measured only 3½ by 4 inches, of which the portrait ate up a good four fifths. Mothers spent hours puzzling over the proper wording, which movie credits (if so blessed) to list, and what other qualifications to feature. As a result the children usually ended up being sold by the year and the pound, pretty much like vintage wine and prime beef.

Virginia Ann Reed appeared as a pretty dark-eyed tot, "32½ inches, 27 pounds. The Baby in *Stella Dallas*." Beneath a picture of Wynonah Johnson's three girls ran the no-nonsense caption: "Johnson: Experienced Troupers." (The oldest was ten.) Reesie's doughty four appeared in a group portrait above a single large-type "Parrish," which implied an established brand name, any of whose products the buyer could trust. Beside the photo of a three-year-old blond girl ran the coy phrase "Baby Darling! That's What They All Say!" (Later, as Jean Darling, she starred in *Our Gang.*) Under a full-length still of a tiny boy, jauntily togged out in checked cap, golfing shorts and bamboo cane, the copy stated: "Jackie Combs, 2 years old, height 32 inches, weight, 29 lbs." And then, in a seemingly desperate attempt to cover all bases, *"Try Me as a Girl!"*

Mothers with large families learned one thing early in their studio apprenticeship: directors preferred one mother and five kids to five mothers with five kids. Such fruitful women represented a sizable saving to studios on everything from transportation and location lodging to box lunches — not to mention reducing by half the inevitable backbiting and quarrels that plagued most sets where more than two movie mothers were foregathered. Such multiple entries also gained the inside track, at the same time increasing their parents' odds of hitting the child star jackpot with at least one out of five.

A mother could also go the route of an agent, but it meant yielding up a full 10 per cent of what little the child might earn. Still, some advertisers were careful to include the line "Courtesy to all agents," which meant that anyone coming up with a job for that player was welcome to his pound of flesh. In Hollywood in the 1920s only two agents specialized in handling children, Harry Weber and Lola Moore. Weber was a long-time "flesh peddler" who had for years divided his efforts equally between big-time vaudeville and films. Lola Moore was a former Universal screenwriter who gradually developed a children's talent agency.

It was Harry Weber who took over Mickey Rooney's career when he ceased being Mickey McGuire and began looking for other jobs. Weber sold him as a character actor, younger than most, but reliable. A ten-day run with Tom Mix in *My Pal, the King* garnered $250 for Nell's boodle bag, less of course, Weber's $25. Next the agent sold a parsimonious producer on the idea of using Mickey to play a midget in a Colleen Moore film entitled *Orchids and Ermine.* Mickey was willing to work for less, he argued, and looked as much like a rich hogman from Walla Walla as any forty-year-old Singer midget around. But as Mickey strutted through one scene, the hazards of a child portraying a midget caught up with him. Biting off the tip of an expensive cigar and spitting it in the general direction of an elegant spittoon, the diminutive big-spending hogman spat out a baby tooth as well. Dismayed, the director halted the scene. But Nell was never at a loss where Sonny's career was concerned. Retrieving the missing tooth, she secured it in place with chewing gum. By delivering his lines with care, Mickey remained a midget for the duration of the film.

Agent Lola Moore was always on the lookout for promising children, and every Friday night she invited applicants to her home to audition. If their singing, dancing, recitation, or other talent passed muster, she took them on as clients and included their picture in a private directory of her own, which she circulated among casting directors. She was highly respected and keenly competitive. If an interview called for street waifs, she thought nothing of changing a child from his Sunday-best interview clothes into the rags she always kept on hand in her closet for just such emergencies. The fancily dressed, made-up children were turned down while hers were invariably chosen.

Lola was protective of her clients, too, more so than most movie mothers. Once she received a peculiar call from Monogram for a very small and compactly built year-old baby. She had such a child, but because the baby's mother was Polish and barely spoke or understood English, Lola decided to go to the studio on the day of the shooting. On the set she found the baby wearing a leather harness and nearby an enormous eagle in a cage.

"The eagle and the child have something to do with each other?" Lola queried the director suspiciously. "Well, it's a trained eagle," the man explained, "and he's been taught to pick up big objects. We are going to have him pick up this child and fly it up there to that little pole." Lola looked at the top of the pole, aghast.

"Why don't you use a rag baby or a dummy?"

"Oh, no, we want it to look real. The baby of course will be frightened when it's picked up, and we want that fear to show."

"Well, you can just get some other baby," Lola cried furiously, snatching up the child and taking off its harness. "You're not going to use *my* baby, so forget it!" And Lola walked off the set, the fretful infant in her arms, shepherding the bewildered mother before her.

Such Poverty Row directors were not the only ones careless of the health or lives of movie children. Because of her spartan training under the great realist D. W. Griffith, Mary Pickford often made outrageous demands upon herself and others in her zeal to achieve lifelike effects on screen. In a 1926 film called *Sparrows*, Mary played a fifteen-year-old named Mamma Mollie, who champions the cause of a group of younger orphans trapped on a mean farm in a southern swamp. The farm, barn, quicksand, and steaming swampland, including a pool filled with several very real and voracious alligators, were all carefully brought together on the Pickford lot.

In one especially dangerous sequence, in which Mollie leads the escaping orphans across a swamp, Mary decided not to use a double for herself or to substitute a dummy for the baby she was carrying on her back. She went through six rehearsals and finally shot it live, picking her way across the pond within inches of the alligators' snapping jaws, barely managing to keep her balance and her footing. When Douglas Fairbanks learned what she had done he was furious, pointing out that with one misstep she could have met a grisly death and taken the helpless baby with her. Mary had not seen the episode in that light at all, but she deferred to her husband's insistence that she show better judgment in the future. As a consequence, she refused to hire that director again, transferring the blame to him for risking her life and that of the child, although, as her own producer, she had the final say on everything. Upon release, the film was touted as "Mary Pickford's Christmas gift to everyone whose heart is young." The mothers whose children had enjoyed a long run on the set of *Sparrows* felt she had already made *their* Christmas. Certainly the mother of the infant on Mary's back was not one to argue with success.

Every alert movie mother recognized the importance of cultivating casting officers and assistant directors. Convinced that good food was the quickest way to a man's heart, some women surprised the assistant on the set with a home-baked pie or cake.

Who could tell, such gifts might win Baby that special bit of business in the close-up with the stars, or at least a call back for tomorrow. A hardy few, with the good looks and temerity to qualify, promised even more personal favors to any official who would open studio doors to her child.

Dancing schools offered yet another possible avenue to opportunity, although they did not attain their real importance until after the advent of sound. And of course the local newspapers were not to be despised. As in any one-factory town, anything concerning the major industry was considered good copy. An annual forecast of MGM's forty-nine or fifty planned productions rated headlines. Films using exceptionally large numbers of extras were written up as news, with the time and place of the interviews included well in advance of the event.

The casting of a Cecil B. De Mille religious epic was a matter of no small economic import to the community's chronically underemployed labor force. It was common knowledge that the meticulous De Mille hand-picked even his sorriest mob scene beggars. Luckily for child extras, he also insisted that every contingent of Roman slaves or band of doomed Christians include a generous sprinkling of dolorous-looking children, to heighten the horrors of bondage and martyrdom.

On such huge "cattle calls," as they were known, two hundred mothers might show up at the studio on the designated empty stage, their entire brood in tow. The children formed ranks while De Mille himself or a trusted assistant walked the length of the lines, peering into every face and singling out the special types desired. During this ordeal almost total silence hung over the assembly, the atmosphere throbbing with hope, jealousy, and fear. When the call was finally filled, the lucky few were marched off to the studio wardrobe to be fitted for their costumes while the rest were dismissed with a terse "Thank you." A heavy pall of disappointment settled over the rejects, muffling their retreat as they grumbled their way back to the front gate.

With close to a thousand young hopefuls streaming into town every day, Hollywood resembled the Old Woman Who Lived in a Shoe. She had so many children, there were just not enough jobs to go around. The awareness of this grim truth kept families competing over what few morsels the studios could toss out in any given month. Children of the same sex, age, or general appearance scrapped incessantly over the best lines, the meatiest parts, or the rare featured roles that came up for their type. At almost any given moment the fortune or misfortune of one child in some manner altered, threatened, or even furthered the career of another. An *Our Gang* member might shoot up unexpectedly almost overnight and need to be replaced by a younger child of the same sex, color, or size. Illness, accident, or even the temperamental outburst of a child star's parent could suddenly clear the way for an unknown whose future had looked bleak only days or hours earlier. Edith Fellows's first break was typical.

Although their distinguished-looking talent scout had turned out to be a fly-by-night confidence man, Mrs. Elizabeth Fellows was both too poor and too proud to return to Atlanta and face her friends. With a nonexistent agent's card in her hand and only a few dollars in her purse, she bought a newspaper and searched the classified section for a job, finding one as a housekeeper in a Beverly Hills home.

Returning home from a long day at work, Mrs. Fellows still found the time and energy to rehearse Edith in her songs and dance routines. As five-year-old Edith now discovered to her surprise, her pigeon toes had not really been the cause of her dancing school lessons at all, but merely the perfect excuse for investing in her career. Her grandmother confided that Edith's parents had both been well-known actors and singers on the eastern stage, and Mrs. Fellows herself had been a singer and songwriter of note. She had aspired to opera in her time and knew many arias by heart. Now, at great personal sacrifice, she paid for Edith's singing lessons. As she rolled Edith's ginger-colored hair in neat curlers at bedtime, she drilled her in whatever songs she had learned that day and told her what life would be like for them once she was letter-perfect. Edith would be discovered, she would become a star, and they would live in their *own* big mansion in Beverly Hills.

Meantime, while she was at work, the ruthless Mrs. Fellows was forced to leave Edith in the care of a neighbor whose small son was Edith's age and sometimes worked in the movies. One day the Hal Roach Studio called him for an interview, and, unable to leave Edith home alone, the boy's mother took her along. The casting director thought Edith was an applicant, too, asked her to audition, and then chose her for the part over the boy. The incident brought the two women's friendship to a stormy end, but it marked the beginning of Edith's painful climb to fame.

Not only were Hollywood children forced by such circumstances to square off against their peers — those who in a less remorseless situation might have become good friends — they found themselves pitted against each other's parents as well. When Edith tried to strike up a friendship with the rising child star Jane Withers at professional school, Edith's grandmother swiftly intervened. "Don't you let me catch you so much as *speaking* to that girl!" she hissed. Edith was stunned. Mrs. Fellows's reasoning, of course, was sound. If the two girls became chums, Edith might confide the details of a part her grandmother had lined up for her, and Jane could snatch it from her.

Contentious though some of the fathers undoubtedly were, mothers were by far the deadlier of the two. The viciousness of their infighting reflected in part the traditional female lack of that saving sense of chivalry, which had humanized warfare among males for centuries. While accustomed to doing battle, men fought not merely for victory but to demonstrate the knightly virtues. Women, when forced to fight, fought strictly for survival and to protect their young. Male warriors might display their magnanimity of soul by restoring a defeated foe's treasured horse and sword. Women sought only to destroy the enemy, giving no quarter and expecting none. In Hollywood such women became predators who struck out at each other's young as fiercely as they defended their own. As a casting director at Universal once groaned, "I'd rather face a saber-toothed tiger than Gloria Fisher's mother!"

Ironically, those to whom these mothers showed the least mercy were their own daughters. Many girls wearied of the relentless striving for the top. Others hated picture work from the beginning but dared not betray such feelings. Mother had long ago set her course as a matter of survival and there was no turning back. In some cases a daughter escaped her fate only through marriage; others actually died in the traces. When Margaret Jones outgrew her baby cuteness, Frieda thrust baby Marcia Mae into harness and drove her so relentlessly that the sensitive Marcia Mae recalls her childhood as a nightmare. When eleven-year-old Beverly Parrish succumbed to diabetes, Baby Helen became the focus of Reesie's star-making zeal. "I used to feel sorry for the Parrish boys," Marcia Mae recalls. "Reesie practically ignored them, except to pocket their paychecks, devoting all her energy and time to making little Helen a star."

Of course the shining example of movie motherhood, held up before these women every day, was Charlotte Pickford herself. Mary was not only idolized by them as their gracious queen, she was regarded as an angel of mercy because for a solid decade her succession of little girl roles provided a continuing bonanza of "cattle calls" and long-run jobs. *Rebecca of Sunnybrook Farm, Sparrows, Little Annie Rooney, Daddy Long Legs,* and half a dozen others required anywhere from ten to a hundred atmosphere children in the schoolroom, orphanage, and other scenes. And always on the set, hovering over her own little Mary with a glass of scalded milk or a tart word of advice, was Mama Charlotte, living proof of what determination, drive, and a hard-working daughter could achieve.

"If I'm not here," Charlotte told a visitor to one of Mary's sets, "I soon get a ring from Mary asking what's wrong, and I put on my hat and coat and come over to the studio." She occupied a director's chair next to whoever was wielding the megaphone on her daughter's film. She put in her ideas for dialogue and made suggestions about production. She faithfully attended business meetings at United Artists, Mary having completely washed her hands of such grubby affairs. Some insisted that, for a time at least, the officious and omnipresent Charlotte actually ran the studio.

Certainly she ran her children's lives as much as any mother ever did. Mary obligingly drank the fortifying glass of hot milk Charlotte prescribed several times a day. She endured Charlotte's jealousy of Doug and her husband's jealousy of her mother with an almost saintly patience. As with Owen Moore, Charlotte made it clear to Mary's second husband that she ran her daughter more than he ran his wife.

Mary's brother Jack, following the much-publicized suicide of his showgirl wife, was named director of one of Mary's films. Charlotte and Mary both felt it would rouse him from depression and lend a healthy sense of purpose to his seemingly pointless life. But Jack's directorial career was short-lived. Despite a certain temporary cockiness, his drinking continued and so, too, rumor persisted, did his dependence on drugs. A second and third marriage, both to former Ziegfeld beauties, foundered in quick succession. At thirty-six, he undertook a transatlantic voyage, ostensibly to restore his ruined health. Three months later he was pronounced dead in a hospital outside of Paris. Those who knew him best claimed he had died from the combined effects of alcohol and drugs. Thus, in death, Jack Pickford joined the equally tragic John Ashworth Crabtree and Percy Janis, all three destroyed by the unbeatable combination of an overpoweringly ambitious mother and a formidably talented sister.

Lottie Pickford alone remained aloof from her sister's career, trying desperately to make a way for herself. But Mary considered her wild and an embarrassment to the rest of the family. Her only accomplishment in either Charlotte's or Mary's eyes was having produced a daughter, Gwynne, Charlotte's only grandchild. Lottie drank heavily and was deeply unhappy both during and between her four unsuccessful marriages. "At least I married them all. I didn't have round heels like your Aunt Mary," Lottie told Gwynne shortly before she died.

But Charlotte, Mary, and Doug conspired to take Gwynne away from her mother long before that day came. In a bitterly fought lawsuit, in which Mary proclaimed Lottie an unfit mother, they gained joint custody of the girl and Mary raised her almost as her own. Later, when radio became a favored source of additional exposure and revenue for Hollywood stars, Mary had her own dramatic show. When Lottie secured a children's program simultaneously, she was virtually told to get off the air by her famous sister. "One Pickford on the radio at a time is enough," Mary shouted at Lottie in an angry exchange that Gwynne remembers well. As Gwynne put it, "Auntie broke my mother's heart."

As her own and Mary's wealth continued to grow, there were increasingly fewer reasons for Charlotte to run to the studio and do battle as of old. She had more money now than she could count, and Mary was many times a millionaire. Fighting to get Mary ahead in the world had meant everything to Charlotte, but now, with nothing left to fight for, she felt useless and almost betrayed by success. In her own palatial Beverly Hills home, crammed with silver service, expensive furniture, and rare antiques, she, too, turned to drink for consolation. Gwynne, who lived much of the time with Mama Charlotte, remembers sitting on the front veranda of the big house keeping a sharp eye out for Mary's limousine. Mary had become a Christian Scientist after her second marriage made it impossible for her to remain a Catholic communicant. Publicly, at least, she scarcely drank at all, and she disapproved of those who did. Gwynne's duty was to signal Mary's approach so Charlotte would have time to clear away all trace of her guilty secret.*

Still, if she had to invent them, Charlotte found ways to remain essential to her daughter's career. When Mary needed a mourning dress for her part as *Little Annie Rooney,* Charlotte dug into an old theatrical trunk to find a remembered piece of black cloth that would be just the thing. The trunk lid fell on one of Charlotte's breasts, and in time a growth developed. Advised that she must undergo surgery or die, she stubbornly refused to submit to the indignity of having a breast removed. As her mother's condition grew increasingly grave, Mary stopped work, and she and Doug moved into Charlotte's beach house to be with her. When death finally came, Mary refused to believe her mother was gone. Totally hysterical, she struck out at everyone around her. She turned on Lottie and Jack (both of whom outlived their mother by several years) and even struck her beloved Doug across the face. As she admitted later, "I am ashamed to say that during those hours I even hated God and said so. I was completely out of my mind."

Charlotte's estate totaled $3 million, a sum that not even mingy Mary Ann had managed to squirrel away in forty golden years. Her will bequeathed $200,000 each to Lottie, Jack, and Gwynne.

---

* For most of the details of the Pickford family's last years together I am especially indebted to Robert Windeler, *Sweetheart: The Story of Mary Pickford* (New York: Praeger, 1974).

The remaining $2,500,000 went to her beloved Baby Gladys —
ambitious and proud, but loyal to Charlotte and submissive to the
very end. Mary, who needed it less than the others, received the
lion's share perhaps because her mother meant to make a statement with her wealth. She had bet on Mary to win in films and
Mary had proved her judgment sound.

After Lottie's death in 1936, the Queen of Pickfair, and the last
member of that hardscrabble foursome who had clawed their way
up from Toronto's fish market to the very pinnacle of success,
loftily described herself as "the sole survivor of a fond and vivacious family that had triumphed so long over the uncertainties
of life." To a degree Mary spoke the truth. Over the cruel uncertainties of poverty, hunger, and hardship Charlotte had triumphed
every time. It was the numbing certainty of security, wealth, and
fame that ultimately did her fighting spirit in. And, in a very
few years, Mary herself was put to a similar test.

12
High Noon in Fort Worth

*Peggy just loves vaudeville. She's like a fire horse
waiting in the wings, just dying to get out on that
stage. She doesn't know what stage fright is. But
then, children don't have any nerves.*

— Marian Montgomery

THOSE WHO MISTOOK Charlotte's passing for the final exit
of classic stage mothers per se were sadly out of tune with the
times. If anything, her death gave renewed impetus to that grim
theatrical phenomenon. Instead of a buoy, marking and warning
others away from the site of the family shipwreck, Charlotte's
posthumous fame served as a kind of sinister pilot boat, leading
unwary voyagers straight into the same kind of whirlpool that
had swallowed up the unhappy Pickford clan.

Indeed, death won for Charlotte the ultimate maternal reward,
for while her aimless last years were lost on the back pages of
yesterday's newspapers (along with Jack and Lottie's well-edited
obituaries), Mary, Charlotte's one glorious and unfading achievement, remained emblazoned across every screen and in headlines
around the world. Beauty, talent, gentility, wealth, fame, social
acceptance, and a happily-ever-after marriage to the handsomest
of men — Mary Pickford appeared to have it all. And the mar-
tyred mother who had so selflessly put her daughter's career above
every other interest deserved to be canonized. Mary's own out-
pourings in print, heaping love and gratitude upon her mother's
memory, made Charlotte the stained-glass model for every aspiring spotlight madonna with a potential child star in her arms.

And still living the stage mother legend to the hilt was invincible Jenny Janis, Charlotte's erstwhile adversary. Between musicals and touring the Orpheum circuit with Elsie, she was nearing the apex of her own brilliant backstage career. Mama Rose Hovick also remained in the ring, having exchanged her Hollywood movie aspirations and "The Pocket Size Pavlova" for bigtime vaudeville and the new billing, "Dainty June and Her Pals." Eleven-year-old June starred in the act with her older sister Louise and a clutch of starving, unsalaried street boys whom Rose had conscripted to work for food, transportation, and theatrical experience. Although Rose talked big time, more often than not she settled for the sticks, even touring Gus Sun's infamous "death trail" more than once. It was a brutal existence for the girls, but one that Rose characteristically justified in terms of the "greater good," a category covering everything from the broadening aspects of travel to the advantages of being financially independent of those irreformable rotters, men. And waiting in the wings of history, so to speak, was yet another shatterproof pair, this one as awesome a mother-daughter team as ever came out of Texas — the state where everything, including ambition, comes on a grand scale. Known to each other as Mommy or Lee-Lee and Virginia or Gee-Gee, they burst upon the rest of the world as Lela and Ginger Rogers.

Lela was one of five pretty Owens sisters who had grown up in Kansas City, Missouri. Her cornflower blue eyes, pug nose, and coquettish smile suggested a helpless clinging vine. But this soft exterior concealed a double-edged sense of self coupled with the fighting heart and staying power of a pit bull. Lela, like Jenny Janis, was a self-liberated woman born before her time. Graduating from the eighth grade, she enrolled herself in business school and at fifteen had a secretarial job. On her eighteenth birthday she married an electrical engineer named McGrath, and after losing their first child in infancy she returned to the marketplace as a newspaper reporter in what was now the McGraths' home town, Independence, Missouri.

In 1911, discovering she was pregnant a second time, the purposeful Lela determined to leave as little as posible to nature and chance. Just as Jenny had done, she deliberately "exposed" her unborn child to uplifting cultural influences — fine plays, great paintings, literature, and what little symphony and opera Independence could offer. If such a highbrow overture seems curiously unsuited to the life of a girl who one day put both the Charleston and swing music on the map, her place of birth was both fitting and prophetic. Independence had come into being, back in 1849, as the jumping-off point for the California gold fields. Lela used it for the same purpose, although adversity forced her to choose a more circuitous route than the early forty-niners.

To no one's surprise, the McGraths' marriage quickly fell apart. Lela supported herself and her daughter, Virginia, by working as a reporter. Meantime, she entered a short story contest sponsored by an amusement park and won first prize. Unexpectedly, a movie producer asked her to convert it into a screenplay. Leaving Virginia, now nicknamed Ginger by a small cousin, with her parents, Lela fearlessly tackled the hurly-burly film world of Hollywood, circa 1916. She found herself writing and collaborating on film scripts starring Gladys Brockwell and Theda Bara. She also supplied stories for such early child stars as Baby Marie Osborne and the popular sister team of Jane and Katherine Lee. Signing a contract with Dianando Studios, Lela was transferred back to their New York office just as the nation entered the Great War. She promptly joined the marines as one of the very first "marinettes," and was sent to Washington to write for *Leatherneck* and to serve as film processor and cutter on Marine training films.

Meantime, Ginger was growing up with no parents and grieving keenly over her mother's extended absence. She rejoiced when, at war's end, Mommy returned home and almost immediately married an old suitor, John Rogers, who adopted Ginger as his own. But marriage was too restrictive for Lela's restless spirit. When the family moved to Fort Worth, she founded a local symphony and, in a calculated move to achieve financial independence and eventual freedom from her spouse, she found work as a drama and entertainment reporter. Her newspaper chores took her backstage in the local theaters, and soon vaudeville folk were visiting the Rogers home, the family now consisting of Lee-Lee and Gee-Gee only, John Rogers having drifted on following a stormy divorce.

Ginger studied dancing and the ukulele at a local dancing school, both accomplishments unexceptional for a fifteen-year-old schoolgirl in the age of "flaming youth." But friends agreed that Ginger danced a truly wicked Charleston with remarkable sass and speed. When the Interstate Vaudeville Circuit announced it would hold a Charleston contest in various cities, with the winner guaranteed booking in their theaters, Ginger made up her mind to enter.

The Fort Worth competition was held on the stage of the Majestic Theater after the last show on Friday night. Some three dozen young contenders were there, prepared to dance their hearts out for the deciding vote, to be judged by the volume of audience applause accorded each contestant. The time was late October 1926, and thanks to a series of swift and terrible events in my own career, I found myself backstage at the Majestic that very same night, rooting for my eleven-year-old sister Louise to win over hoydenish Ginger Rogers, the Fort Worth flash.

Front-office studio shoppers, thumbing through an early spring issue of the 1926 *Standard Casting Directory*, were astonished to note the name of Baby Peggy among the two hundred other Hollywood children listed as available for screen work. Even for its rather cynical readership, the *Directory* resembled a depressing casualty list — every month someone's career turned up missing, wounded, or dead. Now, it seemed, even the kids were beginning to be picked off, a sure sign that the industry was growing older. Tossing aside their directories, many a Hollywood veteran wondered, "Whatever happened to Baby Peggy?"

The grim truth was that Baby Peggy, at the advanced age of seven, was already a has-been, a failure, a sharp disappointment to her family and, most of all, to herself. The $50,000 Laurel Canyon estate was gone. Gone too were the private stables, the Pierce-Arrow, the Dusenberg, and the staff of six. In their place was a rented bungalow not far from Poverty Row and one second-hand car.

Mother was a haggard, distraught shadow of her former self, hovering over Father, who spent his days in a darkened bedroom, only occasionally strong enough to walk to the front door and back. He had suffered a ruptured appendix, complicated by severe peritonitis, at a time when antibiotics were unknown and only the hardiest few survived that ordeal. But his exceptional recovery was followed by a crushing depression, diagnosed then as a complete nervous breakdown. He had twice attempted suicide in his despairing state, and we now kept his favorite .45 carefully hidden in the garage.

"All he needs is hope — some kind of goal, a challenge," the doctor said when he made his weekly house call. "Without the will to live, there is simply nothing medicine can do."

As I followed Mother and the doctor to the front door, I reflected on the terrible events of the past two years and wondered once again where I had gone wrong. Certainly I could not be faulted for lack of good will or not living up to the contract.

A child star's contract was a very sobering legal instrument that most movie mothers, to whom a week's work for their child constituted a career, would have paled to read. My own gilt-edged agreement with Sol Lesser, for example, left small room for error and was shot through with ominous references to suspension "due to illness or injury of the said Peggy." A still more chilling passage touched upon her possible "refusal to work," spelling out the swift and lethal reprisals for such sabotage. Small wonder that parents' palms grew damp as they read these documents, and their already obsessive preoccupation with the health and good will of their child rose to even higher levels of anxiety. Viewed in the light of the contract, a peevish child star's "I won't" assumed the magnitude of a full-scale slave rebellion in the antebellum South. Both threatened the breakdown of an exploitative system.

In an industry built on contradiction, the child star was Hollywood's ultimate paradox. Certainly Jackie Coogan and I were, for although we were both cheerful, tireless, and cooperative on the set, our parents, producers, and most other adults were careful to talk down to us, as though we were appealing but mindless pets. They instinctively turned away our most innocent questions about what we were doing, why, and sometimes for how much with fatuous replies, as though they feared candid answers would give us a sense of self-importance, power, and perhaps even trigger a mutinous refusal to comply. Jack Coogan appeared to flaunt Jackie's ignorance of his own financial worth in public, as though his son's density on the subject somehow justified total parental control over every aspect of his life. Repeatedly, too, total strangers took it upon themselves to advise me that I had the most generous, self-sacrificing parents they had ever met, adopting a threatening "and don't you ever forget it" tone that implied I was a spoiled ingrate on the brink of rebelling and casting my poor family penniless into the street.

Spoiled darlings in the eyes of an envious public, we were actually child laborers working to support our families. Envied as history's youngest self-made millionaires, we were in fact charged with the unenviable task of bringing up our own emotionally immature and insecure parents even as we earned their bread. With astronomical earnings any adult might envy, we were constantly reminded that we had no right to special treatment of any kind. We had obligations, not privileges. We were, in effect, only "doing the chores" like any other boy or girl.

In a universally admired effort to offset the excessive public acclaim accorded us as stars, our parents deliberately withheld the special praise and approval that only parents can give and that are so critical in building a child's self-esteem. We were asking for gratuitous love. They demanded humility, submission, and performance as the price. In the end it became clear that no matter how much we loved our parents or wanted to believe they loved us, our real value to them seemed measured only in terms of performance and earning power.

When Jackie was eight and signed his million-dollar contract with Metro, he was immediately insured for the full amount the interested parties stood to lose in the event of his untimely death. But, as I learned long before I was eight, there are worse things than dying young, insured or not. Foremost among them was the devastating experience of losing the only things that guaranteed attention from one's parents — performance and pay.

Everything seemed to cave in on me at once. After completing my second Lesser film and a brief personal appearance tour with it, I returned to Hollywood prepared to start work on *Heidi*. What none of the family was prepared for, however, was the state of affairs at home. J.G. and my grandmother had divorced a year or so earlier, but he remained in charge of my affairs. Now we returned to find J.G. gone and the servants in a state of mutiny. The always self-righteous and punctilious J.G., who had delivered daily sermons over breakfast on the techniques and merits of propriety and thrift, had eloped with a Texas oil heiress he had met on the veranda of the Hollywood Hotel.

While J.G. was not exactly irreplaceable, especially in Mother's view, he had taken with him the irreplaceable funds of the Baby Peggy Corporation, with which, as vice president, he had been entrusted. Not only had he embezzled all that remained of my movie earnings, he also made off with the very respectable sums I had earned on the road over a period of many months; they had been mailed back for him to bank. The servants' salaries had gone unpaid for three months, and several of Father's most valued insurance policies had been allowed to lapse. On checking more closely, Mother discovered to her horror that even her household crystal, linens, and silver were missing, too. The heiress must have demanded matching funds.

J.G.'s treachery was a blow from which we never fully recovered, either financially or as a family. Father's always shaky confidence in his own judgment was shattered and his faith in business associates utterly destroyed. But he realized that the only way to stem the monetary hemorrhage was to get me back before the camera and to immediately collect from Lesser our share of the two films' earnings. However, when he sat down with Lesser to cut up the pie, he was quietly told that neither film had shown a profit. Father was appalled. How could that be? We had toured with both features and *Captain January*, at least, had never failed to play to standing room only in every theater large and small.

What Father did not realize was that "block booking" was a widespread practice among producers and distributors, and Lesser was among the shrewdest of the lot. Theaters were pressured to buy all of a studio's products, good and bad, in order to obtain the one or two outstanding films turned out each year. The revenues were then spread evenly among them and any percentage split of profits promised a star usually proved nonexistent.

Outraged by what he considered a flagrant breach of contract, Father invoked the "refusal to work" clause and severed all relations with Sol Lesser's studio. Lesser did not seem reluctant to let me go. Rumor had it that he was contemplating something even more lucrative than playing musical chairs with child stars. He was buying the screen rights to Edgar Rice Burroughs's jungle hero, Tarzan. Although Julius Stern had only managed to trade dollars on his version at Century, Lesser felt there was money to be made on the old chestnut. He was very right.*

Divested of both income and savings for the first time in five years, Father turned to the urgent business of collecting royalties from those firms that had used my name. Here another disastrous surprise awaited him. All but one or two had dissolved their companies before royalty claims could be made. In most cases there was not even a legal entity left to sue.

Over the next few weeks the world in which I had grown up — the one my earnings had built for us all — simply fell apart. Everything we owned that could be liquidated was sold. For the first time within memory I found myself idle, not the carefree child's idleness I had long dreamed of, but a tense and anxious time. Among the casualties was our tutor, and Louise's renewed pleas that we be allowed to attend school went unheeded. We were now too broke to afford a private school and Father was too proud to send us to a public one. As a concession to his pride, we had no schooling whatever for more than two years.

Louise and I missed our favorite mounts, but made do with two saddles thrown over wooden sawhorses in the back yard. One afternoon Mother made us lemonade, and, just like ordinary children, we hit upon the idea of setting up a stand on the streetcorner and selling it to the neighborhood kids for five cents a glass. We were having a glorious time when suddenly Father

* Burroughs's son-in-law, Jim Pierce, himself the former Century Tarzan, was given film rights to a Tarzan film by Burroughs as a wedding gift when he married his daughter, Joan. These rights Lesser bought and went on to make some sixteen movies. Over the years they earned three million dollars for author Burroughs (in addition to his earnings from MGM's Tarzan films) and brought an undisclosed fortune to the foresighted Lesser.

came home and ordered us into the house. After upbraiding Mother for allowing me to be seen in such a "degrading" situation, he burst out, "It's bad enough I can't get her a job at any studio in town, you have to let the neighbors think we're so poor she has to sell lemonade on the street!"

Father's reaction reflected his state of panic over my disintegrating career. By now he was convinced that Lesser had "blackballed" him from the industry because of some parting remarks he had made about the producer's origins, all the way back to his pushcart forebears. He had no real proof that Lesser had so retaliated, but he suffered as much as if it were true. Nor did it help to read in the papers that Jackie Coogan's land investment in the Wilshire tract (the very same one from which Father had withdrawn his $50,000) was now valued at over $100,000. And in a prime business block on Western Avenue, Coogan's holdings were reportedly worth another $300,000. In all, his choice real estate totaled $1,500,000, and the Coogans still had "plenty of money looking for bargains in real estate." Both Mother and Father recognized the fine hand of Arthur Bernstein, who had shrewdly placed a blue chip on every square.

When it seemed that things could hardly get worse, the final blow fell. My two front teeth dropped out. In an average family this rite of passage is a sign of growth, and some children even receive a gift from the tooth fairy to commemorate the event. Our Gang's Mary Ann Jackson was considered twice as cute and "typical" without her front teeth as with them. But I was a personality star, therefore not a typical kid at all. To present me without teeth was like serving a wedding cake without the frosting.

"It was bad enough before," I overheard Father telling Mother; "now I'll never be able to get her a job." Glancing guiltily in the hall mirror as I passed, I would cringe at the sight. At off moments I found my parents gazing sadly at me as though I had fallen victim to some disfiguring and terminal disease.

And then, one bright spring day in 1926, a Poverty Row producer who had seen my listing in *The Standard Casting Directory* called me for an interview. Dressed in my best and looking not a day over six, I set out with Father in our secondhand car for the studio. On the way over we agreed I was to look as happy as possible without actually *smiling* at anyone. When we entered the office, a fat middle-aged man in a shabby dark suit came from behind a desk and walked around me several times as though judging a livestock entry at the county fair. At length he returned to his desk.

"Mr. Montgomery, I'll be honest. I can't pay her anything like the kind of money she's been getting, you understand. But she'll do for the Russian immigrant kid in *April Fool*. And even though it's a small part, it's worth it to me to have her name on the credits — you know what I mean?"

As the negotiation progressed, I sat quietly in a carved Spanish-style armchair, eyes discreetly downcast, ankles neatly crossed. I realized the man couldn't afford me, but he also seemed to sense that we could not afford to reject him. He was not a very pleasant man, but it was nice to have someone — *anyone* — want me again.

"Let's say a hundred and fifty for the few days she's before the camera," he offered, spreading his hands. "Okay?"

Father accepted and, relieved that the ordeal was over, I jumped up and dropped my farewell curtsey, smiling broadly. The man stared at my toothless grin, and in a tone of complete resignation added, "Oh, and by the way, you better do something about that hole in her face. I know a credit dentist who makes plates cheap. Could be he can make one for a kid as well as grownups."

Such a possibility had simply never crossed Father's mind, but on the way home we stopped by the dentist's office, where I was told to bite into a mouthful of cold pink wax. "Nothing to it," the dentist chirped as though highly pleased with himself. "I never made one this small before, but when I get through not even her own Mother's gonna know she's wearing false teeth!"

April Fool took only four days of my time, working on a scabrous old stage that made Century's meanest sets look posh. When the shooting was over Father expressed relief, for, as he explained to me, he now had "a job of his own," having signed a contract with director Henry King to double Ronald Coleman in all the riding scenes of a big new Western, *The Winning of Barbara*

Worth. He invested in expensive studio portraits to circulate among the casting offices. Not yet thirty-five, a handsome man who photographed well and could ride with the best, he was making a strong bid for stardom. As for his acting experience, well, he could do what all the other cowboy stars he knew did — make it up as he went along.

Father was happier than I had ever seen him. His working relationship with me was terminated, as though it had never been. Like one of those early Keystone Cop sequences where the film is run backward, Father and I had come full circle: I was once more the child at home, he the working horseman and, most important of all, the breadwinner.

He and Mother also began getting along better than they had in years. One night when they returned from an evening of dining at the Hula Hut, I was awakened by the silvery strains of the popular waltz "Three O'Clock in the Morning." Tiptoeing down the hall to the sunroom, I peeked through the half-open door. Unseen by them, I watched as they waltzed to the ghostly music of the player piano, Mother in a gossamer chiffon evening gown, Father in his tuxedo, both of them drenched in the blue-white moonlight streaming through the french doors. They were deeply in love again.

Returning to my bed, I lay awake a long time pondering what the scene meant to me. While I was relieved that they were happy, the realization that I was no longer essential to that happiness filled me with an unnamed dread, a feeling of being somehow disembodied. Crisis-oriented since I was two, with performance and concern for their welfare my only means of giving or receiving love, I now felt cut off from all human consolation and support. Floating off into the dark sea of sleep I did not cry, but I felt abandoned, clinging to a raft that was myself alone. Fortunately for the adult I would one day become, my sense of identity was uncommonly strong.

A few days later, while on a weekend vacation in Yosemite to celebrate the completion of shooting on *The Winning of Barbara Worth,* Father was stricken with appendicitis. It was thirty-six hours before he underwent emergency surgery. A full six weeks after that he returned home, only to sink into a numbing melancholy, his nascent career as a cowboy star over even before it began, my own ruined beyond reclamation.

One evening in mid-October, when Mother, Louise, and I were around Father's bed trying desperately to cheer him up, the telephone rang. Mother answered and countered the operator's opening question with one of her own. "Long distance? Collect? But operator, we don't know a soul in Fort Worth."

Curiosity seemed to spark Father's first decisive statement and action in months. "Here, give me that phone. I'll talk to her."

"Who's calling?" Father asked, and then he heard a familiar voice on the other end: "Hello, Jack, this is Earl Hanson!" Father accepted the call.

Earl Hanson was one of my parents' more recently acquired foul-weather friends. He was a dapper, razor-sharp promoter and drummer in his early thirties who had done a little bit of everything until Prohibition revealed where his true talents lay. With the glib tongue of a snake-oil vendor and the cold nerve of a counterspy, he had plunged into the business of bootlegging liquor out of Tijuana in the inner tubes of spare tires and the false bottoms of selected automobiles. He had often used our basement as a temporary hideout in exchange for free samples when revenuers were hot on his heels. Not only did Earl buy and sell the stuff, but he consumed it on a truly prodigious scale. When he couldn't lay hands on the real thing, he made do with toilet water and high-grade perfumes much to Mother's displeasure. Despite these minor flaws, Earl possessed a character of such overpowering sweetness and generosity that my parents could not bring themselves to terminate their rather risky relationship with him.

"Earl, what in hell are you doing in Texas?" Father wanted to know.

"Oh, engaged in my usual import-export business," he laughed. "But seeing as how this is your nickel I'll get down to why I'm calling. I know you folks have been on hard times and I took it upon myself to act as your advance man."

"Advance man for what?"

"For Peggy. See, I've got a friend here who's a theater manager and I just booked her into the Majestic Theater opening this coming Wednesday matinee."

Father sat bolt upright in bed. "You did *what?*"

"It's a fantastic break. She's replacing a big name vaudevillian who's sick. If her act is good enough they'll book her for the full forty-two weeks on the Interstate circuit."

"But, Earl, Peggy doesn't *have* an act!"

"Well, get one before Wednesday. She's heading a six-act bill and it pays two grand a week."

There was a long pause, then Father said, "Okay, Earl, consider yourself hired as our advance man. Set up the promotion and publicity and reserve us a two-bedroom hotel suite. Tell your friend we'll be there Tuesday morning in time to rehearse for the Wednesday matinee." In what amounted to a single flowing motion, Father slammed down the receiver, threw back the bedclothes, and swung his feet to the floor. Mother, Louise, and I stared as though he were a corpse risen from the grave.

"Well, don't just sit there! Somebody get me my robe and slippers. We haven't got much time. Let's get moving!"

From that instant chaos reigned. Over the next two days everything we owned was either put in storage, packed to go, or summarily thrown out. Three days after Earl's fateful phone call we were aboard the Southern Pacific rolling toward the Texas plains. But the desert scenery streamed past the windows of our compartment unseen as four of the most inexperienced comedy writers alive set about putting together a vaudeville act. Without so much as an old Joe Miller joke book, we cribbed from comic strips and cartoons and added remembered bits and lines from my old comedies. The act was built around a three-minute screen test I had made for circulation before my teeth fell out. In it I played a little girl in rompers who steals a policeman's motorcycle and rides away. The last frame faded out on the officer on foot, in hot pursuit of both bike and thief. Using the film as a prologue to set the proper "movie star" mood, the act continued the adventures of officer and child onstage. Father, who had always been paralyzed with stage fright, said he would play the policeman. That meant it would be my chore to pull him through every performance.

Earl was at the Fort Worth depot to meet us, nattily dressed as always in a pin-stripe suit with a pink carnation in his buttonhole and matching floral-scented breath. "Welcome to the land of bluebonnets and bourbon!" he greeted us in a mock Texas drawl. "You're already famous here." As we crowded into a taxi with our luggage, he continued to expand on his activities as advance man. "Say, I've plastered this town with posters from one end to the other."

He was right. As we drove to the hotel my name shouted back at me from every other billboard and telephone pole:

> Baby Peggy, In Person!
> Six Big Acts!
> Starts Wednesday
> Continuous Performance

"Yessirree, Peg," Earl said enthusiastically, "Texas is gonna be Comeback Country for you — and for all of us!"

For the first time in my life I experienced genuine terror. Young though I was, my professional instincts were highly developed, and I recognized the difference between a simple "thank you for coming" personal appearance and a high-powered act. It was clear to me I had neither. I had seen a lot of big-time vaudeville during my months of touring — the Duncan Sisters, Eddie Cantor, Al Jolson, Elsie Janis. And I remembered very well the time we saw a rowdy audience become displeased with Elsie. Hooting and throwing peanuts, they backed her against the velvets and finally off the stage. And certainly Elsie knew every trick there was. What if the same thing happened to me?

Only three days earlier I had been worthless, washed up, a discard. Now, for $2000 a week I was expected to perform a feat only slightly less impossible than walking on water — to face an audience without material. Mother, Father, Louise, and Earl were all in the wagon hitched to what they confidently hoped was still a star. Involuntarily I drew back from the cab window. I dreaded what lay ahead. Perhaps if no one recognized me I wouldn't really *be* in Fort Worth at all. The whole thing seemed like a terrible dream, and in one sense it was. From that day forward, for the rest of my life, I was haunted by the recurring nightmare of being forced to go on before an audience without a script, my family desperate in the wings, begging me to come through for them just one more time. In later years I would wake up in a cold sweat, relieved to find it had only been "my dream." But the first time I was only seven, I was wide awake, and the nightmare was inescapably real.

Although we had been under killing pressure for almost a week, the door of our hotel suite barely closed behind us when the first "continuous performance" began. For eighteen hours straight Father and I, with Louise holding the cue sheets, rehearsed the twelve-minute skit over and over again. Father's temper, frayed by months of illness and anxiety, snapped like a buggy whip over a circus pony's head whenever I missed a line.

"Hell, you could do better than that when you were two years old!" he shouted in exasperation, as fright and fatigue took their toll of my once-faultless memory.

"I knew we shouldn't have tried it," Mother wailed, wringing her hands and pacing the floor. "We should have stayed in Hollywood."

On Tuesday morning we arrived at the Majestic Theater to rehearse with the electricians, stagehands, and orchestra. There we found the welcome mat was definitely *not* out for us. The other acts were cold, clannish, and withdrawn; "show me" signals were everywhere. Obviously the vaudeville headliner I was replacing had earned the coveted next-to-closing spot, and everyone on the bill wanted me to know it.

Wednesday at noon we were struggling with the last-minute crises of make-up, costume, props, and music. Shortly before two o'clock I found myself alone on a darkened stage, crouched inside a prop barrel watching the screen test flash the Hollywood Hills and the Hollywood sign before my eyes. Many times over the next few years I would experience the sensation of being adrift inside that barrel, an endless abyss below. But on that first day as I felt the warmth of the spot pour down upon me all I could think about was surviving. Mustering all the courage I possessed, and making certain my upper plate was firmly in place, I rose smiling, ready to face whatever life, vaudeville, and the people of Fort Worth had to hand me.

Twenty minutes later we were taking our bows to sustained and enthusiastic applause. Suddenly, too, the hostile people on the bill gathered around as friends.

"Great act!"

"Freshest comedy stuff we've seen on the Interstate in years!"

At the dressing room door Earl appeared, glowing with excitement and good news. "You did it! Harry Weber was out front and wants to handle the act!"

"Who's Harry Weber?" I asked numbly, almost beyond caring.

"Why, honey," Mother told me almost reverently, "he's just the biggest vaudeville agent there is!"

A week later a long white envelope appeared on my make-up bench. Inside were dozens of crisp ten- and twenty-dollar bills, $2000 in all. We were booked onto the entire Interstate circuit and were "held over" a second week in Fort Worth by popular demand.

Meantime, Louise was nearly hysterical at the prospect of finally being able to shine on her own as a possible winner of the Interstate circuit's widely advertised Charleston contest. She spent every minute between shows rehearsing her routine and sewing the costume she would wear.

Finally, on the big night, Louise was lined up with some three dozen other contenders against the back curtains on a full stage. When her turn came she whirled through her version with spirit and virtuosity. At last it was narrowed down to a contest between Louise and a Fort Worth girl named Ginger Rogers. The applause for both was deafening, but Ginger won by a few decibels recorded on the official applause machine.

Louise was devastated, but she dried her tears and perked up when the winner's mother generously came over to her afterward. "Now don't you worry, honey, you danced real well," she said encouragingly. "You just keep on practicing and you'll be ready for your big break when it comes. That's what Ginger did."

That was my first fascinating glimpse of Lela Rogers in action, not as Ginger's mother but in her other role, herself. She had a positive genius for drawing Ginger's natural rivals into her corner and converting them into zealous partisans. Working from the unassailable premise that Ginger was more beautiful, talented, ambitious, and hard-working than most girls, still, "you too" could be a winner if you really tried. It was a tactic that won supporters to Ginger's cause and did no harm. It also gave many people a blind faith in the power behind Ginger's rise. With her steely, winsome ways, Lela was stage mother, Christian Science practitioner, talent scout, and star-maker all in one. While she never believed for a minute that anyone had been born who could outperform her Ginger, she convinced dozens of her own drama students that they could.

I met many mothers in show business who attempted the impossible. Only Lela Rogers came close to actually pulling it off.

13
Comeback Country

*I wrote her baby talk routines. I wrote songs. I
made clothes. I even carried a sewing machine.
I was a regular Mama Rose, exactly — except that I
did it by cooperating with the circuits, cooperating
with the managers, making them see that what's
good for Ginger is good for them.*

— Lela Rogers, in *Ginger,*
Loretta and Irene Who?, 1976

FROM THE CRUDE "BIT" THEATERS and melodeons of Lotta
Crabtree's youth, vaudeville evolved into America's favorite
family entertainment. The grand old "two-a-day" had reigned
supreme from 1875 until 1920, when most theaters had to begin
running films or close their doors. Subsequently, small houses offered occasional vaudeville with movies, while the big-time ba-
roque palaces staged six top acts plus a first-run feature for eighty-
five cents.

But the price of survival came high. Now, even the proudest
two-a-day headliners found themselves doing four and five shows
between screenings of the feature film, programs quite accurately
billed as "continuous performances." This frenetic pace kept up
until 1933, when vaudeville was finally done in by talking films.
Its passing left some of the country's finest theatrical artists
stranded, talents soon plundered by radio, Hollywood, and nightclubs, the last emerging as an iridescent butterfly from the ugly
"speakeasy" cocoon once Prohibition was repealed. But since no
one dreamed the end was near, confidence ran high during those
final days. I for one, who spent what seemed an interminable

three years in hotels, Pullman cars, and basement dressing rooms, thought vaudeville would *never* die.

From 1926 to 1929 the deadly pattern included three shows on weekdays, a morning matinee, a Baby Peggy look-alike contest plus four shows on Saturday, and five shows each on Sundays, Thanksgiving, Christmas, the Fourth of July, Labor Day, and most Jewish holy days. Having grown up in a totally creative and spontaneous work environment, I found repeating the same few lines five times daily depressingly monotonous. Onstage I suffered frequent mental blackouts from which I would awaken minutes later, exactly on cue, not even Father being aware of any lapse.

But while it was a repetitive existence, it was anything but predictable. To those familiar insecurities experienced in Hollywood, the road added the abyss of being homeless with all the attendant vulnerability and helplessness. Our first Christmas in vaudeville was spent in Dallas. Louise and I enjoyed a nine-foot tree and a mountain of marvelous toys. At week's end the wagons rolled — as they did after every Christmas and birthday. Having played with our toys for only a matter of hours, they had to be left behind. For hotel chambermaids, being assigned to Baby Peggy's suite was the next best thing to winning the Irish Sweepstakes.

Arriving in Little Rock, after only six weeks on the road, Father was rushed from the train to the hospital for emergency surgery, and we were faced with the ruinous prospect of being laid off and stranded in a strange town. Over Mother's protestations that it was impossible, I played the first Little Rock matinee as a single, secretly welcoming this refreshing opportunity to ad lib and cover the policeman's absence with spontaneous and humorous asides. My gamble paid off. I won a standing ovation from the audience and bought enough time from the management to break in Larry Rich, a comedian on the bill, before the supper show. We worked together until Father recovered and returned to the act.

On the road, health itself was a continuous crisis. Mother began each day asking me how I felt and observing anxiously that I looked either feverish or pale. My parents loved me as their child, but they were more concerned with what might happen to us all if the machine that made the money broke down. The change in drinking water from one city to another often laid the entire bill low with severe cramps and diarrhea, an affliction not easily explained to audiences, but one that even children had to deal with. In Buffalo we lost ten precious days to mumps; in Battle Creek we nearly lost me to pneumonia. After that, tonsillitis settled in, but, with my earnings at $300 a day, who could afford time off for a tonsillectomy? "The show must go on" was not the affected theatrical battle cry that decades of Busby Berkeley musicals have made it seem. It was simply another way of saying *"Survive!"* A bewildering array of backstage talismans and taboos aided that survival in a profession where mere mortals needed all the supernatural help they could get. More practical help, however, came to the truly needy from another and far more mundane quarter.

The National Vaudeville Artists' Association staged all-star benefit marathons lasting seven or eight hours, and in a single night often raised as much as $50,000 for sick or jobless artists. Although I worked every NVA benefit within driving distance, one was especially memorable because of an unforgettable encounter with Al Jolson.

When we arrived at the benefit in New York, it was already past one in the morning and my performance would be my sixth that day. George Jessel was onstage, giving his third encore, while Eddie Cantor, Sophie Tucker, and Al Jolson were lined up to follow. Finally, at three, Father went up to Jolson and asked him if he would mind letting me go on ahead of him. My act was short, the hour was late, and I was only nine years old. Jolson shot an unfriendly glance at me, and I found myself looking into the cold eyes of a man who I understood had fought his way out of Hell's Kitchen by dancing for pennies on streetcorners as a boy.

"Sorry," he snapped. "I was a kid once myself. That's show business."

In a sense I could understand Jolson's callous retort, for by then I was familiar with the slum neighborhoods where he had grown up. For several weeks we had descended daily from our luxurious apartment overlooking Central Park into what was to me the terrifying squalor of Brooklyn's slums and New York's Lower East Side. Pushcart vendors, shoppers, urchins, and idlers turned the narrow streets into a surging tide of humanity, filling the air with a cacophony of foreign curses, shouts, and cries. Doing the usual four shows a day, we spent from noon to midnight in this alien world.

The minute they spotted our limousine, street boys of all ages closed in on us from every side. Riding the running boards and rear trunk all the way to the stage door, they screamed obscenities, beat on the tightly closed windows with small, birdlike fists, or silently pressed their faces to the glass and stared in hungrily. One day, as our chauffeur drove slowly and carefully through the teeming streets, I watched transfixed as a buxom woman pushed her six-year-old girl off the curb directly in front of our car. "Go on, Rachel, go!" the mother screamed, a threatening fist upraised. "Let them hit you! We can sue!"

I endured these fearful encounters by holding tightly to Jimbo, my faithful teddy bear, and by trying to keep the ever-threatening children at bay with a frozen smile.

It was only natural, I suppose, that a child celebrity, to whom children had always been strangers anyway, would be frightened of a species that always seemed to come in mobs of two hundred or more and demanded of me everything I had or was. Later I was given a rare glimpse of the other side when I received a deeply revealing and poignant letter from a lady who had been a little girl of six when I played her home town of Salt Lake City. She described in eloquent terms what such child star worship meant to a lonely and unappreciated child trapped in a cold and loveless home:

> What a captivating comet you were, flashing across my bleak sky, sliding off the silver screen onto the Pantages stage, as a real little girl. I stared at you avidly, taking in all that I could in the few brief moments allotted as mine in which to see *you*, not as just a picture, but really *alive*. I felt such a nonentity. I wanted more than anything to be you, to possess your black hair and brown eyes that sparkled fire. I had a little dark fur muff, and when I got home I put it on my head like hair, and I plucked the stick-eyes out of my teddy bear and held them up to the mirror to see how I would look. Brown teddy bear eyes and a dark muff head — Baby Peggy? Well, hardly. So I named my favorite doll

and then myself Peggy after you, hoping your magic would rub off on me. Your confidence, your charm, your happiness and fame — oh, you were *everything* I yearned to be!

Appearances were indeed misleading, and false impressions were imparted not only across the footlights but backstage as well. By this time my parents were unshakably convinced that I possessed a genius for observing any skill, however complex, and mastering it magically from within. Given this false premise, it was obviously unnecessary to train me in any depth or logical order. Dramatic skits, impersonations, songs, dance routines — all I had to do was flash a glance at some other performer and presto! all his expertise was mine. Teaching me something would spoil my "naturalness" was the burden of their argument, and, as I learned, it was an occupational hazard of many children who had been performing so convincingly all their lives that they had even deceived their parents.

Playing just across town, for example, was Dainty June Hovick. She had been on the road for years and not always enjoying my luxuries of big-time bookings and big-time pay. Now, with managers casting about frantically for fresh stage attractions to compete with the threat of talking films, "Dainty June and her Newsboys" was a very old act that was giving at the seams. Agents had as much as told Mama Rose Hovick that Louise and June looked like freaks; going on twelve and fourteen, they still dressed and acted like six-year-olds. Indeed, June was still delivering her threadbare specialty "Nobody Knows Me Number" after all these years. Formal dancing lessons had been left behind long ago in Seattle, and June had been gamely faking her toe routines and all else ever since. Finally in desperation June begged her mother to allow her to take ballet lessons.

"Lessons would ruin you, darling," Rose said — that all too common reply. Rose, now middle-aged, was a small, dark woman with an incredible inner toughness. She had managed to survive by single-mindedly pursuing what she thought was best. It had made her narrow, prejudiced, and virtually blind to any alternatives but her goals as chosen years earlier. "You're a natural dancer, honey," she continued, as though stating an obvious fact.

"But I haven't learned any new steps in years," June pleaded. "I can't go on forever doing those baby 'Pocket Size Pavlova' routines!"

"You're Mother's baby," Rose replied absently as she buffed her nails. "You'll always be Mother's baby."

At this low point the Hovicks were asked to audition their act for Mr. Rothafel at the Roxy in New York, the most prestigious presentation house in the country at that time. To June, the Roxy stage seemed as big as an ocean liner and the theater positively cavernous, especially when empty, with the house lights on and the great Mr. Rothafel himself watching expectantly from the front row. After June and the company finished auditioning the act, Rothafel sent word backstage that he wanted to see June onstage alone.

Painfully aware of her crooked front teeth, absurdly youthful dress, and her bony knees that creaked and cracked every time she moved, June forced herself out onto the giant stage. Rothafel — known to everyone as Roxy — was sympathetic, asking her to sing whatever she wished and then to dance.

When her ordeal ended, he asked her down into the aisle, where Rose joined them. Then Roxy invited them both upstairs into his elegantly furnished suite. Tactful but direct, Roxy came right to the point. He told Rose the act was awful and he was not interested in booking it.

"But we've headlined all over the circuit." Rose bristled. "There *is* no more circuit," Roxy informed her, then added, as if relieved at the prospect, "There will be no more acts like yours." But he was interested in June. "She has future possibilities. She has talent or I wouldn't be wasting my time talking to you."

June sat transfixed, trembling from a combination of chills and nerves, drinking in this wonderful man's kind words.

"But she must be taught by experts to sing and to dance — not just dance so that people think it remarkable she can dance at all. I believe she can do it. Her personality" — he bent his magnetic gaze on the trembling girl — "even now is full of promise."

"I can do better," June babbled wildly, "I know I can learn. I pick things up quickly backstage. I only have to watch two or three times. But, oh, if I had lessons!"

Roxy smiled. "I know you'll work. You're a worker." Suddenly June saw herself on stage in a lavish Roxy presentation, glamorous, glorified — then the vision was shattered as Rose doubled back to the beginning of the conversation. "What about the act?"

"You don't need it," Roxy assured her. "I'll take care of you. We'll draw up an agreement, and I'll personally supervise the development of your little girl."

June was ecstatic. It was as if God himself had stepped down from the clouds to create her all over again, this time beautiful, confident, and, above all, *professionally trained.*

"Give me this little girl for three years," said the famed entrepreneur slowly, "and I'll give you a star."

"A star!" Rose shrilled, rising from her chair. "She *is* a star!"

"Mrs. Hovick, in three years you'll be proud — "

June caught her mother's arm. "Please, Mother, listen to him." But Rose could see only a male monster who wanted to come between her and her baby, for only God knew what perverted and selfish purpose.

"Look at what you've done!" Rose screamed at Roxy. "She's even taking your side against her own mother! How dare you come into our lives!"

Roxy shook his head silently, rose from his chair, and, without a word, left the room. June stared at the door as it closed behind him. "Thank you, anyway," she murmured.

A few months later, in Topeka, Kansas, June fell in love with Bobby, an eighteen-year-old who worked in their act. She had just turned thirteen. When Rose came upon them, wrapped in a curtain in the wings, she dragged June bodily into the dressing room, having fired Bobby on the spot. Once the door was closed, she dealt her daughter a blow that sent June reeling to the floor. Tears streaming down her face, the outraged Rose shrieked so loudly she could be heard above the organist's soft accompaniment of the silent film out front.

"Ungrateful! All my life spent on *you!* Trying to make something out of you — "

June struggled to her feet and looked at her mother threateningly. "Don't hit me."

"Hit you?" Rose cried. "Who do you think you are? I can't even get an audience to accept you anymore. Out there on the stage you're *nothing!*"

Dramatically Rose ordered June out of "*my* dressing room," and when June contested her, she picked up an ivory hand mirror from the make-up bench and struck her a solid blow. For a moment the dressing room was silent except for the combatants' heavy breathing. Then Rose drew herself up self-righteously. "You'll see. God will punish you. He's already started. You're a failure — a failure. After I've spent my whole life on you, too. I can't book you anywhere anymore." Then, gingerly kicking the bits of splintered mirror with the toe of her shoe, she said ominously, "This is your seven years' bad luck, not mine," and walked out.

That night June and Bobby eloped. A year or two later, when June stopped by her mother's New York apartment before entering her first dance marathon, she found Rose engrossed in the skyrocketing career of her other daughter, Louise, now the famous stripper Gypsy Rose Lee. As her mother pasted Gypsy's latest reviews into an enormous scrapbook, June mused aloud, "I remember the scrapbooks you kept on me. All the time we played the Keith-Orpheum circuit, and even when I was Baby June in movies."

Rose looked pained. "Those seem a million years ago"; then she added archly, "And of course none of it was Broadway."

After that June went her own way. She changed her name from Hovick to Havoc — which aptly summed up what life with Mama Rose had been.

My parents entered their second decade of marriage on the road. Their union was as turbulent as ever. Mother was now more beautiful and independent than before. Touring Chicago and New York speakeasies became a way of life for them after theater hours. But Father's jealousy increased in proportion to Mother's attractiveness. One of my recurring terrors was the quite familiar scene of Father accusing Mother of being in love with some handsome hotel manager, band leader, or other passing acquaintance.

What followed was the classic farewell scene. He dragged out his trunk and started packing while they continued to scream insults at each other. Louise lay low while these battles raged, but since I felt such responsibility for keeping the family going I usually went to pieces, crying wildly, begging Father not to leave us alone here in New York, Chicago, Detroit — wherever we were playing at the time.

When we played Milwaukee, in Mother's home state of Wisconsin, she was thunderstruck to receive a call from the hotel lobby announcing the visit of her own long-lost mother. When the gray-haired lady arrived, Mother was so distraught she refused to admit her into our suite, but, with Father and me beside her, confronted the stranger in the hotel corridor instead.

"What do you want with me?" Mother asked icily.

"I only wanted to see my famous little granddaughter with my very own eyes." With that she knelt beside me and clasped me to her bosom. "And oh, what a darling she is!" she cried, sounding exactly like any other Baby Peggy fan. Rising to her feet, she gazed a long moment into Mother's eyes and then said hesitantly, "Well, Marian, you did a good job on her."

Hurt, angry, and in shock, Mother burst out, "You're not my mother! My mother is dead!" Then she rushed back inside our suite in tears, slamming the door behind her.

After a moment's painful silence the lady dabbed at her eyes with her handkerchief, shrugged her shoulders philosophically, and said as if to herself, "Oh, well, at least I got to see my granddaughter." Father and I watched as she turned, walked slowly down the long hall, and disappeared into the elevator. We never saw or heard from her again.

Father still had his dream ranch staked out somewhere in the future, but Mother had no intention of seeing it come true. From people like Lela Rogers, Mother was picking up ideas about what should be done with my career when I blossomed into that tall, beautiful, talented willowy brunette I was certain to become any day now. Lela had set her sights for Ginger on Broadway. "Musicals are where the big exposure is, where the right people see you," she often said. But Mother had never forsaken Hollywood. Like Lot's wife, she was forever looking back at the ruins of my film career, wondering what had really happened. Maybe I *was* only "between pictures" after all — that face-saving ploy that dead theatrical talents traditionally fell back on in Hollywood to keep their career artificially alive when it was already in the grave.

But the news coming out of Hollywood in those days was not exactly cheerful. Early in 1928 it was headlined that Mrs. Arthur Bernstein was suing her husband for divorce, naming none other than Mrs. Lillian Coogan as corespondent. In addition, she was filing a $750,000 suit against the child star's mother for alienation of her husband's affections.

While Bernstein rushed to file a cross-complaint divorce suit, Lillian grew shrill in her own defense and Jack Coogan stoutly defended his faith in his wife and best friend. Local newspapers quoted him as vowing to "fight this thing as nothing has ever been fought before. Here's one bunch of motion picture people that is not going to be made to pay a lot of money just because somebody thinks they will not be able to stand the spotlight!" In public refutation of the charges, the trio appeared at the Ambassador Hotel where, the Los Angeles *Times* reported, "both men danced with Mrs. Coogan in the presence of many celebrities of the motion picture world."

Not in a long while had so sensational a scandal rocked the movie colony. Mrs. Bernstein had hired a private detective, who claimed that during her husband's recent nervous breakdown, when he was cared for in the Coogan home, he and Mrs. Coogan had on several occasions been caught, in dishabille, in each other's arms. It was difficult for my parents to visualize Lillian and Arthur as the stars in such a bedroom farce, but that was really not the point. "It all revolves around the popularity of Jackie Coogan," meowed the Los Angeles *Times*, "for, while the other principals are known in cinemaland, it is through the youthful star that they obtained their rank."

Bernstein, winning his cross-complaint, succeeded in divorcing his wife, and both he and Lillian Coogan testified under oath that no money had been paid Mrs. Bernstein as a settlement. But apparently the scandal left its scars. Only a few years later the Coogans began living apart, Lillian remaining in the Beverly Hills house while Jack Senior spent most of his time at his Pine Valley ranch property near San Diego. No whisper of their separation reached the press, but those who were close to the Coogans maintained they would have divorced had they not been Roman Catholics.

Mother soon learned that Arthur Bernstein was not the only solid rock that could be shaken by an unexpected crisis. When we checked into the Book-Cadillac in Detroit we found a message from Lela Rogers, who was also staying there. When Louise, Mother, and I entered Lela's room, it was apparent that she had been crying long and hard. Lela had always seemed such a forceful woman; I had never before seen her reduced to such a helpless rage — nor would ever again.

"I suppose you've heard what's happened?" she asked, her eyes filling up with irrepressible tears.

"No, Lela, of course not," Mother replied with genuine concern. "What is it?"

"It's Ginger. She's run off with a chorus boy — a common hoofer!"

"*Ginger?*" Mother repeated incredulously.

Lela paced unhappily back and forth while Louise and I began to get the uncomfortable feeling that at least part of this outburst was intended as a salutary lesson to us.

"She didn't tell me — not a word. I didn't even know she *liked* him. And now they're forming *their own act!*"

The boy's name was Jack Pepper, and as I silently constructed their new billing I was inwardly amused: "Ginger and Pepper — The Spicy Two Spot."

Lela felt she had sacrificed her own career to help her daughter, and a girl's perfectly natural instinct for love and marriage had never entered her plans. To Lela, Ginger's defection amounted to cold-blooded, premeditated treachery. Sitting on the edge of the bed, her handkerchief balled into the palm of her small hand, she kept repeating, "I still can't believe she would *do* this to me." Then, rising again, she squared off in front of Louise and me. "Let this be a lesson to both of you. Don't ever run off and break your parents' heart the way Ginger has mine!"

*

Between shows one of Mother's favorite pastimes was to go to the other theaters in town and catch the other acts. All theaters exchanged courtesy passes, so no one ever had to pay to see each other. It was a popular show business tradition that Mother was pleased to make her own.

In this fashion ten-year-old Mitzi Green and her parents, Joe Keno and Rosie Green, came back to see us in New York to ask how one went about making good in Hollywood. My parents acted as though we had walked away from it all because vaudeville was so much better for a child. Later we caught Mitzi's act — she did impersonations very well — and my parents were not impressed. Mother had picked up Lela's penchant for comparing others unfavorably with her own daughter, but she lacked Lela's subtlety and charm.

When we played Indianapolis, Mother heard that Elsie Janis was headlining at the Orpheum. Off we went to catch Elsie's act and, of course, trot around backstage to meet her. Onstage Elsie was a cyclonic performer. Although she sang and danced effectively, the real cutting edge of her talent was still her ability to impersonate. With her long hair piled high and a pink feather boa wrapped three times around her throat, she *became* the Divine Sarah Bernhardt. Then, while the audience looked on, she dismantled this personality, slicked back her hair, put a straw hat aslant her brow, and caught every nuance of Maurice Chevalier's gallic charm.

But as a performer she possessed an added bonus, just as Lotta Crabtree had before her, something that had nothing to do with talent but *where* that talent had bloomed. Throughout Lotta's career, every audience would contain a few scattered forty-niners who had loved her as a child in the camps. Their presence added a magic quality of nostalgia and made each show a joyous personal reunion. In Elsie's case it was the soldiers of the American Expeditionary Force from World War I who provided her with an enthusiastic audience of old friends wherever she played. After her beloved Basil Hallem was killed in 1916, Elsie had thrown herself into entertaining servicemen with compulsive dedication. Even I had heard the legend of the two Janis women at the front, cheering on the troops during the darkest days of the Hun offensive. Elsie sang for her "boys" in hospitals, in tents, in the open fields.

She sought out lost regiments of downhearted, homesick American soldiers sharing every hardship — rain, mud, miserable trenches, even braving the shells of Big Bertha herself. She was dubbed "The Sweetheart of the A.E.F.," their buddy, the first woman ever — with the exception, of course, of Jenny, who accompanied her everywhere — to brave the front. They would never forget her gallantry. To Elsie, every one of them was her lost Basil, and she would often say that those eighteen months in France, singing her heart out for the troops, remained the happiest and most meaningful of her entire life.

Even that day in Indianapolis, some ten years after the armistice, there were middle-aged men in the audience who called out with the old camaraderie, "Hey Elsie, how about giving us 'Hinky Dinky Par-lez Vous'?" The curious chemistry between them gave off light and ignited the entire theater. Elsie produced a tin helmet from nowhere, threw an imaginary rifle over her shoulder, and put every fiber of her square, bony frame into marching across the stage as she belted out "Over There!," "Pack Up Your Troubles in Your Old Kit Bag," and "Give My Regards to Broadway." And then, very slowly, she slid into the first lines of "What's Become of Hinky Dinky Par-lez Vous," pausing to allow the veterans to shout back at her the long-remembered naughty verses. It was an encore that never failed to bring down the house. Wherever she went, their welcome awaited her, making the glorious comradeship of those days come alive again.

Going around backstage, we were graciously admitted into Elsie's dressing room by her Negro maid, Hallie, who had been with her since 1906. It was unlike any other backstage visit I had ever made. Here one of the great mother-daughter combinations in theatrical history was holding court, turning an ordinary star dressing room into a great reception hall. Every corner of the large room was crammed with tall, flared baskets of roses, chrysanthemums, and gladioli in various stages of bloom and decomposition. The place was filled with people come to bid hail or farewell to vivacious Elsie and her scintillating mother. We all moved amid a positively Byzantine collection of exotic birds — screeching parakeets, green and blue lovebirds, and a full chorus of bright yellow canary contraltos in full voice. Visitors had to thread their way around two or three H and M wardrobe trunks standing half-open in the middle of the room and tread a gritty carpet of birdseed flung far and wide by the prima donna inmates of the dozen gilded cages.

Elsie was changing behind a shoulder-high dressing screen, assisted by two French maids. Behind her was an open closet with racks of odd-colored gowns, all of them twinkling with sequins or rhinestones. (One of the first lessons we learned from Elsie was that a bile-colored or chartreuse dress that looked hideous offstage took on an entirely different hue in the spot, to be transformed into a unique color you could be certain no other performer would have.)

Elsie looked much older offstage than on, but then, she was nearing forty. Perspiration poured from her forehead, neck, and bare shoulders. After slipping into a Japanese kimono and feathered satin pumps, she came forward to meet us. She was gracious, outgoing, and obviously loved being surrounded by people. Her mother, on the other hand, impressed me, even in this first meeting, as a woman who felt she was born to preside over others, and even life itself. Jenny was as restless as her twinkling jet jewelry, her eyes darting everywhere, taking in everything as though she were the choreographer of a never-ending ballet. Life for her seemed a grand ball that Elsie's efforts kept going twenty-four hours a day.

Jenny apologized for not being able to spend more time with us, but this was their last day, and they were returning to New York. "Please come see us at the Manor House. There is where we *really* entertain. After all, Elsie has to have two weeks vacation-rest after every six weeks of work — something I've insisted upon ever since she was a child."

Jenny slipped into a velvet coat and deftly inserted into each spacious drooping sleeve a graying and sleepy-looking Pekinese dog. "Come, Ching, don't be stubborn," she said as she slid him, tail first, into his portable doghouse.

We carried a little dog with us on the road, too, as did most show people, but I had never seen a woman *wearing* a dog before. Noting my fascination, Jenny leaned over, her jet earrings dancing. "They go to the movies like this, too," she confided conspiratorily, "and Elsie's two lap dogs do the same. No one even suspects they are there, and do you know, they *enjoy* watching the films!"

Then in a second she was in command again, deploying an army of visitors that seemed forever on the move. "No, no, not those bags. They go with me. Elsie, dear, please take the parakeets, and you, Hallie, don't just stand there, tell the porter we want the thirteen bags, the Victrola, radio, and the five wardrobe trunks loaded at once. Oh, yes, darling, we'll be at the Palace for two weeks — unless, of course, Elsie is held over, which is usually the case, you know. And, Robert, dear, don't forget to write — " Then, as she neared the door, she turned one last time, and I could see the eyes of the two dogs shining out from either sleeve. "Now, remember — you must come see us at the Manor House!"

Later we took Jenny up on her invitation and spent a wonderful day in Tarrytown. Jenny proudly told us how she had built an aviary onto the veranda; Elsie showed us her collection of Chinese artifacts from her tours of the Orient and a magnificent polar bear skin rug a game-hunting admirer had given her. As though reciting a line from a play she said absently, "He wanted to marry me, you know" — and then after a pause — "but Mother knew best."

Not long after that, Elsie fell during a performance at the Palace, breaking a shoulder and a wrist. But when she told Jenny she thought it was time to retire, Jenny talked her into making "just one more trip to Paris" first. Then Elsie started writing short stories and selling them to *Redbook* for a nice fee. When she told her mother she would like to turn to writing, Jenny surprised her with an outrageously expensive string of pearls for her birthday. Elsie was obliged to do the Orpheum circuit one more time to pay for them.

Finally, in April of 1929, Jesse Lasky gave Elsie a job as writer-producer at Paramount. Like Mary Ann, Jenny managed to purchase a Spanish-style bungalow in Beverly Hills as a surprise while Elsie was giving one of her last matinees. After that, Jenny's thirty-five-year party was over.

When Mitzi Green played the Orpheum in Los Angeles, Elsie

caught her act. The little girl with the marvelous impersonations reminded Elsie of herself at that age, and as she was casting Paramount's first musical, *Paramount on Revue*, she signed Mitzi for a part. Just as Chaplin had plucked Jackie from the same stage ten years earlier, Elsie now lifted Mitzi from vaudeville and turned her into one of the first child stars in talking films.

Jenny was not even mildly interested in Elsie's new find. Every morning she waved a brave goodbye from the front doorway as Elsie set out for the studio. Later, Elsie remarked that her mother "only pretended to like playing bridge and living the life of an idle wife." After where she had gone and who she had been, Jenny felt shelved. In June 1930, following a bout with pneumonia, Jenny died quickly, but apparently not unexpectedly. Six months earlier, on New Year's Eve, she had penned a farewell note that Elsie did not discover until after her mother's death. It revealed clearly that Jenny could not conceive of Elsie being really happy without her.

> We have lived fifty-fifty, and I leave content if you will just carry on and be happy. I shall always be near you. Don't get hard ... Don't weaken ... You should be a rich woman, dear, but we have lived without thought of riches and if you will try to be happy, I'll carry on Somewhere, Somehow! My prayers, my love, and all I have is yours. Mother.

After the funeral, which Elsie appropriately referred to as "Mother's going-away party," Mary Pickford came by the Spanish bungalow to comfort her old friend. As Elsie later recalled, they found themselves laughing together when they visualized "Charlotte and Jenny together somewhere, Charlotte saying with her fascinating little brogue, 'Ah, you haven't been a good business woman. That girl should have a million in trust,' and Jenny, eyes snapping, retaliating, 'But *we* have had a wonderful time!'"

Alone in her garden after Mary left, Elsie saw a beautiful black and yellow monarch butterfly hovering over her. "How terrible! Mother will never see a butterfly again!" was her first reaction. Then a sudden calm settled over her. "How ridiculous," she thought. "That butterfly might even *be* Jenny!"

As she noted in her memoirs: "To this day that butterfly or one exactly like it rules my garden." A few years later, when she led me into that pleasant retreat for the first time, the butterfly had indeed "become" Jenny and was casually introduced to me as such. "You see," the deeply tanned Elsie said as she relaxed and took the sun. "Jenny's still here, taking care of me."

14
Dancing Will Make It So

*Shirley's film career was thrust upon us. We
never thought of it.*
— Mrs. Gertrude Temple, 1934

W HILE THERE WERE SOME — especially movie producers —
who regarded Santa Monica as an insignificant suburb of
Hollywood, good for beach locations and not much else, its pride-
ful residents did not share that view. Here plain folks plied their
trades all day, and when sundown turned the western skies a
fuchsia pink beyond the black silhouettes of sea bluff palms, they
returned to small, unpretentious homes. No Hollywood hijinks
here, no Brown Derby restaurants or wild hotel parties. Santa
Monica was a perfectly sane place to live, and to perfectly sane
George and Gertrude Temple, newlyweds in 1913, this neat-as-a-
pin community seemed the ideal place to settle down.

The men in George's Pennsylvania Dutch family had traditionally practiced medicine. But when the Temples moved from
Fairview, Pennsylvania, to California, where change was in the
air, George broke the pattern by going into banking instead. At
Polytechnic High School in Los Angeles he met the quiet daughter
of a former Chicago jeweler. Their tastes proved identical, modest
and conservative, and when Gertrude turned seventeen they were
married.

Over the next five years the couple had two sons, and George
was promoted to branch manager of his bank. When they celebrated their fifteenth anniversary, the Temples owned a one-story
stucco house with a minuscule mortgage on it and a sensible, low-

priced car. Always a careful man, George felt he could provide better for two children than three, and so the Temple family was considered complete. If anything about the phantasmic movie town next door interested or attracted Gertrude, that devoted wife and mother gave no outward sign. But in 1927, nine years after the birth of what she had supposed would be her last child, Gertrude found herself pregnant again, and a striking change took place.

It may be that Gertrude Temple, like many other women in America's increasingly youth-oriented culture, felt herself over the hill at thirty-two, her youth forever flown and with it all opportunity for adventure and personal recognition. Whatever wrought the change, she felt an irresistible urge to realize her own girlhood dreams of a theatrical career through this unborn child. She hoped fervently for a daughter, and, as she stated the case in print six momentous years later, "long before she was born I tried to influence her life by association with music, art and natural beauty. Perhaps this prenatal preparation helped make Shirley what she is today."

Shirley Jane Temple, born April 23, 1928, was not only the girl her mother had prayed for, she was singularly pretty and gifted as well. As soon as the golden-haired cherub could toddle, she gravitated toward the family Victrola and radio, dancing and singing to their music as airily as any born fairy star. Although the Depression lay heavy on the land, the Temple home was a snug harbor of conservatism and security, despite several salary cuts that hard times had levied on the bank. There was no foolish spending, no fripperies, in George Temple's home.

This made Gertrude's request that Shirley study dancing all the more difficult to broach. Granted, George adored his little daughter, but dancing lessons at a dollar a throw seemed an almost sinful luxury. Still, Gertrude persisted. She only wanted to give Shirley the pleasure of dancing with other tots her age, an argument that George could not totally ignore. With her brothers so much older than she, Shirley was being raised almost as an only child. George did not want her spoiled, and the boys were already doing their fair share of that. Maybe Gertrude was right. But the dancing school itself was "over there" in Hollywood, and he wanted no part of the movie world for his child.

"Movies?" Gertrude chided him. "Why, the idea is absurd." And then, with a humorous twinkle in her eye, she added, "Of course, if the movies come after her with a big fat contract, well, that will be different!" George enjoyed a good laugh, for if ever there was *not* a stage mother it was shy, retiring Gertrude Temple.

By the early 1930s talkies were a reality, musical movies were all the rage, and it seemed that every mother in America wanted her child to sing and dance. The Depression notwithstanding, dancing schools sprang up everywhere like mushrooms following a rain. In far-off Liddy, Oklahoma, a hamlet of five hundred souls, the housebound wife of the town banker gazed at her beautiful hazel-eyed daughter and told her, "Darla, you're my ticket out of Liddy." When Darla turned three, Mrs. Hood talked her husband into paying for expensive dancing lessons in distant Oklahoma City. Twice a week she drove the three-hundred-mile round trip to Kathryn Duffy's Dancing School. After six months Miss Duffy pronounced Darla "ready" and won Mrs. Hood's permission to take the tiny girl to New York. Years later Darla asked her mother why she let her go with a virtual stranger on so long a trip; Mrs. Hood responded, "Honey, you had stardust in your eyes and I knew you were going to be somebody."

Miss Duffy and her star pupil stayed at the Edison, and one evening in the hotel dining room the orchestra leader handed Darla his baton and asked her to lead the band while her proud teacher looked on. In that same dining room was a roving talent scout for Hal Roach Studio, searching for just such a little girl to play the lead in a proposed *Our Gang* musical film. Without so much as calling Darla's mother, Miss Duffy agreed to his offer of a screen test in a New York studio. Then she telephoned the good news of Darla's acceptance to Mrs. Hood in Liddy. "They want her in Hollywood right away," the practical Miss Duffy explained. "She can't come home first."

That was the last Darla saw of Liddy and the last Liddy saw of Mrs. Hood. Upon arriving in Hollywood, she signed Darla to a nine-year contract with Hal Roach, and a year later, having given up his job and home, Mr. Hood joined them.

While the dancing school boom hit every town and city in the country, none was better prepared to meet the challenge than Hollywood, which boasted some of the oldest and most professionally run schools to be found anywhere. This proved a fortunate coincidence, for they were confronted with at least twenty times more pupils than those in other towns. Almost every dancing school in the Los Angeles area had gotten its start, or at least kept going, on the strength of the movie industry's needs. Long before all-singing, all-dancing films were possible, studios relied on the support of expert dancing masters. At Century, even I had to take a few quick lessons from Ernest Belcher, a pioneer in the business, in order to get through a dancing sequence. Grown-up stars did the same. Whenever Cecil B. De Mille wanted to make a hundred idolators dancing around a golden calf look graceful — if not entirely believable — he sent for Ernest Belcher or the Russian refugee Theodore Kosloff to choreograph his extras' drunken orgy.

Indeed, De Mille's needs were so considerable and constant that in 1931 he built a three-story, $300,000 building on Western Avenue to house the Ernest Belcher School of the Dance. It boasted 30,000 square feet of floor space and trained an annual enrollment of between 1500 and 2000 pupils. In addition, Belcher wrote a nationally syndicated column on dance techniques, and each summer he conducted a month-long intensive course especially for dancing teachers, who flocked to him from all over America and carried his methods back with them to the hinterlands. In this respect, Hollywood dancing studios exported as well as imported talent.

Belcher's nearest rival was Mrs. Ethel Meglin, who had taught dancing in her native Cincinnati and had come to Hollywood with her husband for her health. Because she missed teaching, she soon took on several neighborhood children as nonpaying pupils. Later, lacking proper space, she approached Mack Sennett, whose studio was directly across the street from her home, and asked permission to use an empty building on his lot. He rented it to her for twenty-seven dollars a month. Arriving to give her first lesson, she discovered that Sennett had generously erected an enormous sign across the entire building spelling out ETHEL MEGLIN STUDIOS. The sign put her in business and she began charging for lessons.

She started out with a total of thirty pupils, but new applicants turned up every day. Almost without exception their mothers were using the sugar bowl money to pay for the lessons, and all of them were anxious for the dollars to start flowing the other way. Put simply, when would Mrs. Meglin find them stage and movie jobs? Loew's State Theater in downtown Los Angeles was noted for its ambitious stage productions, and during Christmas week they often showed kiddie revues as a break from their usual lavish presentations. Pressured by her pupils' frantic mothers, Ethel Meglin approached Fanchon and Marco, the producers of these shows, about hiring her "Demi Tasse Revue" for the Christmas holiday. She was told that thirty children would not adequately fill their stage; a San Francisco Company, the O'Neil Children, usually got the job because they had one hundred youngsters. Calling Fanchon's bluff, Mrs. Meglin promised one hundred and one kiddies, one more than the O'Neil troupe. Still skeptical, the producers insisted upon seeing her act first.

Returning home, Ethel called in her thirty pupils and their mothers, asking them to bring their sisters, brothers, and playmates to her studio for free lessons in exchange for padding the act. The place was bedlam for a solid week, children running in and out at all hours, mothers waiting in cars up and down the street, and rehearsal rooms so few and small Ethel had to take her pupils in shifts. When Ethel's troupe auditioned, Fanchon and Marco were amazed. They booked her for two weeks at Christmas and gave star billing to "The Famous Meglin Kiddies."

It was to Ethel Meglin's school that Ethel Gumm brought her three girls, Virginia, Jane, and Frances, when the Gumms finally moved from Grand Rapids, Minnesota, to the small desert town of Lancaster, some eighty miles northeast of Los Angeles. Frank Gumm had agreed to sell the New Grand back home, but had been unable to find its replacement in Hollywood, as Ethel so much desired. So in 1927 he purchased the Lancaster, which enjoyed the sole distinction of being the only theater in town.

There the Gumm girls again took up their curious double lives. All week long they attended school like ordinary children, but on weekends and vacations they went on the road with their mother, playing every small-town benefit or vaudeville show they could find.

When money was especially tight and bookings scarce, Mrs. Gumm played the piano at the Meglin Studio in exchange for singing, dancing, and acrobatic lessons for the girls. After all, out here in California the Gumms were in effect starting all over again, both as a family and as a sister act. Thanks to Mrs. Meglin's efforts, the Gumm sisters made some of their very first "big time" appearances at the Los Angeles Orpheum and Loew's State theaters as part of the Ethel Meglin Kiddie Revue. By then Mrs. Meglin was well on her way to making a fortune with her "wonder kiddies." She eventually had forty franchized Meglin Dance Studios throughout the country with a total of ten thousand pupils.

Although Mrs. Meglin later pointed with pride to Judy Garland, née Frances Gumm, as one who got her first professional training as a Meglin kiddie, it was Shirley Temple who focused nationwide attention on the Meglin School. Mrs. Temple took Shirley there to study dancing sometime in 1931. After that, nothing was ever quite the same in the sane Temple household.

Shirley proved an outstanding student who worked hard, had a mousetrap memory for routines, and seemed to enjoy every minute of her time with Mrs. Meglin. Not long after she began her dancing lessons, a studio talent scout made one of his intermittent raids on the Meglin nest of fledgling child stars. His name was Charles Lamont and he scouted for Educational Films, one of the lesser lights along Poverty Row but still able to pay my old director Alf Goulding the $1250 weekly salary his considerable comedy talents commanded.

Because it was a cold, rainy day, Gertrude Temple had brought Shirley to dancing school in her play overalls. After looking over the well-dressed cream of Ethel Meglin's current crop, the talent scout suddenly glanced under the piano in the rehearsal hall — there was three-year-old Shirley, hiding. She was exactly the right size, height, and personality for a series of *Baby Burlesks* the studio was casting, and Lamont told her mother to bring her around for a test. When Gertrude got home and told her husband, the conservative George "hit the ceiling," to use his wife's words. Three days later, Shirley was hired at $10 a day. "When I told George that, he hit the ceiling again — with joy!"

The *Baby Burlesks* were, in fact, taking a page out of the earliest Baby Peggy comedies, for while they featured children, they were aimed at an adult audience, which could appreciate their satirical thrusts at the leading film hits of the day. *The Runt Page* was a spoof of *The Front Page. Pie-Covered Wagon* parodied *The Covered Wagon,* and in *Kid'n Hollywood,* Shirley was put through very similar situations as those employed in my own *Peg o' the Movies* of a dozen years earlier.

Unfortunately the *Burlesks* were in very poor taste, all the children being required to appear in diapers fastened with giant safety pins. They were also rough-and-tumble affairs in the worst tradition of Poverty Row's disregard for the safety of children. Shirley was made to ride in a cart that was hitched to a blindfolded ostrich. To start the scene, they yanked the blindfold off the bird, and his frantic efforts to shed himself of his burden terrified Shirley. As a lady explorer in darkest Africa, she was chased by a band of Negro extras playing cannibals, who were unexpectedly tripped by an invisible wire and sent sprawling in all directions. Shirley and the other toddlers were frightened and all of them reduced to tears.

In *Polly Tix in Washington,* four-year-old Shirley played a call girl, decked out in black lace panties and bra, mouthing dialogue that was better suited for delivery by Mae West. But by then Mr. Temple's bank was on the verge of being closed, and Shirley's forty dollars a week was no laughing matter.

One evening Shirley and her mother went to see the most recent *Baby Burlesk* previewed, and in the lobby afterward an assistant director from Fox hailed them. He introduced them to a songwriter who was searching for a little girl to do a big production number in a new musical, *Fox Movietone Revue* (later retitled *Stand Up and Cheer*). Because the Burlesk series spotlighted Shirley's polished song and dance skills, the songwriter felt she was perfect for the part. But to make sure he rehearsed her carefully, and a few days later, in costume, he took her on the set to audition the number for the Fox vice president Winfield Sheehan. Mr. Sheehan did not yet know it, but in Shirley Temple he was looking at a miniature Fort Knox who was destined to bail out the barely solvent Fox lot beyond his wildest dreams.

Shirley's rendition of "Baby Take a Bow" was flawless. "It was perfectly done," the exacting Gertrude said. "Even I was thrilled. Harold Lloyd . . . standing in the back with me was saying, 'My God! Another Coogan!' "

At this point in Jackie Coogan's career, Lloyd's remark was not intended to imply the curse it might later have been mistaken for. Compared to my own childhood, Jackie's seemed singularly serene, with the possible exception of the unhappy Bernstein-Coogan scandal. But that never cast a shadow on his public image, however it may have affected him as a son. His earnings, like his career, were phenomenal. A 1923 poll had rated him the number one box-office star, with Rudolph Valentino in second place and Douglas Fairbanks a poor third. His Metro contract of that year gave him a $500,000 bonus to leave First National and a million dollars over the next two years for a modest four films. Throughout 1924 and 1925, Jackie was said to earn $22,500 a week, continuing to star in MGM features until 1928, when his contract expired. As one Hollywood wag quipped, "Senility finally got him at thirteen."

Still, Jackie was far from a fallen star. Appearing with his father at London's Palladium that same year, he earned $5000 for a single week. Two years later, making his first comeback as a youth of fifteen, he starred in Paramount's *Tom Sawyer* at $10,000 a week. By 1933, back under contract to MGM, his paycheck had dwindled to $1300 but this was at the very nadir of the Depression. Needless to add, the product royalties had never ceased flowing into the Jackie Coogan Corporation coffers throughout the lucky thirteen years he had been a star, while his real estate holdings rivaled those of Mary Pickford.

Jackie and I had met up again in the early spring of 1929 at Chicago's popular supper club, the College Inn. I had just retired from vaudeville, while Jackie and his father were en route from a private eastern academy to Hollywood, where he was to be enrolled in a miiltary school. He was fourteen at the time and quite handsome, with short brown hair, a trim figure and the poise of someone much older. I was a worldly ten. When he first came to our table without his father and asked me to dance, I did not even recognize him.

Most advantaged youth of that era were well versed in the art of ballroom dancing, and Jackie and I were no exception. As we glided onto the floor, the management became aware of our presence and ordered the white floor-show spot to follow us. Immediately all the other couples drifted to the sidelines, leaving us alone dancing to the seemingly endless strains of "Lover Come Back to Me." We had started out talking to each other, asking how and where we had been over the years. But the unexpected public exposure petrified us, and when we finally left the floor to smiles and applause we were both scarlet with embarrassment.

While Jackie and I had been on the dance floor, Jack Coogan joined my parents at our table. As he told it, he and Lillian were very disappointed in Jackie's performance at school. His grades were low, he wasn't "taking to school," and he had "absolutely no sense at all where money was concerned." Curiously, it was Jack Coogan himself who a few years earlier had ordered Jackie to tear up a $10,000 check that Douglas Fairbanks had gratefully paid him for the story idea of his very successful film *The Black Pirate*. One did not take money from friends, Coogan had told his son, not even in payment for something, and Fairbanks was certainly a friend. Jackie's parents had impressed upon him that he was rich and "fixed for life," but, as Mary Ann used to say about Lotta, since Jackie had everything he wanted, he had no need of money. What Jackie seemed to need desperately, even then, was a sense of his own worth in his parents' eyes. But fearing that such approbation would be the final drop of praise that turned his head, they did not give it.

While the Coogans continued on their way to California, we entrained for Laramie, Wyoming, where, some thirty-five miles outside of town, Father had purchased a fifteen-hundred-acre dude ranch. The purchase price for this Montgomery fiefdom was $25,000, and not much more was left of the $200,000 I had earned during my three and a half years in vaudeville. The modernization of the still-primitive 1880 ranch buildings was to be financed through sizable contributions from three New York investors scheduled to buy into the project in the fall of 1929.

Father, Louise, and I all loved the place. Here Father would regain his lost self-respect as his own man. But Mother felt hopelessly marooned. Despite its insecurities, she had enjoyed living on the road. She loved city life, nightclubs, change, and the incessant travel that went with vaudeville. To add to her unhappiness, Mother now found herself with no other fixed goal in life but me and my career. Over the years that I had headed the family financially I had become her alter ego, the vicarious means by which she participated in an otherwise unobtainable life of luxury and excitement. Throughout her marriage, friendships had been about as lasting as one turn through a revolving door. Circumstance had rarely served up the same person twice, and as she loathed letter-writing, the few friends she might have kept were scattered by the constant winds of change. While Mother did not demand quite as much hoopla along the way as Jenny Janis did, she had been badly spoiled for any other life but the theater. And I remained her only key to that world.

Knowing she had lost the battle, she was determined not to lose the war. One way or another she would get out of this godforsaken spot and back to the civilization that was show business. But she found herself up against many of the same obstacles that had kept Mary Ann helpless so long in Grass Valley and Rabbit Creek. The distances to town, to neighbors, and to the nearest city worthy of the name were almost insurmountable. She did not drive, and Father had convinced her that women were temperamentally unsuited to do so. Still, to her credit, she tried. She cheered herself by recalling how up to date the ranch would be when all the investors had pooled their shares.

That first summer at the ranch was the most carefree and happy time that we as a family ever knew. Louise and I even attended school for the first time in my life. It was a one-room cabin that had served the youngsters of covered-wagon immigrants passing through on the nearby Overland Trail to Oregon. In the schoolyard I picked up ancient Sioux and Arapaho flint arrowheads, and suddenly history became not merely a subject to be studied but a trail to be followed. I was determined to become a writer, perhaps as much for the protective privacy it afforded as for the satisfaction of working with words. During my years in vaudeville I had written steadily — songs, stories, and plays. My parents never took these efforts seriously, but I did.

On October 29, 1929, I celebrated my eleventh birthday. Father gave me my very first saddle horse, and in far-off New York the stock market crashed. Our eastern friends were financially ruined, and the money they had planned to invest would never be forthcoming. Worse still, the first mortgage payment fell due.

In desperation Mother and Father decided to drive to Denver and personally appeal to the banker who held the notes of foreclosure. Louise and I went along. Mr. Hay proved a far cry from the stock landlord villain in old homestead melodramas. Going over the family's assets, he decided that I was the most promising and marketable collateral we possessed. He strongly urged my parents to take me back to Hollywood and reenter me in films, where I could earn far more than was needed to save the ranch. To make what he saw as a seemingly effortless feat simplicity itself, he kindly loaned us $300 of his own money to finance the trip.

It speaks volumes for the shape of the economy at the time to state that we in fact were able to make the twelve-hundred-mile trek from Laramie to Los Angeles, and even install a caretaker at the ranch, on this slim advance. But Mr. Hays's faith in me was tragically misplaced. After beating on dozens of doors in Hollywood, we finally found an agent blind enough to take on a gangling country girl with crooked front teeth (that saving upper plate had cost me dearly in the end), a broomstick figure, and three left feet. Louise and I were enrolled in a dancing school run by two old friends and refugees from vaudeville, the Mosconi brothers. Although they were barely eating, they cheerfully offered to put our lessons on the cuff. Peggy's sure to make it in talkies, they kept saying. Nothing that kid can't do. She's a born trouper.

Actually, I was a sacrificial lamb. If I didn't offer myself on the altar of fame, we would all likewise perish. Recognizing what an awkward, scarecrow creature I was in those in-between years, facing a camera was tantamount to standing before a firing squad. But there was nothing I would not do to save the ranch. I loved it as I had never loved anything in my life before. It had brought me peace, rest, privacy, and security. However, no one in Hollywood asked me to make the supreme sacrifice, our money ran out, and after six months we returned empty-handed to the ranch.

The following summer we resorted to serving chicken dinners all day each Sunday, hoping to make the ranch pay off as a roadside restaurant. The four of us killed, plucked, cleaned, cooked, and served hundreds of white leghorns from our own flock. It was like doing five shows a day all over again, this time with feathers. Between Sundays Mother insisted that Louise and I rehearse our time-steps and the tap routines the Mosconis had taught us so we would be ready when our chance came. When our tap shoes wore through at last, Louise and I rejoiced, but Mother was not so easily defeated. She made us insert cardboard soles inside our shoes and replace them as they, too, wore through.

But our polished time-steps notwithstanding, it all came to nothing anyway. We lost the ranch to the bank and were forced to auction off almost everything we possessed from the Beverly Hills furniture to the saddle horses. In June of 1932 we loaded into a Model A Ford sedan and a small trailer the little that remained from the $2 million I had earned over my first ten years and once again headed back for Hollywood — just one more family displaced by the Depression, with a dancing child they knew could make a fortune in films.

15
Growing Pains

*I stopped believing in Santa Claus at a very early
age. Mother took me to see him in a Hollywood department store, and he asked me for my autograph.*
— Shirley Temple

W HILE THE POSTWAR FASCINATION with children had focused on the moral power of their innocence, the post-
Depression fixation took a somewhat different turn. During the
prosperous twenties, both blue-collar worker and multimillion-
aire honestly believed they had built a solid future for their
posterity. For many, the Depression swept away even the illusion
of security.

Some parents tried courageously to conceal from their children the full extent of the family's financial plight. Others discovered, to their surprise and relief, that most youngsters when
confronted with the awful truth responded with an unquenchable
confidence in the future that their elders found inspiring. It was
the inspirational quality of their children's faith that gave renewed hope to parents almost ready to succumb to economic
disaster. And in Shirley Temple, Hollywood and the American
public found the perfect symbol of youth's boundless optimism.

Children cast in the Dickens mold had been traditionally helpless, exploited by their elders, and often plagued with ill health,
which brought about their early and powerfully redemptive death.
The new child that Shirley symbolized not only underscored the
deceptive strength of virtue, but she actually got things done when
adults seemed incapable of effecting change. Shirley was anything

but passive. Pouting, scolding, singing, dancing her way through every film, *she* did the cheering up, *she* was the savior. If wistful little Jackie Coogan had been a skyrocket, bubbly, bossy Shirley Temple was a Roman candle.

The writer Irvin S. Cobb, who had publicly rhapsodized over Jackie during his angelic childhood, now extolled the wonders of this newest gift from God.

> Darling, when Santa Claus bundled you up, a . . . joyous doll-baby package, and dropped you down creation's chimney, he gave to mankind the dearest and sweetest Christmas present that ever gladdened the hearts and stirred the souls of this weary old world. Through your . . . natural artistry, millions upon millions of children have been made to laugh, and millions of older folks have laughed with them.

In 1934, Shirley's performance in *Stand Up and Cheer* had audiences all over America doing just that. Fox immediately negotiated a seven-year contract at $150 a week. That same year the studio shrewdly loaned out their small gold mine to Paramount, where she made *Little Miss Marker*, a second box-office bonanza. In the bargain she earned her home studio $1000 a week. Miffed when they were not cut in on any of the loan-out fee, the Temples considered breaking with Fox, but they finally settled for a revised salary of exactly that amount. It proved a wise compromise for both the studio and the Temples. At her peak Shirley averaged about $100,000 a year; Fox pocketed a tidy $6 million from her pictures annually.

Early in Shirley's career, a familiar Hollywood figure strode confidently into the Temples' hitherto untroubled lives: Arthur Bernstein paid them a call. He offered to take over the headaches of managing Shirley's affairs, promising to put his years of child star experience at their disposal, for a reasonable consideration, of course.

"He came over here to the house with Mrs. Coogan one day," Gertrude told author J. P. McAvoy in an interview, "and walked up and down waving a check for a million dollars in my face. He told me he had just gotten that much for Jackie and we ought to let him handle Shirley, because we didn't know anything about the picture business and we would certainly be cheated if we didn't let him take care of us. Practically every agent in town had been after us, and we didn't know which way to turn."

Arthur Bernstein's advice was to increase Shirley's earnings ten-fold by booking her in personal appearances and radio broadcasts between pictures, thereby raising the salary she could command for films. Resistant to the disrupted home life that all this added exposure would entail, Shirley's parents declined, using as their excuse that she was already under contract to Fox. Impatient and seemingly irritated by their naiveté, Bernstein declared he could "handle" the Fox contract for them.

"Bernstein talked and talked until we were dizzy, and then in desperation we called our family doctor, and asked him to come over and advise us because he was the only professional man we knew." George Temple's inherited respect for the medical profession paid off handsomely. As Gertrude Temple explained, "He has been advising us ever since. Of course, we have a lawyer now who helps us, but weren't we lucky to have such a sensible doctor!"

As Shirley's fame grew, she quite effortlessly earned as much or more from endorsements than she might have by going on the road. Her name and picture appeared on every possible product from dolls and drinking mugs to dresses and soap figurines. On the Pintner-Cunningham IQ test she breezed in like the thorough-bred she was at 155, a cool twenty points ahead of the mere genius level of 135.

Mrs. Temple became a fixture at the studio and was paid $150 a week to act as her daughter's coach and sole hairdresser. She alone set and brushed the famous Temple ringlets. She rehearsed Shirley in her lines before bedtime each night, followed by a quick run-through after breakfast in the morning. Shirley arrived on the set letter-perfect every day, apparently needing only her mother's familiar "Sparkle, Shirley, sparkle!" from the sidelines to turn in one dazzling performance after another.

Now it was Gertrude Temple's turn to be the model child star's mother, advising others how to raise the perfect child. In *Parents' Magazine* she described how she was bringing up Shirley.

"I wanted her to be artistic. I was determined she should *excel* at something." Mrs. Temple went on to state that Shirley's training was entirely her domain, without any interference from her husband. "When I speak, she minds. There is no argument, no pleading and begging. I have never permitted any impudence, crying or display of temper. I have also taught her not to be afraid of anything...I began this training very early and it means constant vigilance. I soon learned not to let my affection make me too lenient..." *

Despite their greater prudence in handling money, both Temples shared my father's stern attitudes toward the performing child. When the distinguished photographer George Hurrell was assigned to do a series of portraits of Shirley, she came to his studio with her mother. It was a lengthy session, and he realized Shirley was tired. "She must have been tired all the time because of her hectic schedule. I remember once she fell asleep when I was changing a background." Touched, Hurrell photographed her that way before she awakened. During another sitting, when she was being strictly disciplined by her mother, the sympathetic Hurrell tried to intervene. He only tried it once, for Mrs. Temple warned him sharply, "You tend to your photography, Mr. Hurrell, and I'll tend to my daughter."

Nevertheless, Mrs. Temple consistently referred to Shirley's work as play, comparing it to every child's love of dressing up and make-believe. The only difference was that Shirley did it in front of the camera. She invoked this theme when relating how Shirley came to make a certain film. "Some time ago, she read ... *The Little Princess.* 'Mother, I'd love to *be* the Little Princess,' she said to me. Darryl F. Zanuck made it possible for Shirley to actually become the Little Princess on the screen. Where else but in the magic world of pictures could a little girl have so fabulous a wish come true?"

At the height of Shirley's fame, President Franklin D. Roosevelt counted her a valuable national asset in the country's economic

* C. J. Foster, "Mrs. Temple on Bringing Up Shirley," *Parents' Magazine,* October 1938.

recovery. "It is a splendid thing that for just fifteen cents an American can go to a movie and look at the smiling face of a baby and forget his troubles." How could the *Daily Worker* prevail against such solid arguments for the American dream?

As for Shirley herself, she went on record as saying, "I can't wait till I grow up. I don't exactly know why I want it so much. I think perhaps I have had enough of childhood. I think you have more fun when you grow up. I don't know why, but there is more . . . isn't there?"

Still, during the fairy-tale years both Shirley and her mother knew well who they were, with or without each other. When a reporter was interviewing Mrs. Temple about Shirley's daily activities, Shirley endured it for a time, then broke in impatiently, "Why don't you interview me? I'm the star." And Mrs. Temple, when told the President of the United States wanted her famous daughter to visit him at the White House, asked matter-of-factly, "Why can't he come here?"

Shirley's income enabled the Temple family to move from their little stucco house to a more spacious and secure mansion, still in staid Santa Monica. For a time Mr. Temple was pleased that customers were switching their accounts to the branch bank he managed just so they could brag that Shirley Temple's father was their banker. Soon, however, George was forced to retire to become full-time banker for his daughter.

In spite of all attempts at normalcy, the entire Temple family was gradually drawn into the vortex of Shirley's fame. Her older brothers became responsible for keeping their sister's scrapbooks up to date. While they teasingly called her "La Temple," there was no escaping the fact that she was the breadwinner for them all. As Judy Garland said years later about the men in her life, "They all got into the Judy Garland business," so even the sensible Temples found themselves in the Shirley Temple business.

George Temple was not the only banker with a child star vying for his role as breadwinner. Darla Hood's father spent an entire year trying to bring himself to give up his secure and promising position in the bank in Liddy. Knowing well that movies were a fly-by-night business, he was certain that Darla and her mother would come back as suddenly as they had gone. But finally, faced with the prospect of permanent separation from his wife and daughter, he opted to make the move; surely he could find a similar position in Hollywood. Disenchantment awaited him. The only job open was for a teller in the Bank of America at $25 a week. Not only was he starting at the bottom, but his five-year-old daughter was earning six or seven times more than he.

Dickie Moore's father was another case in which the combination backfired even more cruelly. At eleven months, Dickie had been discovered by a studio secretary who lived next door to the Moores in Hollywood. A veteran of many starring roles before he was seven, he signed a one-year contract with Hal Roach with a starting salary of $225 a week, far more than any other Gang member in history. Later he left Roach to earn as much as $2000 a week in major films. At the same time his father found himself out of work, going from door to door seeking a job. A highly paid banker before the Depression, he now found the only openings were for tellers. Swallowing his pride he applied, only to be told he did not qualify. It wouldn't be fair, his would-be employers explained, because with his little boy earning so much in films he did not need the money. There were plenty of other jobless fathers with entire families to feed.

Although Mother remained an inveterate moviegoer, she viewed the rise of such new child stars as Dickie Moore, Shirley Temple, Darla Hood, and Mitzi Green with a jaundiced eye. When Mitzi won the part of Becky Thatcher in Jackie Coogan's *Tom Sawyer*, she declared it an outrageous injustice and wept all day. Shirley was "too sweet," Jackie Cooper a flash in the pan. The night that Deanna Durbin debuted on the Eddie Cantor radio show, I felt relieved. Mother's jealous recriminations of other children forced me to view their success as my failure. But Deanna's singing voice was so singular and spectacular that not even Mother could bring herself to say I could do the same.

When RKO began casting for the four coveted leads in the first talking version of *Little Women*, Mother was determined that I would nose all the others out to win the part of Beth. Unfortunately we had no agent at the time and did not know anyone with influence at the studio. But Mother was rapidly sharpening her movie-mother claws.

"I've got it!" she announced one morning triumphantly. "You'll write a letter to Mary Pickford."

"But Mother," I hedged, "I hardly consider that I even know her."

"Well, she knows you!" Mother shot back. "And what she says goes in this town. She's the industry's real queen — everybody has to kow-tow to her. And if she tells RKO to let you play Beth they wouldn't *dare* say no!"

Although all my professional instincts told me not to, I dutifully sent off my cheeky letter, requesting that Miss Pickford please intervene with whoever ran RKO to grant me my life's wish of playing Beth. Tears could not make it through the mails or they would have been enclosed.

At that point in Mary Pickford's life she had far more critical things to concern her than playing bountiful queen to an aging child star. Following Charlotte's death, a growing estrangement developed between herself and Doug. In constant dread of growing old, Fairbanks distracted himself by world travel and the still reassuring game of hobnobbing with the rich and titled, managing to be away from Pickfair most of every year. Mary's long and illustrious career was also nearing its close. She missed her mother's encouragement and pined for her husband in his continued absences. Only the youthful actor Charles "Buddy" Rogers, who in 1927 had played opposite her in *My Best Girl*, offered comfort and companionship.

But despite her own sorrows, Mary had the good grace to reply, on embossed Pickfair stationery, too. Generously assuring me that "your talents alone should suffice to win you the role of Beth," she wished me well. It was all a very elegant way of saying no, there was nothing she could do. As I was about to consign the bad news to the wastebasket, Mother snatched the letter from my hands.

"Don't you dare throw that away!" she snapped. "Paste it in your autograph book — there's a blank page between Lindbergh and Elsie Janis!"

*

Ever since our return to Hollywood, life had been a sickening roller-coaster ride of high expectations followed by heartbreaking disappointment. The beginning had been auspicious enough. Immediately after our arrival in June 1932, we stopped by the United Artists studio to visit Douglas Fairbanks. Fresh from a workout in his private gym and a dip in his indoor pool, he was tanned to a deep mahogany and exuding good health, and he welcomed us to his dressing room. While he enthused about his latest venture, a travel film that would take him around the globe, he insisted the still man be called in to take pictures of us together. Publicity is what got things done in Hollywood, Fairbanks said, and if I was interested in making a comeback, there was no better way to lure the mice to the cheese. It worked. The pictures made all the papers.

I was snapped up as a "hot property" and put under contract for a series of shorts starring former vaudevillians James and Lucille Gleason. Their ambitious project extended over two years and called for me to appear in twelve two-reel shorts, a New York stage play, and a feature film, all based on the same lovable folksy characters. I would play the teen-age girl next door at a starting salary of $150 a week. The deal was everything Lela Rogers had advised Mother to be on the lookout for — a perfect mix of Broadway and Hollywood.

If talkies were not ready for me, at least I was ready for talkies. I memorized the entire script, and before reporting to the Griffith Park location for the first day of shooting, I checked in at Max Factor's new studio on Hollywood Boulevard to be made up by professionals. I entered the booth at 7 A.M., the thirteen-year-old tomboy called for by the script. What emerged an hour later was the body of a teen-age girl fitted out with the head of Medusa. But no matter. No one on the set even noticed. Mrs. Gleason scrapped the first script and wrote a second one on the spot, the sound man said we all recorded like Admiral Byrd broadcasting from Little America, and the director walked off the set.

Before the second short could even be made, the company ran short of cash and replaced me with an unknown who was glad to work for only $40 a week. Father retaliated by suing the producers for half a million dollars, claiming breach of contract and irreparable damage to my career. Historically, my lawsuit's only distinction is that it was the first in a long train of similar legal battles involving child stars and their families. It also told wary producers that Baby Peggy's parents favored litigation as a way of settling contractual disputes, not a trait likely to win friends among studio heads in Hollywood. As in the suits that followed it, the lawyers on both sides were the only real winners. But until it came to trial, the strategy advised by agents and publicity people was to make it appear that I was a young lady of wealth and leisure whose last concern was money. Under no condition should I accept a bit part or, God forbid, take work as an extra. The only way to keep the price high was to make sure the merchandise did not get shopworn. Like virtue, this was a doctrine more easily preached than practiced. We were literally starving. Our rent was not paid. The electricity, water, telephone, and gas were regularly being turned off in a variety of combinations.

When it seemed that I could not go on another day refusing extra work, my agent persuaded Uncle Carl Laemmle to give me a screen test for a possible contract at my former home, Universal. Reporting to a small office bungalow on the lot, I was told to make my selection from a stack of old shooting scripts. Remembering how Uncle Carl liked tears, I was determined to avoid vapid tests in which the leading man offers the ingénue a box of candy and she kisses him. After all, I was a serious actress, and I wanted something that would show Uncle Carl I possessed fire and depth. I settled on a scene from Margaret Sullavan's recent hit *Only Yesterday*.

The handsome young stock actor assigned to play opposite me picked up his sides and we began rehearsing. The scene was a meaty one: a young woman, about to bear her lover's child out of wedlock, meets him when he comes back from war and is told he is to marry another. As we got into the dialogue the actor grew impatient with my delivery and interpretation, saying, "No, honey, not that lightly. Don't you realize what has *happened* between them?" While he considered it a purely rhetorical question, to his astonishment I replied, "Not really."

He paused and stared at me, then proceeded more cautiously. "Do you know *how* and *why* she is pregnant with this man's child?" I could feel my face turning red, but I had to shake my head in mute admission of my ignorance. Hollywood may have been a sinkhole of sex and sin to others, but I had managed to come through it all with a virgin mind. Whether I was simply too preoccupied with surviving or merely a slow starter, I had lived fourteen years without even suspecting that something more came after the Crawford-Gable fade-out kiss. It was only fitting that I should be told the facts of life by a twenty-three-year-old actor during dress rehearsal. By the end of this session my head was so full of portentous information I was emotionally paralyzed. When I got home, I asked Father to take me to see Lela Rogers.

Lee-Lee and Gee-Gee were back together again and living in Hollywood, Ginger having shed Jack Pepper after a few months as his partner. Since we last saw Lela, weeping in the Book-Cadillac in Detroit, Ginger had become, successively, a vaudeville headliner, the second lead in a Broadway show, and had played bits in several minor films. Her part in Warner Brothers' successful musical *Forty-second Street* had finally put her in line for movie stardom. Lela and Ginger now shared a three-level Spanish stucco perched on a cliff in the Hollywood Hills. While Ginger worked at the studio, Lela set up shop as agent, drama coach, business adviser, and all-around mother confessor to a gaggle of struggling young newcomers to Hollywood. In her "spare time" she ran the Hollytown Theater, an experimental workshop and showcase for the talents of her most promising protégés.

As I waited my turn in the living room with Betty Furness, Ginger's young cousin Phyllis Fraser, and former child star Baby Marie Osborne, Lela was counseling a tearful Dick Powell in the large dining room. Later she explained in high dudgeon that Warner's was paying "that poor boy" $75 a week while making millions on his musicals. Well, she would fix that. I never doubted she would. I only hoped she could fix me.

While I was too shy to go into the real problem, I asked her advice on how to project emotions and generate tears without falling back on my childish mechanisms. With her usual diligence and pragmatism she got right down to the nuts and bolts of acting. "All Ginger does is go off into a corner of the set a few minutes before a big scene." Obviously, if Ginger did it, that was the right way. "It's not necessary to know the whole script or even the whole character in depth. Just bite off a scene at a time. That's the way movies are made, and that's the way to make the system work for you."

When I reported to Universal the next morning at eight, Wardrobe issued me a straight, tight-fitting gown that was made of layered silk fringe from neck to toe. I looked for all the world like a walking floor lamp. There were dozens of other people taking tests on the same set, and the crew ran them through like sheep, not even changing light setups from blond to brunette. I waited. I went into a corner of the set, got hold of the scene, and cried. I kept it up off and on all day long until, at six-thirty, my name was finally called. By then I was as dry as a stone, incapable of shedding a single tear.

When Uncle Carl viewed the test he was dismayed. He was not upset by the silly fringe dress. He was not even concerned that I did not shed real tears. "It's not good, the 'Baby' being an unwed mother," the strait-laced Uncle Carl told my agent coldly. "My God — and her not yet fourteen!"

The "Baby's" comeback at Universal went aglimmering.

The Pasadena Playhouse was a highly respected drama school where one paid for lessons and was permitted to appear in professional productions. I could not afford the course they offered, but in the summer of 1933 the Playhouse directors decided to stage a new play, *Growing Pains,* by the author of the successful Broadway hit *Skidding,* Auriana Rouverol. *Growing Pains* was in fact what today would be called a pilot for the Andy Hardy series. The playwright later sold a variation on the same plot to MGM, and movie history was made from its puffery.

There were only two adult roles in the cast, the mother and father, but the play offered a baker's dozen of juicy parts for teenagers. As a result, the night of the first Playhouse auditions looked like a class reunion of graduates from *The Casting Director's*

Album of Screen Children. Although it was made clear at the outset that no salaries would be forthcoming for either rehearsals or performances, all the applicants and their parents blindly subscribed to the old Hollywood belief that a good performance, even if gratis, could win "exposure" and that once-in-a-lifetime break. It was pure gravy for the Playhouse, which, notwithstanding its free ride, charged the going price for seats. Most of us who landed good parts moved Heaven and earth just to get to Pasadena.

Fifteen-year-old Trent "Junior" Durkin, a fine actor from the New York stage, was wasted on the typical Andy Hardy–small-town boy lead, but the rest of us were grateful he stooped to take the part. It was Junior, in his very own car, who picked up six of us every day for two months as we waited on various street-corners all over Hollywood.

The playwright's daughter Jean Rouverol played Junior's sister, and the rest of the cast included Dawn O'Day, a veteran screen actress at fourteen, Leon Holmes, who had worked with me on Poverty Row in *April Fool,* and fifteen-year-old Dick Winslow Johnson, the eldest of Wynonah Johnson's five "experienced troupers." Throughout the play's run, Jackie Coogan was a backstage fixture. He and Dick Winslow and Junior Durkin were close friends from their days together making *Tom Sawyer* and *Huckleberry Finn.* Mickey Rooney also hung out at the Playhouse with us, needling Junior unmercifully about his part, never dreaming that one day he himself would rise to stardom in virtually the same thankless role.

For once, working for nothing paid off. Jean Rouverol was pulled out of the show to be given the lead in Paramount's *Eight Girls in a Boat.* The sixteen-year-old stage veteran Charlotte Henry, who got up in the part on one day's notice, replaced her, only to be herself discovered by Paramount to star in *Alice in Wonderland.* Two weeks later I landed a part with Jean in *Eight Girls in a Boat,* earning $50 a week and all expenses paid on location at Big Bear, an expensive lakeside resort. It took almost sixteen weeks to bring the picture in, but the long run enabled me to put my family back together again financially. By then, too, Mother and Louise were working regularly for Central Casting as extras. Father had given up trying to find Hollywood financing for another dude ranch and had rejoined his old coterie of cowboy friends. Once more he was riding, doubling, and doing stunts as though nothing had happened over the thirteen years since they parted company at Mixville.

It was not that easy for me to find a world where I belonged.

16
Under the Hollywood Sign

*Everything moved in funny ways. I was a child
actor making money before I went to school . . .
Then I was in my teens. That's supposed to finish
a child actor. Temple, Jackie Coogan and the rest
went downhill after puberty. But not me . . . I became bigger than I'd ever been and the money came
faster than any ten children could spend it.*

*Finally I was a man . . . I could vote. I could
marry. But in manhood, in my immature manhood, I made my childish mistakes. It was almost
as if, never a child, I turned childish as a man.*

— Mickey Rooney, *An Autobiography*, 1965

ON THE SOUTHWEST CORNER of Hollywood Boulevard and
Western Avenue an office building housed an institution indispensable to the making of motion pictures, Central Casting.
Right next door to it on Hollywood Boulevard a second building
housed an equally vital but less well known establishment, Lawlor's Professional School. Here on the second floor a hundred and
fifty harassed movie children from toddlers to teen-agers struggled
to get what passed for an education. Lawlor's was not yet ac-
credited by the state, tuition was $25 a month, studying was every-
one's spare-time activity, and the place looked like the prop department's idea of a school. But compared to the alternatives it
was seventh heaven.

About one third of Lawlor's enrollment was comprised of former
child actors and stars like myself, all trying to navigate the treach-
erous reefs of adolescence toward a landfall of adult fame. An-

other third were as yet undiscovered children, snatching at every extra job and scrap of dialogue in an effort to pull themselves up to stardom. In my time nearly a dozen of these plucky youngsters made it: Mickey Rooney, Judy Garland, Jane Withers, Charlotte Henry, Betty Grable, Gower Champion, Juanita Quigley, Anne Shirley, Virginia Weidler, and Edith Fellows.

Sandwiched in between were some three score luckless juveniles destined to make it big only on the neighborhood beer-hall circuit. They danced and sang bawdy songs for $5 a night in "queer joints" such as the infamous B.B.B.'s Cellar and similar dives on Santa Monica Boulevard and lower Western Avenue. They came to school each morning half asleep and only began waking up at noon. They had never been famous, nor would they ever be. Worse still, they knew it. But they were the sole support of their families, and perhaps that is why the welfare authorities seemed to be willfully blind to their existence.

Lawlor's great virtue was that it offered Hollywood children a refuge where they would not be regarded as freaks by teachers and classmates. As a freshman at Fairfax High, I had been buried alive for six months in a class for severely retarded children simply because I had never learned algebra. Whenever Louise and I worked extra we received a demerit from the office for being absent. Matching time had to be spent in a detention hall with other delinquents whose crimes ranged from smoking in the restrooms to acknowledged vandalism. When Judy Garland tried to enroll at Hollywood High, the vice principal informed her coldly, "Children like you should not be allowed to go to school with *normal* children!" Small wonder we all preferred serving our time at Lawlor's.

The education of movie children had always been a contradiction in terms. After all, any five-year-old who can earn $2000 a week without being able to read and write does not appear to have a handicap, especially to his or her parents; obviously the child did not need an education. To most movie parents school was simply an obstacle, to be gotten around with the maximum speed and minimum time. Traditionally, parents and studio bosses conspired to sabotage the efforts of welfare workers and teachers on the set, whom they regarded as their natural enemies.* The more time the children worked the more money they earned and the sooner their career got off the ground; this was the parental position. Directors and producers likewise considered time spent on schooling as money thrown away — in addition to the teacher's salary they were required by law to pay. In consequence, the four hours supposed to be set aside for children's schoolwork on the set were more often than not observed in the breach. So-called play or rest periods of some two hours daily were nearly always ignored and plowed back into production time. When we did study, we had to do so under almost impossible conditions, usually right on the set. Nevertheless, dedicated women warriors such as Fern Carter, Mary McDonald, and a lady known only as Mrs. West were more than equal to the challenge.

Mrs. Carter was for years the regular teacher of the Our Gang members. She even accompanied Darla Hood, Spanky McFarland, and Buckwheat when they went on a personal appearance tour. To Mrs. Carter fell the unpleasant task of trying to explain to a worried Darla why Buckwheat and his mother had to ride in a different Pullman car and stay in special hotels on the road. When Mrs. Carter finished with the white children's lessons, she made the long trek back to Buckwheat's car, where she instructed him in antiseptic isolation from the rest of his long-time friends.

Mary McDonald ran the Little Red Schoolhouse at MGM. Among her world-renowned students were Roddy McDowall, Margaret O'Brien, Elizabeth Taylor, Mickey Rooney, Judy Garland, and briefly Freddie Bartholomew, the English-born star of *David Copperfield* and *Little Lord Fauntleroy*. When the studio noticed that fraternization with the others was causing Freddie to lose his clipped British accent, a commodity every bit as priceless as his acting skills, he was pulled out of school and assigned a private tutor, Mrs. Murphy from Ireland. Thereafter, Freddie and his regular stand-in, Ray Sperry, studied together in a makeshift booth

* As recently as 1973, when youthful Linda Blair was slated to star in *The Exorcist*, California Child Welfare authorities refused permission to let a child her age appear in such a film. The girl's mother, siding with the studio, agreed to shoot it in more lenient New York State.

on the set. Even Ray emerged from these sessions speaking like a British lord.

Mrs. West taught at various studios, but at Paramount she won industrywide acclaim for having faced down the great Cecil B. De Mille himself.

"I didn't like the way you played that scene," De Mille told Dickie Moore one day after a take. The always proper and polite Dickie, who felt unusually tired and irritable, responded with an offhand "Who cares?" Infuriated, De Mille raised his arm to strike the child when he suddenly found himself confronting Dickie's avenging angel, a wrathful Mrs. West. Planting her ample-bosomed figure squarely between Dickie and De Mille she declared in tones that rang across the quiet set: "You lay one hand on that child and *this picture doesn't move!*" The best allies some children had were their fearless studio teachers.

The head of Lawlor's school was a woman cast in the same Amazonian mold. Viola F. Lawlor, or "Mom," as she insisted on being called, was a plain, large-boned Yankee from Concord, New Hampshire. Pure American Gothic on the outside, her innermost soul was committed to Hollywood, and movie children were her weakness. Her special favorites were Mickey Rooney and Frankie Darro, both boys from broken homes. Mickey was still doing bits under the aegis of Harry Weber. Frankie was a star, a veteran of the rough-and-tumble Mascot serials that costarred him with Rin Tin Tin and won him a special place in the hearts of Saturday matinee audiences everywhere.

Although the curriculum at Lawlor's was so informal as to be almost nonexistent, Mom liked to think of herself as a strict disciplinarian. "Don't think you're going to lord it over anybody here just because you were Baby Peggy!" was her frosty welcome to me. Whenever there was an uproar in the study hall, which was often, she could be seen striding purposefully down the long corridor, breathing fire and preparing thunderbolts. But if she discovered that it was Frankie dancing on the library table wrapped in a tablecloth, or Mickey standing on a desk doing an imitation of Lionel Barrymore or Clark Gable, she relaxed and signaled them to go on with the show. Folding her arms and smiling, she enjoyed the performance as much as if she had bought a ticket.

One day she confided to me that she spoiled Frankie because she felt so sorry for him. His mother, the former Italian aerialist who had never worked again after her nervous breakdown in Long Beach, now lived in the apartment house across the street from the school. Since the Darros were separated and Frankie lived with his father, the only way she could catch a glimpse of her famous son was at the movies or when he entered and left the school. After that I always watched for Mrs. Darro, and sure enough, every day as school let out the curtain would be drawn back from the window and for a brief moment her face would appear. To me it was the most poignant of scenes, made even more so by its setting against the backdrop of the slate-gray Hollywood Hills. It represented only one among thousands of similar personal tragedies being played out under the uncaring gaze of that forever tipsy Hollywood sign, whose increasingly grimy letters seemed about to fall off the scrubby mountainside.

One entered Lawlor's by ascending a rather grand-looking staircase that, like the school itself, had seen better days. At the first landing it branched into two separate flights, the right one leading directly up to Mrs. Lawlor's desk, the left into the lobby or waiting room. This open area was sparsely furnished with two sagging sofas and a round coffee table on which were scattered several well-thumbed copies of *Billboard* and *Variety*. Some mothers brought their children to school and waited to take them home; others only dropped by to take them on auditions or interviews. A permanent fixture in Lawlor's lobby was Mrs. Lavinia Ruth Withers. A plump, good-natured woman who passed the hours happily with her knitting, she told all who cared to listen the cause of her contentment.

Lavinia Ruth had been forbidden a career of her own, but she made certain that any daughter of hers would not be so denied. When George Withers proposed, she consented only after he agreed that any child born of their union would be allowed to go on the stage. As if predestined to fulfill her mother's dream, when Jane came along she was fairly bursting with talent. At four she headed her own radio program in Atlanta, billed as "Dixie's Dainty Dewdrop." In 1932 Lavinia took the Dewdrop out of Dixie and brought her to Hollywood, confident that stardom could be plucked there as easily as oranges from a tree. Upon arrival, Jane became a Meglin kiddie and was as loyal as she was ambitious. When a rival dance studio opened up on Sunset Boulevard directly opposite Mrs. Meglin's school, Jane darted across the street and, in full view of the owners, spat on the sidewalk in front of their door. Racing back to Ethel Meglin she announced, "Now they know what *we* think of them!"

Lawlor's waiting room was equipped with that absolute necessity in Hollywood, a public telephone. One day Lavinia Withers received a call saying that Jane had been chosen to play opposite Shirley Temple in *Bright Eyes*. Another child might have hesitated to take on the reigning queen. Not Jane. She left Lawlor's and continued her schooling on the Fox lot. There, or on loan to other studios, she made a total of forty-seven pictures over the next twelve years, a record even Shirley Temple could respect. When she quit films in 1947 it was to marry a Texas oil millionaire.

Dawn O'Day was another who received a historic call in that shabby booth. I stood outside as she picked up the phone, and suddenly her face went white. When she emerged she was like someone in a dream. "That was the front office at RKO," she said. "Mitzi Green's mother demanded a salary raise on the first day of shooting on *Anne of Green Gables*. The studio refused, and she and Mitzi just walked off the set. They've given me the lead!"

Overnight her name was changed to Anne Shirley, the name of the movie's heroine, and fan magazines started calling for home layout interviews. "Please don't let them come around to my place," she pleaded with the studio. "They mustn't see where I live." She lived with her widowed mother in a mean studio apartment above a dime store. When the RKO publicity man saw it he blanched, called the studio, and told them to find Miss Shirley a house. They rented a pretty cottage in a nice part of Hollywood, and that night a crew from the prop department settled in to paint, furnish, and decorate the place. Anne and her mother were moved. The following day a beautifully gowned and groomed Anne Shirley received her interviewers in the dream cottage that was the overnight creation of RKO. Lovable, hard-working Dawn

O'Day, with the classic driving mother and impoverished child-hood, had been touched by Hollywood's Cinderella magic more completely than anyone I have ever known. With one stroke she became a star.

At Lawlor's, age was everyone's problem, especially for girls. While younger children such as Shirley Temple and Jane Withers both had a year shaved off their age by the studios, those of us who had just turned thirteen or fourteen strove to look sixteen convincingly. Studios were required by law to provide a teacher on any set that had a player under sixteen, so unless the script called for several children, it did not pay to hire a single underage child. In that case a hard-bitten twenty-three-year-old stock girl, under contract for a flat fee, was given a fresh coat of paint and made to shed her false eyelashes and play the part of the sweet young thing. As a consequence, Lawlor's had the oldest teen-aged girls in Hollywood. We came to school most of the time dressed in high heels, long gloves, slinky gowns, and picture hats, afraid a rush call or unexpected interview might come through and those of us who were fifteen or younger would not appear old enough to fool the casting director.

The well-known Weidler clan alone could manage to be the right age every time. There was a Weidler child in virtually every grade at Lawlor's from kindergarten to high school, and at least one, three, or four on any set where children were called for by the script. Only one of this hard-working family of eight ever made the grade to stardom — seven-year-old Virginia, who became Paramount's resident child star in 1934. Three years later MGM bought out her contract, and she joined the elite group in that lot's Little Red Schoolhouse. Even after her big break, the Weidler cavalcade was never without work. "If I live long enough," one assistant director prophesied, "there's going to be a Weidler who's the right age for *every* role, *from the cradle to the grave!*"

School hours at Lawlor's only took up half a day — usually the least profitable ones at that, since interviews were rarely held in the early morning hours. There were about ten rooms scattered around a main hall, and most of them were equipped with wall mirrors, practice bars, and pianos. By one o'clock the classrooms had been cleared for action, the desks and chairs pushed back against the walls. For the rest of the afternoon and evening those who had been scholars turned into troupers, everyone practicing their juggling, tap routines, ballet, opera, blues singing, piano, violin, trumpet, diction, nip-ups, and contortions.

The shows put on twice a year by Lawlor students were a far cry from the average amateurish school production. Mickey or Frankie served as MC and stand-up comic, often aided by Sidney Miller, one of Mickey's lifelong sidekicks. Jane Withers glimmered through her tap numbers, and an incredibly innovative dancer, fourteen-year-old Gower Champion, fairly ricocheted off the walls in routines that he created and rehearsed with infinite patience every day after school.* Edith Fellows sang the Jewel Song from *Faust* in a voice that was uncannily vibrant for an eleven-year-old child. And, of course, after the Gumm sisters enrolled, Mom Lawlor always put Judy in the star position on the bill.

On her first day at Lawlor's in early 1934, Judy was a quiet, plain little girl whose dresses were a trifle too long and obviously homemade. She looked too old for a child, but she did not yet have the body of a woman. Mom brought her into our study hall, introduced her, and then asked her if she would sing a number for us. Ethel Gumm settled herself on the bench, and Judy clambered onto the top of the old upright piano. When she crossed her legs, I noticed the limp, worn taffeta bows on her tap shoes. They reminded me of my own tap shoes, whose soles had several times worn through, and what they told me about her made me want to cry. I thought it was needlessly cruel of Mrs. Lawlor to put this obvious amateur through such an ordeal; after all, she knew we were an audience of hardened professionals, and this was a poor little kid from the godforsaken desert town of Lancaster.

But we had misjudged both Judy and Mom. After Ethel Gumm swept through the introductory bars of the popular "Blue Moon," an incredibly rich voice charged with a mature woman's emotional power was flooding the room: "Blue Moon / You saw me

---

* Gower later chose as his partner Ernest Belcher's graceful and gifted daughter, and they rose to joint stardom as Marge and Gower Champion.

standing alone / Without a dream in my heart / Without a love of my own . . ."

When Judy finished there were tears of pride in Mom's eyes, and every student in the room was applauding wildly and cheering the forlorn little newcomer. Even then Judy was a professional's professional. At our annual Lawlor shows, staged at the Wilshire Ebell Theater, we kept giving Judy encores that sometimes kept her singing until two o'clock in the morning. She seemed unable to say no to an audience.

When Lawlor kids got together in each other's cramped Depression-era apartments, our idea of a good time was doing what we did for a livelihood. Not even necking was preferred above our all-time favorite pastime, staging impromptu blackouts and musical shows. Mickey and his shadow, Sidney Miller, shared the nicest apartment in the better part of Hollywood, and it alone was big enough to serve our purpose well. Mickey also knew a good many blackout skits from his father, Joe Yule, whom Mickey had found and brought to Hollywood once his own career began getting under way. When Yule was not working at MGM as an extra or bit player, he served as the star comic in a burlesque house on Main Street in Los Angeles.

After the blackouts came the song and dance numbers, usually put together on the spot. One reason we all worked so well together is that everyone understood and used the same nonlinear, purely visual language of movement we had been taught by Ernest Belcher, Ethel Meglin, or the Mosconi brothers. Dance routines were like scripts, comprised of hundreds of variations on a few basic steps and the sequences that stitched them together. When Shirley, Jane, Mickey, or Judy went into rehearsal on a set with a dance director, they merely had to learn his script, composed in a common shorthand they had mastered long before they knew their alphabet. At a party, we could put together a chorus line in minutes with Mickey calling the shots. "Okay, start with a basic time step, then a soft shoe segue into the Charleston, a backward drag and a windmill . . ."

Sometimes the police were called in to break up these marathon parties; they were not wild but they were loud. The neighbors who complained did not realize they were turning off a million dollars' worth of talent performing gratis right in their own back yard. Innocent though these gatherings were, they gave us all a much-needed outlet for severely repressed emotions. They allowed us to play together in the only way we could conceive of recreation, as a reprise of our work. We had neither the time nor the taste for the football rallies and proms that occupied average teen-agers. The fierce competition between us in the daily struggle for bread made our friendships precarious and vulnerable to the demands of our careers. Only when we staged our own shows could we be noncompetitive, completely free of the contentious and divisive spirit generated by parents and others on the set.

While I felt more at ease with Lawlor kids than with others of my age, I saw them as living, working, and playing inside a huge, transparent bubble that to me symbolized the motion picture world. Already exilic in temperament and attitude, I stood outside that globe, which held most of them willing prisoners throughout their lives. My own form of creativity required this self-imposed isolation because I could not subscribe to the well-known Hollywood credo that success in any other profession was almost the same as being "between pictures." The only way I had so far been able to cope with my traumatic experiences was to project them away from myself, becoming a spectator to events as well as a participant. This enabled me to walk around an experience, gain perspective on it, and sometimes even laugh at its absurdities.

As the acknowledged center of the motion picture world, Hollywood had originally attracted — and in a sense been invented by — rugged individualists drawn from strongly diverse and antipodal cultural backgrounds. Each racial and social contingent had gradually found its own way to get around, work within, and finally triumph over the once predominant native sons. But after two decades of enforced confinement to one geographical area and total commitment to a single commercial cause, these formerly venturesome and innovative souls had crystallized into a narrow, chauvinistic, and defensive society that demanded conformity of all its members.

By the mid-1930s, Hollywood had managed to purge itself of the few remaining madcaps and mavericks, silent screen stars and directors, whose once innovative talents were now regarded with as much embarrassment as their once reckless private lives. A mantle of almost puritanical respectability had settled over the studios. Absolute conformity to the rules laid down by what was now loftily referred to as "the industry" was held to be the supreme virtue. Those unwilling to put the industry first did not deserve a place within its hallowed precincts. A star's moral, psychological, and professional proclivities automatically became studio property, to be safely locked away with the long-term contract as soon as the ink was dry. Old-timers who could no longer adorn this society with an attractive presence, or whose personal failure cast a disfiguring shadow across its beatific public image, were expected to have the good grace to remove themselves from the scene. Silent screen beauties who had aged, male stars whose voices failed to pass the sound man's sex-appeal test, and child stars who had outgrown their baby charms were all uniformly labeled "has-beens." Without compassion or regret, they were consigned to the professional equivalent of potter's field. Those who had not already made a mint in real estate made haste to marry money. If all else failed, then an open gas jet, a long westward stroll into the Pacific, and running one's auto engine in a closed garage were quite acceptable ways of making a dramatic exit. Friends and studio heads could lament how "temperamentally unsuited" the late great one really was to the high calling of Hollywood fame. Gossip columnists could speculate on the reasons why. The industry was never held accountable.

I now found myself — together with Jackie Coogan, Marie Osborne, Philippe de Lacy, and the original members of Our Gang — listed as among Hollywood's youngest has-beens. It was our peculiar destiny to spend our adolescence in this throwaway society that equated our growing up with passing into oblivion. During this difficult period of transition — confusing even for so-called normal children — we were required to make the passage from child to adult while fighting for survival on several levels at once. Committed to making a comeback in films, we had to conquer an overriding sense of failure and guilt. Hoping to keep or gain the respect and love of our parents and peers, we were also seeking desperately for a new self-image to replace the prosperous one we had outgrown. But throughout this search for self-esteem, we were forced to read our own professional obituaries as they appeared regularly in the Sunday supplements of the day. The Hollywood editor who was hard-pressed for news on a slow weekend (when no adult has-been had obliged him by ending it all) knew he had us to fall back on.

"Where Are They Now?" keened the poignant headlines.

> Baby stars win fame but soon fade away. One of Hollywood's most ironic stories concerns the fate of an old-time baby star. Now she is grown up and grateful for even a $5 a day call as an extra, because she needs the money badly. When she does get a bit, it is never for the role of the popular co-ed friend of the heroine or the beautiful slave girl. Instead she plays the homely young thing who is the forlorn wall flower at parties.*

Jean Darling, Mary Kornman, Marie Osborne, and I could all look at each other and wonder which one of us the writer was describing. Not one of us was unattractive.

It was disquieting to read that "other actors and actresses have ancestors. Baby Peggy, however, is unique. She descended from herself." In an article showing then and now photographs of famous baby stars, my childhood portrait was topped by a solid black square where the now picture should have been. The eerie caption read, "Disappeared completely." According to these writers, we, who had been judged child prodigies a decade earlier, were now discovered to have been quite ordinary children who had merely reached their intelligence ceiling prematurely. Others preferred the handy catch phrase "burnt-out genius" to explain our fall. As the years and the Sunday supplements passed and the litany of fallen child stars grew, these Sunset Boulevard pundits went on to paint an equally bleak future for Shirley Temple, Jane Withers, Jackie Cooper, Freddie Bartholomew, Deanna Durbin, and others, as though relishing the prospect of their inevitable downfall.

One day, I dropped by a Hollywood portrait studio to pick up

* Los Angeles *Times* Sunday Magazine, May 12, 1935.

some new professional stills needed to further my budding career
as a ingénue. The middle-aged clerk who handed them to me
leaned over, and as if giving in to an irresistible impulse, blurted
out, "How does it feel *to be a has-been at sixteen?*"

There is no question that a great deal of what went wrong with
many of us in later life — the multiple marriages, the drinking,
bankruptcy, nervous breakdowns, and attempted suicides — had
its roots in our singularly painful adolescent years. Most of us
were cut off completely from the normal give-and-take social relationships of the average teen-ager. We could not make small
talk with people our own age. Nearly every one of us was an innocent where money was concerned, having handed over every
cent we earned to our parents since we were infants. And in
many cases our parents worked to keep us ignorant of financial
matters, not even showing us how to make out a check or deposit
slip on our own.

To compound our handicaps, most of us subscribed subconsciously and wholeheartedly to the ideal that romance cures all
life's ills, which was the overriding message of virtually every
movie we ever saw or worked in. If other children of our generation grew up watching movies and were deeply influenced by
their false values, those of us whose childhoods were marinated
in Hollywood sentimentality were even more addicted to the lie.

When Darla Hood and Elizabeth Taylor were young school
friends on the MGM lot, even Darla was struck by Elizabeth's
penchant for movielike solutions to problems. If Darla read her a
story and it did not end happily, Elizabeth would interrupt her
and say, "Oh, don't end it that way. I want it to end *happily.*"
We were all movie addicts, seeing at least four films a week in
our neighborhood theaters. And we believed what we saw on the
screen every bit as devoutly as the moviegoer who had never been
initiated into the mysteries of the back lot.

When Anne Shirley and I talked about the right man coming
along, we meant a typical screen lover who would solve all our
problems with a kiss and a deep, all-encompassing embrace. We
honestly believed that marriage would be a perpetuation of that
deliciously stunned state in which we found ourselves right after
Gable's image faded from the screen and just before the house

lights came up: an unreal and forbidden libidinous ecstasy. Meantime, I fell in love with every actor I played opposite while living by a positively Victorian sex code more suitable for Elizabeth Barrett Browning than a girl growing up in wicked Hollywood. All my affairs of the heart followed the classic Scarlett O'Hara–Ashley Wilkes pattern of faithful frustration.

Now I planned out my entire life to the smallest detail. The blueprint required that I devote the next fifteen years to becoming rich enough to put my parents beyond necessity — with a ranch in the West and a house in Hollywood. (I was intent on making them *both* happy.) This meant I must become a great actress, completely dedicated to a successful career on stage and screen. Then, after thirty, I would leave it all and begin a life of my own. Only then would the man of my dreams be permitted to "sweep me off my feet" in the grand tradition of the Victorian novel. Above everything, I would *never* allow myself to be lured into a premature marriage simply because I was lonely and unhappy at home. So much for the New Year's Eve resolutions of a sixteen-year-old girl, reared on the Hollywood version of love and marriage.

17
A Child's Garden of Reverses

In the little world in which children have their existence, whosoever brings them up, there is nothing so finely perceived and so finely felt as injustice.

— Charles Dickens, *Great Expectations*

THE JACKIE COOGAN whom I met once again backstage during the run of *Growing Pains* behaved very much like a young millionaire. He was, of course, impatiently marking time until his twenty-first birthday, when he would come into his fortune and "own the store" himself. Throughout the early spring of 1935, columnists remarked on the imminent watershed event when the Kid would finally inherit his earnings. Meantime, they pointed out, his tuition at the University of Southern California, his living expenses, and his pocket money were all provided by Jackie Coogan Productions, Inc.

Anticipating his son's October birthday by several months, Jack Coogan surprised Jackie with his very first automobile, a trim sporty Ford coupe with a rumble seat. To celebrate the event, he also arranged to give a party for Jackie's young Hollywood friends at his Pine Valley Ranch in San Diego County. Invited to spend a day dove-hunting in nearby Mexico with Jackie and his father were his closest friends, Junior Durkin, Dick Winslow Johnson, and a youthful playwright, Robert Horner. Junior's sisters Grace and Gertrude, along with several other girl friends, would be among the guests at the party to follow on Saturday night and Sunday at the ranch house.

On Friday, May 4, just as he was preparing to leave for San Diego and the Coogan ranch, Dick Winslow Johnson received an unexpected call from Western Costumers. MGM had arranged a special Saturday fitting for the uniform he would wear as a young midshipman in *Mutiny on the Bounty*. From babyhood, Wynonah Johnson had trained her five youngsters to put picture work first, and the MGM job promised a long run. Though he was bitterly disappointed, Dick called Jackie to say he could not come. As it turned out, Wynonah's early training probably saved her son's life.

Late Saturday afternoon, Jackie, his father, Durkin, Horner, and the ranch foreman, Charlie Jones, started home from their Mexican expedition in Jackie's new car. Jack Coogan was driving; Jackie and Jones shared the rumble seat with several packs of wild doves — a respectable showing for their efforts and a rare delicacy for the guests at the next day's dinner.

A San Diego resident, Guy Holmes, who was driving north on the circuitous La Posta grade only minutes from the Coogan ranch, noticed a car hugging the center stripe and approaching him at a terrific rate of speed. As Holmes later told a San Diego *Union* reporter, after passing him the Ford coupe swerved sharply to the right and Holmes's companion glanced over her shoulder to see it fail to make the curve and plunge over the embankment. Holmes immediately turned around and sped back to the scene, where he found the coupe had hurtled end over end down the boulder-studded slope to a deep ravine below. As Holmes started down the hillside he was met by a hysterical Jackie coming up. "Please help me!" he cried. "My father is badly hurt!"

Holmes helped Jackie carry the unconscious Coogan to the shoulder of the road, where he made a pillow for his head with his own jacket. Meantime, Jackie returned to help Junior Durkin, who was also still alive, but cruelly injured. Robert Horner and the ranch foreman had both been killed instantly. When Jack Coogan was lifted into the ambulance a Catholic priest administered the last rites. By then Junior Durkin was already dead. Minutes later the elder Coogan expired in the arms of the postmaster of the Pine Valley store.

Shaken by the multiple tragedy he had just witnessed, Guy

Holmes stood at the highway's edge, gazing down at the wreckage as the bodies of Horner and Jones were carried up. There in the twilight's afterglow he noticed an eerie, almost bizarre touch to the mournful scene. Scattered over the rock-strewn hillside and all around the battered coupe lay the still forms of dozens of pale gray doves, mute reminders of Jackie Coogan's lost innocence.

As soon as the news reached Hollywood, my parents and I rushed over to see Arthur Bernstein in the offices of the Coogan Corporation. Arthur was grateful for our sympathy, but was besieged by calls and visitors, talking on two telephones at once and trying to carry on a conversation with us simultaneously.

"Lillian's taken Jack's death very hard," Arthur confided. "Thank God Jackie escaped with only a broken rib and a few cuts. But it's the lawsuits I worry about. Jackie swears a brown car with two women driving on the wrong side of the road forced them off the bluff. Others at the scene say Jack was speeding. All I know is that if anyone set out to prove Jackie was driving, damage suits could ruin us all and bring down the entire corporation." Money seemed predominant in Arthur's mind because, as he told us in confidence, the corporation had secretly given Jackie $300,000 in advance of his birthday and he had "gone through it like water. But then, as you know," Arthur added irritably, "the kid never did know how to handle money." At that time we had no reason to question the truth of his statement. He cited it as the self-fulfilling prophecy of Jackie's lifelong financial ineptitude as seen through his family's eyes.

Mrs. Lawlor let out classes so that we could attend both the Coogan and Durkin funerals. For those of us who had not yet looked upon the face of death, these solemn events represented a a very sobering rite of passage. The fact that all three Durkin children were orphans and Junior had been the family breadwinner only heightened the grief we felt at his loss.

Ironically, however, the subject that came up most often over the weeks that followed was how Junior's sudden death at seventeen had snuffed out such a promising career. "Imagine the films he would have made if only he had lived!" was a recurring theme. One excellent role that Junior was already signed up for was the juvenile lead in MGM's *Ah, Wilderness!* The part went by default to Mickey Rooney.

Mickey and his mother, the indefatigable Nell Carter, had fallen on some very hard times. In 1932, with the movie industry in the doldrums, Mickey and Nell had taken to the road in their own act but were caught in the disastrous collapse of vaudeville. Escaping from that wreckage with barely enough money to make it back to Hollywood, they subsisted for several years on the lines, bits, and small parts Mickey could find. Finally, in 1935, when MGM needed a tough kid to play gangster Clark Gable's younger brother in *Manhattan Melodrama*, they remembered Mickey. He was remembered again when MGM was casting about for Junior Durkin's replacement in *Ah, Wilderness!* After that, as Mickey proved a perfect all-American foil for Freddie Bartholomew's proper English lads, the two boys were cast together in a series of successful films — *Little Lord Fauntleroy, Lord Jeff, A Yank at Eton,* and *Captains Courageous.**

When MGM decided to bring to the screen Auriana Rouverol's play *Skidding* — which they may have bought with Junior Durkin in mind because he had scored in a similar role in her *Growing Pains* — Mickey once again fell heir to a typical Durkin role. Produced under the title of *A Family Affair*, in which Mickey played the part of Andy Hardy, the picture was a resounding box-office hit. Over the next six years MGM made something like $20 million on its fourteen Hardy films, which all told cost them a mere $4 million to produce.

Although Jackie had come through the calamitous auto accident unscathed, he soon had to face a very different kind of tragedy. Five months after his father's death, the New York *Evening Journal* bannered the news: JACKIE COOGAN GETS MILLION ESTATE TODAY AS HE COMES OF AGE. The article went on to say that the former child star's father had years ago established a trust fund for his son. Reading similar headlines in the Hollywood papers,

---

* Ironically, Jackie Cooper's career was adversely affected by the popularity of Freddie and Mickey on his home lot of MGM, and in 1937 Louis B. Mayer offered to renew his contract only at a much lower salary than he had been earning. At fourteen Cooper began free-lancing.

I winced in pain. While I rejoiced for Jackie, I could not deny the piercing pangs of envy I felt. If only my own father, whom I, too, had idolized from childhood, had cared as much for my welfare, how different our life would be now!

I was doubly sensitive at this time, for Lyon's Van and Storage Company had just auctioned off five trunks containing all my albums, clippings, costumes, even a few early films. The firm was merely trying to recoup at least the value of the trunks to compensate for our long unpaid storage bill. But I knew that whoever bought the trunks would have no use for their contents; in the Hollywood of 1935 virtually no one was collecting movie memorabilia. We all begged Father to contact the buyers and request the return of my collection. But Father was too proud to expose his poverty to public view, so everything was lost. At twilight, standing alone on the front porch of our bungalow court apartment, watching the tall palm trees bend before an oncoming storm, I cried bitterly. I could hear Mother's oft-told story of my discovery at Century, when her companion, the extra Margaret, had encouraged her to put me in pictures. "Just think, Marian, she'll have a college education, world travel, and all the rest!" Now I did not even have a record of my career, a loss that outraged my sense of history more than my ego.

My envy of Jackie's windfall proved shortlived. When his father's will was filed for probate, Jackie learned to his dismay that according to a 1926 document, Jack Coogan had willed everything to his widow, the estate reverting to his oldest son *only* if Mrs. Coogan should die first or "perish in the same calamity." No trust fund could be found. A year and a half after Jackie's twenty-first birthday came and went, Lillian Coogan became Mrs. Arthur Bernstein in a simple ceremony on New Year's Eve. In so doing, she also became president of Jackie Coogan Productions, Inc. With his mother married to his business manager, Jackie's fortune was no longer legally his.

In 1938, after two years of agonizing over his plight, Jackie sued his mother and stepfather for all his childhood earnings, estimated at between $2 million and $4 million. By then he was married to a rising young starlet and Lawlor alumna, Betty Grable, who encouraged her husband to fight for what was rightfully his. As the youthful Mrs. Coogan was quick to tell the press, "the 'Millionaire Kid' didn't have enough to take me out dancing, let alone get married!"

The trial dragged on for months amid the bitterest kind of accusations and acrimony. Among the items that Lillian Coogan Bernstein was forced to surrender to the court was a $2500 pocket watch that Jackie said a fan had given him years earlier; he claimed his stepfather had appropriated it as his own. In retaliation, Lillian recounted how Jack Coogan, shortly before his death, had told her son, "If you had money you'd be completely haywire in two months."

But Jackie stoutly defended his father, to whom he had been deeply attached. "He always had my best interests at heart," he wrote in a magazine article in which he also expressed his conviction that a trust fund would be found. "He knew that I would always share everything I had with my dad, that I would never let him down. I had a right to expect as much from him. He wouldn't have failed me." Even as I read the words, I could see Jack Coogan standing before our mantel in the Laurel Canyon house, acting out Arthur Bernstein's latest Jewish joke — " 'Ah-ha!' says the old man, *'that's the first lesson. In business don't even trust your own father!'* "

The Coogan Corporation, valued when the trial opened at $700,000, was gradually trimmed down by legal fees and other costs to a mere $250,000, which was split between the contending parties. But it proved no victory at all for Jackie. His marriage to Betty Grable broke up under the strain of the trial, and he was convinced that Arthur Bernstein, who had many relatives and friends in the industry, had him blackballed from every studio in town. To everyone's astonishment, a year later Jackie was reconciled with his mother and returned to live at home with her and his stepfather.

The last time I saw Arthur was shortly after Pearl Harbor, when the Japanese residents of the West Coast were rounded up and sent into internment camps for the duration of the war. We bumped into him in downtown Los Angeles, and he said he was very busy buying up store fixtures and other display equipment from the businesses owned by Japanese merchants who were forced to sell out. He said he was "making a killing" out of the situation, picking up very costly merchandise "for peanuts." Six years later, on January 1, 1947, he was found dead in his room at the Gilbert Hotel, a block south of Hollywood Boulevard. A brief item in the Los Angeles *Times* stated that he had died of a heart attack and described his last occupation as an executive of the Mike Lyman restaurants. He was survived by his widow, Lillian Coogan Bernstein. But the major portion of the article was devoted to the years he was closely identified with the career of former child star Jackie Coogan.

A friend who accompanied Jackie to Arthur Bernstein's funeral recalled him gazing a long while at the figure of his stepfather in the open coffin. Characteristically, Arthur was sharply dressed, even for this last solemn occasion. As they stood together, Jackie's friend heard him whisper through clenched teeth, "I'll be damned! The son-of-a-bitch is wearing a pair of my own best slacks!"

The only constructive thing that emerged from the ruins of Jackie's career was the so-called Coogan Act, a bill to protect the earnings of child actors, which required that parents put aside at least half of such earnings. Those concerned with the welfare of the current crop of child stars were reassured, in some cases quite falsely so. Jane Withers's mother was salting her daughter's income away at the rate of $1000 a week. Shirley Temple's parents were living on their own earnings — Gertrude was by this time being paid $1000 a week for her services — and investing every cent of Shirley's salary. Jackie Cooper, whose career rivaled Coogan's at its height, had a wise mother who was determined to see that her son's fortune was not squandered. Judy Garland's mother, Ethel Gumm, widowed by Frank's sudden death in November 1935, at the very outset of Judy's MGM career, was said to be taking good care of her daughter's fabulous income. Unhappily, in that case the report was untrue. But Judy was not alone in this ominous circumstance. Two other child stars, Edith Fellows and Freddie Bartholomew, suffered similar indignities at the hands of greedy relatives.

As a precocious and handsome child of three, little Freddie had been given by his parents to his paternal grandparents, to be raised under the tutelege of his ambitious Aunt Cissie. Realizing the child possessed exceptional talent, Aunt Cissie drew up a contract whereby Freddie was divided into three equal parts. The first $2500 of his earnings in any given year would go to her, plus a third of anything that remained. The grandparents, in exchange for his education and support, would receive another third. The remaining third was to be set aside in trust for the little breadwinner himself. His father signed this curious family pact without even telling his wife about it, laying no parental claim to any of their son's potential earnings.

In 1934, when Freddie was ten, watchful Aunt Cissie learned that MGM was searching for an English boy to play the title role in *David Copperfield*. Telling the other shareholders in the firm that she was merely going to visit relatives in New York, she took Freddie, left England, and made a beeline for Hollywood. There, as she had expected, Freddie captivated MGM officials, who quickly signed him to a seven-year contract. He received $175 a week in *David Copperfield*, a sum that rose to $1000 as MGM put his career into high gear. Aunt Cissie prudently went to a Los Angeles court to ask that she be made the boy's legal guardian, explaining to the judge that she had had exclusive care of him since he was three.

Back in London, when they heard what had happened, first Freddie's mother, then his father, and after that both grandparents took ship for America, proclaiming their love for the lad. At the same time they demanded their fair share of his earnings. The result was interminable litigation that kept Freddie in court at least twice a month over a three-year period. By the time he was fifteen and his career was nearing its close, some twenty-seven separate lawsuits, filed by members of his family against each other — all at Freddie's expense — had squandered virtually every cent of the one million dollars he had earned over his productive five- or six-year career.

Six months after the first Bartholomew lawsuit, Edith Fellows found herself the unlikely center of a family squabble over her movie fortune. Since the age of five, Edith had known nothing except work, deprivation, and brutal poverty. Night after night, with both the electricity and gas shut off for lack of payment, she and her jobless grandmother had sat by candlelight, bundled up against the cold. The telephone remained the one amenity still in service; in Hollywood its payment always took priority over every other household bill. Having dabbled in spiritualism in her youth, Mrs. Fellows now put her mediumship to practical use, urging Edith to join her in beaming all their powers of concentration on the telephone to *make* it ring. Eerily enough, Edith recalls, nine times out of ten the instrument seemed to respond to their psychic command, Central Casting calling to offer Edith work as an extra. And so they had existed, literally from day to day, until 1935, when Edith was awarded a long-term contract at Columbia.

Although she was now earning almost $1000 a week as her studio's answer to the child star craze, life under her grandmother's rule was just as harsh as ever. Studio chief Harry Cohn himself had to admonish the parsimonious Mrs. Fellows to invest in a decent wardrobe for Edith, now that she was a star. At home she was not allowed to run, shout, or play with other children. "They will steal away your personality," her grandmother warned, or "Your voice must be saved for your singing."

Understandably, Edith came to regard the people at the studio as her real family, their affection compensating for her own mother's abandonment in infancy and easing the severity of life at home. Unexpectedly, one evening she responded to a knock on the apartment door and opened it to two strange women. One of them proved to be her mother, the other her maternal grandmother. Both were bent on winning custody of little Edith from Mrs. Fellows on charges of kidnapping. As Edith's mother told it in court, the child had been spirited away from her, and she was only here in response to the call of mother love. Money, of course, had nothing to do with it.

For several weeks Edith worked mornings at the studio and spent her afternoons in court. She felt a stranger to her mother, and although her grandmother had been a hard taskmistress, Edith loved her, was loyal, and wanted her to win. The legal battle, however, proved a costly one. The judge ruled in favor of Mrs. Fellows, Edith's mother once again disappeared from her life, but her lawyers relieved Edith of several thousand dollars.

When she was seventeen her contract at Columbia came up for

renewal, but by then it was 1940, movie trends were beginning to change, and Edith was dropped. However, one property, bought for her earlier, was still on the studio's shooting schedule, and they borrowed Jane Withers from Fox to play the lead. This was especially ironic because, earlier, Edith had hoped to win a small part in this film for Jane, her dearest friend. Now, in a cruel turnabout, the director of the picture called Edith and asked her to take the minor role of the heroine's teen-age friend.

"I'll take it," the usually meek Edith told him with unexpected spirit, "but only if I'm paid the same salary I was earning as a star." To Edith's astonishment the director agreed.

Despite the circumstances of her return, Edith was glad to be back on her home lot and was warmly welcomed by the people she still considered her studio family. On the last day of shooting, Valentine's Day, the studio teacher and Edith's long-time friend came over to her. "Honey, I just wanted to forewarn you. The crew members have prepared a big Valentine surprise for you and will present it themselves. I didn't want you to puddle up and cry and spoil it for them."

When Edith saw them coming, carrying a huge pink board cut out in the shape of a heart with the words TO OUR LITTLE SWEET-HEART written across it, she had to summon all her self-discipline to keep back the tears. Then, as it reached her, the little procession passed her by. Turning to see where they were taking the Valentine surprise, Edith saw them present it to Jane Withers instead.

In the fall of 1935, nearly every former child actor and actress still in Hollywood found work as extras in MGM's production of *Ah, Wilderness!* I was among them. The still man was careful to snap us, both singly and in groups. "Former child star makes comeback in major adult role in the forthcoming film *Ah, Wilderness!*" went the standard caption for these publicity photos, with only the appropriate change of name. Although none of us had a line of dialogue, the publicity department made it look as if we were starring. It was a familiar form of studio exploitation to which we had long been taught to conform. If we were cooperative, our parents counseled us, the front office would feel obligated to remember us when a really good part came along. It never seemed to work that way.

On that set I met a handsome young auburn-haired extra who claimed to have been a graduate of Our Gang. His rather old-fashioned courtly manners matched our turn-of-the-century costumes and my own proper Victorian mood. When the six-week run on the picture ended, I was in love with Gordon and he with me. The only jarring note was that he was also in love with show business and dreamed of one day becoming a star. The last thing I wanted was marriage to a man whose heart lay in Hollywood. Still, marriage had its attractions, and over the next three years, on every clandestine date, Gordon held it out as a tempting means of escape from a very unhappy home life.

I was understandably weary of working in a profession I had not chosen and one in which I was regarded more as an effigy in a wax museum than someone on the threshold of womanhood. But until I kept my vow to set my parents' lives to rights, I refused to even consider my personal happiness. In fact, I was incapable of doing so. I had emerged from the child star experience with an overpowering sense of guilt. Without the divisive factor of my career, I was convinced my parents would have enjoyed an idyllic life together. I felt equally responsible for Louise's confining and friendless childhood, which would never have been except for the demands of my career.

But while I worked and prayed for the big break that would put us all back on easy street, my parents seemed bent on each other's destruction. They quarreled violently and incessantly, they separated on an average of twice a year, and each vowed to take the other to court, where in a sensational divorce trial one would be publicly branded as the culprit who had squandered my fortune. To save our own sanity and in a desperate move to bring our parents together again, Louise and I ran away from home as soon as I turned eighteen. Our ruse worked. Declaring that Louise and I had indeed been the root of most of their disagreements, they reconciled.

Although no longer living under my parents' roof, I found I still could not free myself from the lifelong pattern of wanting to make them happy by giving them money. Perhaps I still needed to feel essential to their happiness in order to feel loved. Whatever prompted the guilt, when Gordon suggested we write a musical based on my own compositions, I felt he had hit upon the magic formula that would free me at last. A successful play would establish me as a writer and composer, someone completely divorced from Baby Peggy. It would give my parents the long-promised comeback and in doing so clear the way — and my conscience — for seeking happiness in a marriage of my own.

Unable to find an angel to back us, but with the soaring hopes of the very young, we set about writing, scoring, casting, producing, directing, and even acting in a musical play of our own. Opening night was set for September 23, 1938, which also happened to be Mickey Rooney's eighteenth birthday. In a typically magnanimous gesture, Mickey bought an entire block of seats and promised to bring his "gang." Lela Rogers bought tickets and vowed she would be there, rain or shine. Elsie Janis proved an equally enthusiastic booster.

I had not seen Elsie since our last visit to the Manor House in 1928. Now I found her living like a recluse in her Beverly Hills home. Following Jenny's death, she had married a young actor half her age, and when that union dissolved, she had withdrawn almost entirely from the Hollywood scene. But she seemed genuinely glad to see me, and when I introduced Gordon to her as my fiancé, she couldn't have been happier.

"How perfectly wonderful for you both!" she said, as she led us into the garden. "You must marry at once!"

"Well," I ventured, "my parents are very much against it." I did not add that they had been against my dating anyone.

"Don't let anything stand in your way," she said firmly. "Love is a call no one should ever deny."

Elsie was the only person I knew who approved of the match and went so far as to encourage it. I took it as a good omen. Her presence in the fifth row center on opening night seemed another promising sign, as was her opening night telegram: PEGGY DEAR, LOVE TO YOU AND THE BOY AND GREAT SUCCESS TONIGHT. Perhaps she was remembering that night so long ago in London when she and Basil had stood onstage together as he recited her poem before he left for France.

"Musical drama contains excellent songs," was *Variety*'s opening comment. "Peggy Montgomery, the Baby Peggy of yesterday's screen, conveyed a natural performance as the girl of the west . . . play consists of a prologue, two acts and is studded with five singable tunes. Title song stands out. Music was provided by Dick Winslow and orchestra."

Despite this and other kind reviews, we could not lay our hands on enough money to raise the curtain a second time. Still unwilling to marry Gordon, I gave in to my parents' pleas that I come back and live with them. It was my final effort to be the ideal daughter they claimed I had never been.

18
Rites of Passage

The war, and especially the post-war period, shattered a lot of make-believe and unchecked platitudes. My pictures, written for me like so many variations on the theme of the concocted Durbin personality, were a series of failures. To this, more than anything else, I owe my luck of being able to jump off unharmed. Yes, I was lucky. Deanna Durbin was dead, and my own life really began.

— Deanna Durbin, in Norman Zierold,
The Child Stars, 1965

THE FIRST RULE of living under Father's roof was that I never see Gordon again. At three I had found Father just and fair; at twenty his demands seemed dictatorial and cruel. But characteristically I submitted, until the day I accidentally bumped into Gordon and he offered to drive me home. Father met us on the front steps of the apartment and demanded that I choose, once and for all, between Gordon and my parents. I rebelled, got back into the car, and drove with Gordon to his parents' home. Three days later we were married.

Gordon found work as a bartender in Beverly Hills while I set myself to a serious study of music and writing. A radio, on which I could tune in to symphonies, and an old upright piano, which I rented for ten dollars a month, and on which I determinedly taught myself to play and compose, were my most cherished possessions. But after six happy months Gordon was fired, the radio and piano were both repossessed, and we moved into a single room in a moldering old mansion above Hollywood Boulevard.

Jobs were scarce in 1939, and we literally went hungry for days at a time. Although I tried to keep our situation secret, someone sniffed a gossip column item and tipped off Walter Winchell, who admonished Hollywood producers to "do something" about the shocking plight of million-dollar Baby Peggy starving in an attic. Winchell's column caught the sharp eye of a Mr. Lynn at RKO, who had a B movie badly in need of promotion. In headlines he assured Winchell he was giving me my big comeback chance — a leading role in his forthcoming film, which he was careful to name. Mortified by the publicity, which naturally reflected on them, my parents called me frantically. Although they had not spoken to me in the year since my marriage, they now insisted on paying up my long-delinquent Screen Actors Guild dues so I could accept the comeback role.

Mr. Lynn interviewed me in RKO's commissary in the presence of two reporters, one from the Associated Press, the other representing UPI. Over a thirty-five-cent studio lunch, these gentlemen asked how it had felt to starve and to be eating a "square meal" at last. Although furious and humiliated, I was so desperate for work that I responded as I had been trained to — with a smile. After the reporters left Mr. Lynn leveled with me. There was no part, the picture was in the last day of shooting, but thanks anyway for giving out the interviews. To show me his heart was in the right place, he handed me a check for seven-fifty, saying, "The same as if you'd worked extra all day." And then he added grandly, "Mind you, that doesn't count lunch. *That was on me!*"

I was livid but helpless to retaliate. However, the publicity had stirred up some interest, for MGM called Mr. Lynn later that day asking to see his "test" of me, as they were considering me for the part of the native girl in *White Cargo*. Covering himself, Lynn deviously told them my nonexistent test had been "so awful we had to throw it out. You wouldn't want to use her in a newsreel!"

Learning of this conversation from a friend at MGM, Father stepped back into his role of Mr. Baby Peggy and filed a damage suit for $300,000 against Lynn and RKO, a move that generated still more headlines. As a consequence, I received a call from one of Ernest Belcher's most respected competitors, who headed a combination drama and dancing school and said he wanted to see that we both "cashed in on all this free publicity."

When I entered his office the distinguished, white-haired old gentleman got right to the point. "What I want is your name and your presence. You interview the mothers, you audition the kids. Whether the kid's got club feet or a doorknob in his forehead, you tell the mother, 'Your kid's a born child star — and *I* ought to know when I see one. Just needs the rough edges knocked off the diamond.' That's where I come in; I sell her the package of lessons for two hundred bucks, payable in advance, and after that who cares? You get fifty bucks a student, just for suckering the mothers. Is it a deal?"

Fixing him with a long, hard look, I told him icily, "Frankly, I'd prefer to starve."

"That's your privilege," he said without batting an eye. "I can always get Jackie Coogan. He's hungry too."

Soon after I returned to my rooming house, Father called with the news that RKO had offered to settle out of court for $500. I was ecstatic.

"Oh, how wonderful!" I cried. "Now I can buy a piano and still have something left for food and rent!"

"What in hell are you talking about," Father shot back irritably. "We're not settling for chicken feed. We're going after the full amount. After all, don't forget, *they've ruined your career!*"

I hung up the telephone in the dingy hallway, walked into my room, and closed the door quietly behind me. I could feel a hurricane of rage and grief tearing through me, but I was afraid to cry for fear I would never stop. I felt as though a long-delayed time bomb had finally detonated somewhere deep inside and what little self-esteem I still possessed was disintegrating all around me. At that moment I hated my parents, my sister, my husband; I loathed everyone and everything that was even associated with Hollywood. But the most terrifying thing of all was that my wrath simply refused to be directed against any of them. Instead it turned inward, beaming its murderous rage toward someone I had come to hate more than anyone else in the world

— Baby Peggy. *She* was the one who had done it all to me. She was the one who kept me captive, without any self of my own. She was the one I would have to destroy if I was to survive.

The war proved to be a watershed, a global trauma that changed the moviegoing public's tastes dramatically. The stunning loss of Corregidor, the fall of Bataan, and other crushing military defeats in the first weeks after Pearl Harbor turned countless sentimental Americans into hardened realists.

Millions of GIs, encountering honest-to-God orphans scrounging for cigarette butts and survival in the rubbled streets of Rome, Paris, and Berlin, would never again be impressed by Hollywood's saccharine, smudgeproof waifs. Newsreels and chilling photographs showed the real victims of war: children maimed, burned, abandoned, or dead. Everywhere one was confronted by the stark and brutal images of worldwide holocaust.

Only five-year-old Margaret O'Brien, in her starring role as the London evacuee in MGM's *Journey for Margaret*, seemed capable of reaching out to the American people as compellingly as the wartime headlines. With her wispy voice and dark eyes that seemed to mirror the ravages of war, she symbolized the new era's vulnerable child, growing up in a world threatened by wholesale devastation. After Margaret's outstanding career, there were individual children such as Elizabeth Taylor, Patty Duke, Hayley Mills, and Tatum O'Neal who scored personal acting triumphs, but their careers were no longer a part of the American child star cult. Once again, attitudes toward children had changed.

The typical postwar couple was decidedly family centered, but not vicariously so. The word "togetherness" came to imply everything that went with the baby boom: television, backyard swimming pools, station wagons, and a college education all around. With so many children at home — many families averaged four and five each — and with the rising interest in child psychology and child-rearing techniques, the average parent had about as much of little people in any given day as he or she could handle. They didn't need child stars anymore. After half a century of redemptive suffering on the American stage and three sugary decades in Hollywood, the child star era drew to its close, a victim of profound social change. And, as if to underscore the fact, *Variety* listed in its 1941 obituaries the death of Cordelia Howard MacDonald. The original Little Eva, America's very first child star, was ninety-one years of age.

With typical rigidity, the motion picture industry found itself totally unprepared for the postwar social revolution. Most studio heads had never left Hollywood, and their view of the world from inside the big glass bubble that was the industry appeared the same after the bomb as it had before.

They failed to comprehend that their once priceless product had finally been called by its real name — escape entertainment — and was almost universally rejected by moviegoers. "Gable's Back and Garson's Got Him!," MGM's challenging postwar cry to audiences, was a weak match for the steamy realities of such European films as *Open City* and *The Bicycle Thief*. As a consequence, the film capital was a shambles when dozens of former child actors began drifting back to the only home they knew — Hollywood.

While over the years psychologists and sociologists had written volumes about the dangerous influence movies exerted on the youngsters who frequented them, not one word had been written about the crippling effects that an entire childhood spent working in films could have upon a person. The very same experts who were marveling at our remarkable IQs when we were three and four were conspicuous by their absence now that we were young adults, trying to put together a mature image from the jagged pieces of a shattered child star. None of us had been trained to do anything but sing, dance, and act; we had no other trade, and virtually all of us had been seriously shortchanged on education. Yet, in what other postwar industry could so many (or even one!) twenty-five-year-old job applicants bring over twenty years of experience to their profession?

Unfortunately, the last thing Hollywood or the moviegoing public wanted in a former child star was professional maturity. In a sense, our fans regarded us much as they did the dolls made in our likenesses. Bought to please, divert, and amuse, a Shirley Temple or Baby Peggy doll could be cuddled at will, laid away for a time, and then brought out and played with again. Dolls never change. We, by growing up, had changed: we were now strangers to our fans, adult usurpers whom they subconsciously blamed for robbing them of the children we had been and whom they adored. One matronly moviegoer in 1948 put this sense of outrage and betrayal into words. After deploring the fact that Deanna Durbin had grown up, she declared to me in all seriousness, "That was a *positively wicked* thing for her to do!"

The readjustment to postwar Hollywood was more difficult for male child stars than for the girls, perhaps because American society exerts more pressure on men to prove themselves. Many had seen wartime duty, and military service, by its very nature, tends to level men, stripping even the most well adjusted egos of their sense of individuality. To former child stars, accustomed to public adulation, being sheared of their personality was an especially brutal experience. In some cases they seem to have been singled out, either through jealousy, envy, or just plain meanness, for cruel and unusual punishment.

When Jackie Cooper joined the navy, his commanding officer's greeting was an ego-crushing, "So you're Jackie Cooper, eh? Well, if you think you're going to get away with anything here, you're in for a big surprise!" It was a foregone conclusion that all child stars were brats. And when Jackie Coogan served as a glider pilot, he had grave problems of adjusting to what my sister had always referred to enviously as "the real world of normal people." With his ex-wife Betty Grable being the wartime pin-up goddess and every serviceman's secret sweetheart, Jackie made the mistake of trying to become one of the gang by telling them what it was like being married to her. An outraged fellow pilot decked him on the spot.

"One thing I was never prepared for," Jackie Cooper told a reporter in 1975, "was to be lonely and frightened in my twenties."

Cooper's mother, who died two weeks before Pearl Harbor, had carefully set aside most of her son's earnings, so when Cooper came out of the service, money was no problem, but his personal life and his career were shattered. Twice married and divorced before 1949, Cooper began drinking, driving fast cars, and unconsciously tearing himself apart. In 1951 he picked up a book entitled *The Will to Live.* The author, Dr. Arnold Hutschnecker, was not a psychiatrist, but he had made a deep study of psychosomatic medicine and counseled persons who had fallen into patterns of self-destruction. Seeing a fair description of himself in the book, Cooper contacted Dr. Hutschnecker in New York, and spent the next three years talking out the frustrations and conflicts that had built up in his childhood. In 1954 he married Barbara Kraus, a New York advertising director, whom he has described as "the most understanding person I have ever known." He went on to head his own production company, and a long list of television successes, both as an actor and a producer, have placed him beyond any sense of competition with himself as a child.

Like Cooper, Jackie Coogan also opted for staying on within the movie industry. He has been widely quoted as uttering such cynical statements as: "We're all in it for the money, so consequently it all comes down to what's good or bad for the pocketbook." Or (after the Coogan trial): "I found out then that the only thing anybody respects in this world is a dollar. Without money you're nothing." Or: "Looking back, [my career] has just been another way of making a living. It's the only way I know." Still, when his little daughter Leslie was four, he entertained heady dreams of making her a star. "The world is ready to take another child star to its heart," he told a reporter in 1958, "and I am convinced that Leslie could be the one. I'm training her to be natural, to be herself. I don't let her play with other children. They only remind her that she is a child . . . When we are ready to start production I will form my own company, and if Leslie is as big a star as I think she will be, I believe she should collect $400,000 on her twenty-first birthday. Public adoration is the greatest thing in the world."

Some years later, in his Palm Springs home, Jackie ran his own rare print of *The Kid* for a visiting reporter and showed him his collection of fifty scrapbooks, each one larger than a coffee table, each with at least a hundred pages of clippings covering his career. Jackie has been before the cameras steadily since 1919, and despite the sad fact that his earnings were squandered and his childhood fame never recaptured, over the years he has managed to earn what he terms a respectable living for his family as a television and screen character actor.

Lillian Coogan Bernstein is a brave, cheerful lady in a wheelchair who now lives in the San Fernando Valley with her youngest son, Robert. Interviewers find her pleasant and cooperative, and when she recalled for me her days as Baby Lillian with the California Stock Company, she seemed to rekindle the happiness those memories held for her. Family reunions are held quite frequently in her apartment, with Jackie and his third wife and children driving from Palm Springs to Hollywood for these occasions.

A few years ago, Jackie told a reporter that the one thing of which he was proudest was that he has never been beaten at Scrabble, not even when playing in professional tournaments. But after a long moment of reflection, he recanted. "No, that's not what I'm proudest of. Everybody's got their pride. No matter what I do now, I was the first. Nobody can take that away from me." *

Freddie Bartholomew, Dickie Moore, and Frankie Darro all returned from the war to discover that there was no market for their talents as actors. Freddie went on to carve out an entirely new career for himself in public relations, rising to become vice president of Benton & Bowles, an advertising agency in New York. And in a successful second marriage he found the warm family life denied him in his own childhood. Dickie also turned to another trade. After an unhappy first marriage he sought the help of an analyst, eventually reconciling himself to his childhood image, remarrying and becoming public relations director of Actors' Equity. Frankie remained within and on the fringes of the industry, working for several years as a regular on Red Skelton's television show before opening his own bar, the Try Later. The name was an ironic tribute to Central Casting's all-too-familiar admonition to extras calling in for movie jobs.

*

* Aljean Harmetz, "Jackie Coogan Looks Back with Pride," Los Angeles *Times*, April 2, 1972.

Before the war, Mickey Rooney was one of MGM's biggest stars. Then, while he was away, Ava Gardner, who as the most beautiful woman in the world seemed to symbolize the movie industry itself, rejected him by filing for divorce. With his height permanently frozen at five feet two, it was obvious to everyone that he would never become Clark Gable's replacement. Moreover, the MGM to which Mickey returned was on the brink of a palace mutiny. The young star now wanted parts with "guts," knowing he would have to act his way back up to the top, but the studio saw him only as a kid who could "mug" or as an aging Andy Hardy. The old, irrepressible Mick, pestering the girls and always onstage with a claque of friends and "gophers" standing by to applaud his perpetual performance, was still there, but with a difference. The new Mickey had held a soldier's hand while surgeons amputed his leg. Experiences like that enlarged one's perspectives.

In 1951 Mickey's father, Joe Yule, Sr., said of his son, "He had too much success without any hard knocks." Mickey's adult years proved that the hard knocks had merely been saved up for later. From 1946 to 1956 Mickey was virtually without a job. By his own admission a man who remarries compulsively because he cannot bear to be alone, Mickey has married seven times. During one tormented two-week interlude between jobs and wives, he took a room in Houston's Shamrock Hotel and, under heavy sedation, lay in a state of emotional collapse.

In 1956 he lost $55,000 with cold dice in a single night at Las Vegas. Ten years later he declared bankruptcy on almost half a million dollars' worth of debts, $97,000 of which was owed the Internal Revenue Service. A merciful judge ruled that he could take the tax money from his own trust fund, set up in his teens. After earning and spending a mind-boggling fortune of $12 million, Mickey was solvent once more and back at work when fate dealt him still one more stunning blow. In 1966, Barbara Thomason, his fifth wife and the mother of three of his six children, was murdered by a jealous lover, who then killed himself, in the bathroom of Mickey's Beverly Hills home. Still, from every tragedy Mickey bounced back. Not yet sixty, and with nearly six full decades of show business behind him, Nell Carter's scrappy Sonny remains an incredibly active, popular, and always reliable performer.

In 1948, I joined the cavalcade of former child stars descending upon Hollywood. Gordon had been drafted into the army, but served as entertainment director for the troops at Fort Ord, in northern California. I set up housekeeping there, but he was rarely home, having become the golden boy entertainer he had always longed to be. The sad truth was that he had married Baby Peggy, not me. The marriage barely outlasted the war, and I almost did not survive its collapse.

It was not the marriage — which had been unhappy almost from the start — but what it symbolized that struck at the roots of my still uncertain ego. As it did to so many other child stars, marriage had represented a psychologically imperative "comeback." It must prove to everyone (most of all ourselves) that, washed up though we might seem at eighteen or twenty, we were actually well-qualified, intelligent adults who could make a smashing success of what a great many people told us was the most important career in life — matrimony. Although I had fought to keep from being drawn into an immature and unsound union, once committed, I put into marriage the same whole-souled dedication and romanticism I had formerly expended on my career and in trying to make my parents happy. I was a born fixer-upper, still playing the eternal child star role to the bitter end, as though I were a mechanical doll someone had wound up at the age of two. Pointing the way to happiness was what I was programmed to do. Not to do it meant to self-destruct.

I believe the terrible sense of failure that we child stars carried over from adolescence made the failure of our marriages a far more devastating experience than outsiders might imagine it to be. Divorce only reprojected on a still wider screen the original breakdown of our childhood image. I, for one, had no idea who I was or where I was going. All I knew was who I had once been, and that — to use a trite show business term — was a tough act to follow. To compound our problem, none of us realized what was happening to us, and each of us thought our problem was unique.

When nineteen-year-old Deanna Durbin married assistant director Vaughn Paul on April 18, 1941, her big church wedding was a major social event. By then already miserable in my own marriage, I envied Deanna, so radiant in her wedding pictures, so happy with her groom. But two and a half years later they were divorced. Like so many child stars she had been overprotected, while parents, directors, and studio heads made all the decisions for her. At twenty-seven, she turned her back on a second marriage and a remarkable film career, which had earned her $2 million over a ten-year period, and fled Hollywood for Paris. There she spent the next few years trying to find out who she really was.

In a third marriage she became the wife of a French film director and began a self-imposed exile from Hollywood, refusing all interviews. Known only as Madame David to her neighbors in the village of Neauphle-le-Château outside of Paris, she at last found the happiness that Deanna had been promised in the rousing musical fade-out of every Durbin film. And from her retreat she later wrote a letter containing some profound truths about the child star experience:

> My fans sat in the dark, anonymous and obscure, while I was projected bigger than life on the screen. Fans took home an image of me and studio press agents filled in the personal details. This worldwide picture of me came back stronger than my real person and very often conflicted with it. How can a young, unformed girl fight this publicized image of herself while still groping for her own personality? I represented an idealized daughter to millions of frustrated fathers and mothers. They could, with their tickets, purchase twice a year new stocks of sweetness and innocence.*

In 1945 seventeen-year-old Shirley Temple was given away by a proud George Temple to John Agar in another spectacular Hollywood church wedding. As I had Deanna, I now envied Shirley her strong, protective husband, her approving parents, and the immense financial security she enjoyed. I had followed her career with more than usual interest ever since we met in her dressing room at Twentieth Century–Fox back in 1936. She was eight years

* Quoted in a 1958 article by Garvin Hudgins in the New York *Post*.

old at the time, and while we waited for photographers to snap us together for publicity stills, she was busily talking to the studio café on her own private phone, imitating her mother's voice and ordering an outrageous assortment of desserts. In another child I would have found the performance bratty. Shirley managed to make it witty, spontaneous and conspiratorial.

Never having been the family breadwinner out of necessity, it was obvious that Shirley had escaped many of the pressures that had been brought to bear on most child stars. I also found George and Gertrude Temple unique among movie parents: they did not seem intent upon perpetuating Baby Shirley into her own old age. When she turned thirteen, they enrolled her in one of the most elite schools in the area, an old-fashioned finishing school dedicated to turning out faultless socialite hostesses, wives, and mothers. The Temples gravitated toward California's "old money," never choosing friends among the new rich of the movie industry. They entertained, Sunday after Sunday, the same close friends and always at home. Shirley's friends were not professional children but the daughters and sons of people of established means.

While Shirley was prepared to head the Junior League, her husband John Agar was attracted to the glitter of show business, a profession the Temples preferred to call "the entertainment world." When Shirley realized that, however unintentionally, Agar might be using her as a steppingstone to a career of his own, her disenchantment with herself may well have been as great as her disillusionment in her husband. The last thing she wanted to believe was that he might have married Shirley Temple and not "Shirl." For someone with such a strong self-image, it must have taken a truly shattering experience to put Shirley behind the wheel of her car one night with the avowed intention of driving off a cliff. As she drove, blinded by the burning tears of this, her first real heartbreak, she remembered the family doctor whose counsel had once saved her career from falling into the hands of Arthur Bernstein. Slowly she turned the car away from the sea bluffs and toward the refuge of the doctor's home. This incident, so out of character with everyone's image of sunny Shirley, was related to the judge when she tearfully sued Agar for divorce in 1949.

Later, on vacation in Hawaii, she met handsome, dark-haired

Charles Black, son of the president of the Pacific Gas and Electric Company of San Francisco. The elder Black was said to be one of the richest men in California. Shirley was unaware of this when the couple met on the beach, and she was delighted when young Charles, who was obviously not a movie fan, mistakenly assumed she was a secretary working on the island. Married in 1950, the Blacks had two children, and everyone's dimpled darling went on to become socially active and politically involved Shirley Temple Black. As a career woman of exceptional intelligence and capabilities, Shirley continues to make headlines. But her childhood image remains enshrined in the hearts of her ever-loyal fans.

It seemed that nearly every one of the former child stars I met on my return to Hollywood had some disheartening story to tell. Even Anne Shirley, my closest friend from our Lawlor days, was a divorcée. At twenty-five she retired from films, confessing that she had never wanted to be an actress or a star. Her mother had wanted it for her so she could tell everyone she was Anne Shirley's mother. But at least Anne had her earnings intact. Others had not been as fortunate.

Edith Fellows, who had been working on the New York stage, returned to Hollywood in 1944 for her twenty-first birthday and to collect her childhood earnings, held in trust by a California bank under the terms of the Coogan Act. When the great day came, the bankers ushered Edith into an imposing board room with a long conference table and ceremoniously handed her a check. It was made out for exactly $900.60. She mistook it as the staid banker's little joke, for that was the amount she had earned every week while she was starring at Columbia. Laughing good-naturedly, she chided them, "Okay, now where's the rest of it?" When they told her that was all there was, Edith was stunned. Intuitively she knew that a great deal of money had vanished into thin air — or into someone else's pocket — but how could she prove it? Her grandmother was dead. There was no studio family anymore. With her $900 stake she returned to the East to make her living on the stage.

Tragic though it was, Edith's story had a familiar ring that made it almost commonplace. Darla Hood had retired at twelve, having earned $750 a week during a remarkably long career of six years with *Our Gang*. Her parents had bought a lovely home, and as Darla herself admitted, she did not begrudge them that or any of the other things they had bought with the money she had earned. But it seemed to Darla that they had not quite done right by her. "Would you believe it?" she told author Walter Wagner in 1975. "For all my years of work in the Gang, I've never seen a single dollar."

While both Mother and Father were relieved that Gordon was out of my life, they still had no understanding of the crisis I was going through. At thirty I desperately needed help and guidance, but first I had to find a way to support myself. One day Father said he had found the ideal job for me. It seemed that Roy Rogers was looking for someone to answer his fan mail. "You want to be a writer," Father said, "so that should be a natural spot for you." Seeing the stricken look on my face, he added, "And who knows, being right there on the Republic lot, you might be discovered all over again!"

I knew then that I had to get out of Hollywood and put a safe distance between my parents and myself or face a serious mental breakdown. I was already at the point where merely hearing my old vaudeville theme of "Baby Face" played on a café jukebox would send me fleeing into the street, where I would run several city blocks, crying hysterically, as though pursued by some nameless terror I could not escape.

Moving to Santa Barbara, I sought help from the only source I knew and could afford — the Catholic Church. Earlier in my search for sanity I had become a convert: the Church offered continuity, security, wisdom, and strength, virtually everything I lacked. An experienced Franciscan priest became my patient spiritual director, a task that entailed listening to me talk out my problems and fears over a two-year period and pointing out practical ways in which I could build a life of my own. I changed my name, took over the management of the Franciscans' gift shop in the old mission, and became a historical research assistant and public relations writer for the canonization cause of Father Junípero Serra.

In Santa Barbara I also met my present husband, a mature and understanding man who is an artist and art historian. Sharing a deep interest in Mexican history, we took up a ten-year residence in Mexico following our marriage in 1954. I can easily understand how Deanna Durbin found happiness in an obscure French village. I, too, found peace in a completely foreign environment. The enormous, protective distance from Hollywood and my parents, and the new perspective that the Mexican life and culture gave me, greatly helped to integrate my two warring selves. I no longer sought to destroy the troubled child within, but set out to befriend her. After all, Baby Peggy was only the shell of the Golden Egg, a shell that had to break if I was to emerge. With that ordeal ended, she could be pieced together again.

19
On the Golden Stair

Hello Central,
Give me Heaven,
'Cause my mother's there.
You will find her
With the angels
On the Golden Stair.
— Popular song, c. 1900

WHILE GREAT NUMBERS of Hollywood's children cast about for ways to earn a livelihood outside the industry, most of the movie mothers who had brought them west during Hollywood's golden era wanted only to remain. Three such pioneers, still doing business at the old stand, were Reesie Parrish, Freida Jones, and Wynonah Johnson. Although their hard-working youngsters had helped these determined mothers to "get the wagons through" in the darkest days of the Depression, after the war most of them were glad to quit. Baby Helen Parrish chose marriage over a career, Bob Parrish became a film cutter and director, and his brother Gordon, an executive with the Coca-Cola Company, the firm that had first brought the family to Hollywood. Ironically, both Mr. Parrish and Mr. Jones had long ago bowed out of their respective families' lives and disappeared without a trace.

For many years Freida Jones expended all her efforts to make daughter Marcia Mae a star, but gifted actress though she was, Marcia Mae was so unhappy and bitter over what she considered her lost childhood that she left films to begin a long, lonely search of self-discovery through the help of Christian Science.

And so, with their children flown, Reesie and Freida concentrated on their own careers, becoming perennial extras in Central Casting's thinning ranks. They worked together steadily over the next thirty years, and when Freida died in 1976, Bob Parrish thought his mother would be desolate. Reesie *did* miss Freida, but, as Bob told me, "luckily the very next day she got a call from Central Casting to do a bit, playing a powder-whitened corpse in a coffin. Mother was elated, and we drove her to the studio in style, just as though she were the star of the picture." Reesie died only a few months after her dearest friend, still on call at Central.

Although Wynonah Johnson had never had the good fortune to become the mother of a child star, her five little troupers had put in their time. Dick Winslow, dropping the family surname, emerged as a successful character actor, appearing in a featured role in John Wayne's movie *The Shootist* in 1976. Having mastered every instrument in the one-time family band, on occasion he can be seen at Disneyland or Knott's Berry Farm, amusing the youngsters with his walking one-man band. But if none of Wynonah's children became child stars, they escaped some of the sorrows of stardom too. And Wynonah won a special place in movie history when, in 1942, she was honored as the Hollywood Movie Mother of the Year, no mean accomplishment in itself, since the other mothers had to vote her in.

My parents, too, remained tenaciously attached to Hollywood. Only after Father's lawsuit against RKO came to nothing did Father and Mother both resign themselves to the fact that Baby Peggy could not be resurrected. Free of that albatross, they put together a totally new life in the Hollywood of the forties and fifties.

Mother now had her social life served up to her on a daily basis by Central Casting. She spent her days on different sets but with the same friends she had known, and with whom she had worked extra, for years. They and the studio provided all those essential social activities that most women find in their home, family, school, church, and club. Location trips broke what outsiders might have mistaken for monotony, with occasional jaunts to interesting racetracks, mansions, and resorts. And in a remarkable gesture, Mother had in fact ceased to be Marian Baxter Montgomery, the starry-eyed girl from a small Wisconsin town. In 1950, when she learned that I had changed my name, she immediately picked up the discarded Peggy Montgomery and had herself relisted at Central Casting. In effect she had at last become the star she had always wanted to be.

Father, also, found a life tailored to his own physical and psychological needs. He and his lifelong cowboy friends were enabled to ride their make-believe 1880s' range for another twenty-five years, thanks to that unique time warp that the industry's product and its almost limitless resources made possible. The cowboys, too, spent several weeks each year on location, being flown to such rugged outposts of their natural habitat as Durango, Colorado, and Sidona, Arizona. Moreover, they were paid well, and could indulge their passion for poker, winning or losing from each other what they referred to as "calf money." This was tax-free income, with which they euphemistically promised themselves they would buy "a few weaner calves and start a little spread." No nineteenth-century cowboy adrift in the twentieth could have asked for more.

While only a few old-timers could remember the forceful Charlotte Pickford in her Hollywood heyday, the empire that her determination helped to build continued to live on at Pickfair. Mary retired from the social whirl after the war almost as completely as she had from her career ten years earlier. Married happily to Charles "Buddy" Rodgers since 1937, following an agonizing divorce from Douglas Fairbanks, close friends said she still dreamed of her beloved Doug and often cried out for him in her sleep. The doll that David Belasco gave her when she played Betty Warren in *The Warrens of Virginia* is still cherished in her upstairs bedroom, while in the living room a life-size painting of little Mary in her prime dominates an entire wall. Pickfair is perhaps the last grand estate in the triumphant tradition of Mary Anne's Attol Tryst and Jenny Janis's Manor House.

For a time Mary stubbornly tried to keep United Artists going, but she was infuriated by her long-time partner Charlie Chaplin's lack of business responsibility and his failure to even show up at meetings. And her patriotic soul was outraged when he chose to live abroad. Later, when Chaplin returned to Hollywood in 1973 to accept a special Oscar, Mary flatly denied his request to visit her at Pickfair. She described him to one interviewer as "a cheap ham fat comedian" who had been overrated by the press. She had indeed come full circle in her attitude toward Chaplin. As for her own film legacy, in September 1965, the erstwhile Gladys Smith told Kevin Brownlow in London, "Maybe it's a form of gratitude, I don't know. But I will not put my films on television. I will not do anything to that young girl who made everything possible for me. I will not exploit her."

Of all the mother-daughter relationships to be sundered by the child star experience, perhaps that of Judy Garland and Ethel Gumm was the most tragic. When Judy began her career at MGM she and her mother seemed close. Judy's money built a mansion for Ethel in Stone Canyon. Later, however, when Judy began having trouble keeping up with the day-and-night shooting schedule of musicals and started taking pep pills and other stimulants to keep her on her feet, their relationship changed. Her mother, too, pushed for performance. Ethel became a kind of studio spy, checking on her daughter's activities and reporting directly to Louis B. Mayer. Judy felt her mother had betrayed her, and her attitude cooled still more. In 1952, after her own marriage to William Gilmore failed, Ethel took her case to court, claiming that Judy should support her, as she was now a very wealthy star.

"Judy has been selfish all her life," Ethel told reporters glibly. "That's my fault. I made it too easy for her. She worked hard but that's all she ever wanted, to be an actress. She never said, 'I want to be kind' or 'loved,' only 'I want to be famous.' " It never occurred to Ethel that she was the one who had given her daughter such values, if indeed Judy truly subscribed to them. The gulf between them widened.

On January 6, 1953, Ethel was found dead in a parking lot at the Douglas Aircraft Company. She had taken a $60-a-week clerk's job when Judy, then married to Sid Luft, had failed to set up a fund for her mother's living expenses. To rub more salt in Judy's wounds, columnists were quick to point out that while Judy was pulling down $25,000 for one week in a New York concert hall, her poor mother had been taking home a little more than a dollar an hour from the plant.

On her part, Judy seemed as eager to place the blame for her problems at Ethel's doorstep as Ethel had been to pin the responsibility for her troubles on Judy. Not long before her own tragic death in London in 1969, Judy had created a fantasy figure of Ethel, in several interviews likening her role in her daughter's life to that of the Wicked Witch of the West, who had appeared as the incarnation of cruelty and evil in Judy's first starring film, *The Wizard of Oz*. Perhaps it was the only way Judy had of fending off the ghosts of her childhood that haunted her to the very end.

In 1961, when my sister wrote to me in Mexico that Father had only a short time to live, Bob and I decided to make the long journey back to Hollywood and take our nine-month-old son, Mark, with us. I felt sure that seeing his new grandson would make Father happy, for over the years he was always urging me to "settle down and have a family like any normal woman." Mother found Mark adorable, but she admonished me to "get as much pleasure as you can out of him while he's still a baby. That's the *only* age when kids are a joy. After that they're nothing but heartaches and grief." I nodded knowingly.

With the entire family gathered to celebrate Father's seventieth and last birthday, I cast about for some very special gift that would somehow reflect my own desire for a complete reconciliation. Through my friends John and Dorothy Hampton, of Hollywood's Silent Movie Theater, I was able to arrange for a private showing of one of my early Baby Peggy films. Louise and her three grown children came, as did several of Mother's old-time extra friends and a scattering of grizzled cowboys. For an hour Father was carried back into the world of five-day wonders, and there were tears of gratitude in his eyes.

But later, back in their apartment, while playing with the baby, Father suddenly sat bolt upright in his chair as though he had just seen something that had not been there seconds earlier.

"Marian, just look at this kid," he said to Mother. "Why, he's the image of Peg when she was his age. He'd be a natural to star in movies and television!"

As I felt myself stiffen, Mother replied, "You're absolutely right, dear! Why didn't we notice it before!"

Although I was having difficulty even breathing, I felt compelled to speak as I moved protectively toward Mark. "Oh, no," I said as if warding off a blow, "I would never permit such a thing!"

"But why not?" Mother said almost petulantly. "Just think of the residuals he'd get from commercials. Why, he could pay his way through college and travel around the world on his own money when he grows up. Just because *you* don't like the industry doesn't mean you've got the right to deny your only child *all that!*"

After Father's death, Mother lived alone and continued to take extra work for almost a decade, but in 1971 she entered the Motion Picture Home. Bob and Mark and I also returned to the States and settled in the San Diego area that year, so I made every effort to visit Mother regularly. The Home is a well-run, cheerful place, with a comfortable lounge dominated by a large oil painting of director John Ford above the fireplace. It is an institution to which everyone in the industry has contributed, and to me, at least, it represents the distilled essence of early Hollywood. Here as on the set extras gather, as though on a perpetual call-back for tomorrow. Here as always the conversation centers on the studio world, and some of the old class barriers prevailing on the set have been lowered. A director, a producer, a script girl, and an extra woman may now share the same table, but a front-office man can still put down a creative Academy Award–winning director with "Don't tell me about your Oscar. You only directed the picture. I *own* the film!" Any other setting for Mother's last years would have been unthinkable.

One day when I was visiting her at the lodge of the Home, I was admiring the impressive larger-than-life studio portraits of famous old-time stars lining the walls of the dining room. Mother interrupted me.

"Do you know what all those people — Judy Garland, Clark Gable, Spencer Tracy — have in common?" she asked.

"MGM?" I ventured.

"No. *They're all dead!*" She fairly spat out the words. "We don't like looking at them anymore."

On my very next visit the beautiful photo blowups had been taken down and replaced with a completely new set of relative newcomers to Hollywood.

"I see you noticed the improvement," Mother remarked cheerily. I nodded.

"But, Mother, you didn't know any of these people. They were never old friends like the others were."

"I know that, but who cares?" she said offhandedly. "These have something in common, too. *They're all alive!*"

In 1976, the last time Mother was well enough to leave the Home, I took her to lunch at the fashionable Calabasas Inn nearby. Even at eighty she was still a slim and attractive woman, in immaculate white slacks and bright red blazer. As we sipped our martinis — forbidden on her diet at the Home, but always indulged in when we went out — she once again told me how badly she felt about the loss of all my childhood earnings. As usual, I told her not to worry about it. She could never comprehend why I considered the lost fortune the least part of a child star's problems.

"I felt especially bad before your father died," she went on. "When he presented you with that note for two thousand dollars, with all that interest — I just couldn't believe he would demand money from you, of all people!"

True, at the time I had been deeply hurt. Father had loaned me the sum, out of his movie location poker winnings, or "calf money," to help me finance a small business of my own a few years prior to my second marriage. I had foolishly believed it was a gift, even a chance for him to feel he was making up to me in some way. But, wanting to leave Mother as well fixed as possible when he died, he had not only listed this debt as part of his estate to be collected, but he had added on 5 per cent interest over the many intervening years. Reflecting on his motivation though, I felt the gesture was more desperate than mean. As I tried to explain it to Mother, "After a lifetime as Mr. Baby Peggy, owing so much to me, his ego wanted to make sure that when he died *I* owed *him* something, and not the other way round." She shook her head, still baffled by the curious twists her marriage to Father had undergone.

Trying to change the subject to something less painful, I pointed out that the view from our table — overlooking giant California oaks and the neatly clipped golf course that rolled on for miles — was actually the old Hidden Valley location site.

"Remember when this was that remote little hideaway where the cowboys used to make their endless chases with John Wayne, Errol Flynn, and Roy Rogers?"

Mother set down her glass and looked at me quizzically. "But you can't remember *that* far back! Why, honey you're not *old* enough!"

When I reminded her of my real age, she shook her head in disbelief. "But that's impossible. You still seem just like a little girl to me!"

Mother's remark, indicating her complete blindness to my maturity, jolted me back to Mary Ann Crabtree and the way she had continued to refer to Lotta long after she had grown old, as though Lotta were still the reigning fairy queen of the camps. And Lotta had, perhaps unconsciously, striven to keep her mother's curious illusion alive. But after Mary Ann's death, Lotta's desire to express her gratitude and honor her mother's memory became almost an obsession, as though no amount of money, gifts, or performance could ever adequately expiate her debt. She commissioned a $20,000 stained-glass window of angels in flight as a public tribute to her mother. Made in Europe and shipped back to New York for installation in any church that would accept it, Lotta was shocked to discover no church in the city would have it, even as a gift. Therefore, in 1915, when her beloved adopted city of San Francisco invited "the California Diamond" to preside over an official Lotta Crabtree Day, she was determined to use the occasion to make a crowning public statement about Mary Ann.

Standing beside the carved stone water fountain she had presented to the city years before, and with the streets roped off for blocks around, she faced the largest audience of her life — and her last. With her carefully prepared speech in her hand, the sixty-eight-year-old Lotta began, "Dear Friends" — and then she suddenly burst into tears at the overwhelming tribute the vast crowd accorded her. As she wept silently, thousands of voices took up the familiar chant: "LOTTA! LOTTA! LOTTA!" In her shimmering yellow silk gown, not unlike the human sparkler she once had appeared in the smoke-clouded bars and theaters of the gold camps, Lotta made one last gallant effort to utter those all important words she had written: "What I am, what I have been, what I was, I owe entirely to my mother. My mother was the most wonderful woman that ever lived — and I want the world to know it." But completely overcome, Lotta threw aside that carefully prepared speech, bowed her head, and murmured only "Thank you" to her thousands of chanting fans.

Lotta's feelings toward Mary Ann were far more ambivalent than she probably ever realized, and because she was denied children of her own she lacked the key that might have freed her from her mother's overpowering personality and given her a fulfilling life of her own. For me the key was my three-year-old son. While absently watching him play contentedly in his sandbox one day, I was suddenly flooded with an inexplicable sense of consolation and well-being, as though an aching void had been filled and all the broken parts inside of me had been miraculously mended. By merely doing what was pleasing and proper to a child his age, he had unwittingly bestowed upon me the healing gift of the childhood I never had.

Not surprisingly, nearly every former child star I know has displayed a fierce desire to protect his or her own children from the limelight. Perhaps we do it, not merely for the sake of our children, but because we know instinctively that we need their carefree and happy childhoods every bit as much as they do — probably a great deal more.

Acknowledgments
Bibliography
Index

Acknowledgments

I WISH TO EXPRESS my appreciation to the following childhood friends whose early years were spent on studio sets and who were kind enough to share their recollections with me: Barbara Perry Babbitt, Margaret Jones Brown, Jean Rouverol Butler, Marge Champion, Frankie Darro, Charlotte Henry Dempsey, Johnny Downs, Edith Fellows, Alf Goulding, Jr., Marcia Mae Jones, Arthur Kahitsu, Lola Roach Larson, Gertrude Messinger, D'Arcy Miller, Louise Montgomery Moore, Robert Parrish, David Sharp, Anne Shirley, Ray Sperry, George Weidler, Dick Winslow, Jane Withers, and Marie Osborne Yeats.

I also owe a special debt of gratitude to the following pioneers and professionals of the motion picture industry who generously granted personal, written, or telephone interviews: Lillian Coogan Bernstein, Lee Hanna, Freida Jones, actress Babe London, Western star Colonel Tim McCoy, former MGM schoolteacher Mary McDonald, Ethel Meglin, Lewis Milestone, Marian Baxter Montgomery, Catherine Moore (widow of Owen Moore), Ethel Fishback Palmer (widow of Fred Fishback), long-time assistant director Willard Sheldon, former MGM casting director Bobby Webb, pioneer film producer Julius Stern, his wife, Edith Stern, and silent screen star Blanche Sweet. Nancy Voorhees, a school chum of Shirley Temple, was especially helpful in giving insights into Shirley's adolescent years and the daily life of the Temple family.

I am indebted to Christopher Cook of the British Broadcasting Corporation, who, in the summer of 1975, conducted in-depth interviews with several former child stars including myself for the BBC's documentary series "Yesterday's Witness in America," entitled *Babes in Hollywood*. The perceptive and thought-provoking questions he asked me during the five days of intensive interviewing and filming of the Baby Peggy segment caused me to rethink many aspects of the child star phenomenon.

Richard Lamparski was unfailingly helpful in locating sources, and film historian Kevin Brownlow assisted me in countless ways. In the areas of film history and uncovering rare photographs, those who have contributed include the Academy of Motion Picture Arts and Sciences, Bart Andrews, Richard Bann, Eddie Brandt's Saturday Matinee, Loraine Burdick, Ed Cogan, the Lotta M. Crabtree Estate, Bob Cushman, David Dempsey, Larry Edmunds Bookshop, the Harvard Library Theatre Collection, June Havoc, Ed Hutshing, Wayne Martin, Robert Parrish, Ray Sperry, Bruce Torrance, and Dick Winslow. I am also grateful to research assistants Kristan Caruso and Joan Cohen, and to the University of California at San Diego Librarians Phillip Smith and Fran Ness for their skill in helping me locate many facts, photographs and documents. Lois Strachan provided valuable insights into the attitudes of youthful fans toward famous child stars.

My editor, Joyce Hartman, deserves my heartfelt thanks for being an editor in the truest sense of that word. Last but not least, I am grateful to my husband and son for their unflagging encouragement, patience, and perseverance in keeping our household running during the more than five years it has taken me to research and write this book.

Bibliography

Anderson, Jean. "Hollywood's Great Child Stars: Where Are They Today?" *Family Circle,* October 1976.

Ariès, Philippe. *Centuries of Childhood: A Social History of Family Life.* New York: Alfred A. Knopf, 1962.

Basinger, Jeanine. *Shirley Temple.* Pyramid Illustrated History of the Movies. New York: Pyramid Communications, 1975.

Best, Marc. *Those Endearing Young Charms: Child Performers of the Screen.* New York: A. S. Barnes, 1971.

Brownlow, Kevin. *The Parade's Gone By.* New York: Alfred A. Knopf, 1969.

Burdick, Loraine. *The Shirley Temple Scrapbook.* New York: Jonathan David, 1975.

Cameron, James. "You Had the Cutest Little Baby Face . . ." *The Listener,* September 30, 1976.

Cary, Diana Serra. *The Hollywood Posse: The Story of a Gallant Band of Horsemen Who Made Movie History.* Boston: Houghton Mifflin, 1975.

Chaplin, Charles. *My Autobiography.* New York: Random House, 1964.

Chaplin, Charles, Jr. *My Father Charlie Chaplin.* New York: Random House, 1960.

Chaplin, Lita Grey. *My Life With Charlie Chaplin.* New York: Bernard Geis Associates, 1966.

Cooper, Jackie, as told to Roger Kahn. "Unfortunately I was Rich." *The Saturday Evening Post,* March 25, 1961.

Dahl, David, and Barry Kehoe. *Young Judy.* New York: Mason/Charter, 1975.

DeMause, Lloyd. *The History of Childhood.* New York: Psychohistory Press, 1974.

Dempsey, David, and Raymond Baldwin. *The Triumphs and Trials of Lotta Crabtree.* New York: William Morrow, 1968.

Drinkwater, John. *The Life of Carl Laemmle.* New York: G. P. Putnam's Sons, 1931.

Eels, George. *Ginger, Loretta and Irene Who?* New York: G. P. Putnam's Sons, 1976.

Essoe, Gabe. *Tarzan of the Movies.* New York: Citadel Press, 1973.

Fairbanks, Douglas, Jr., and Richard Schickel. *The Fairbanks Album.* Boston: New York Graphic Society, 1975.

Fenton, Robert W. *The Big Swingers.* Englewood Cliffs, N.J.: Prentice-Hall, 1967.

Foster, C. J. "Mrs. Temple on Bringing Up Shirley." *Parents,* October 1938.

Gardella, Kay. "Jackie Cooper: Surviving Stardom." New York *Sunday News,* August 31, 1975.

Garland, Judy. "There'll Always Be an Encore." *McCall's Magazine,* January–February 1964.

Gish, Lillian, with Ann Pinchot. *Lillian Gish, the Movies, Mr. Griffith, and Me.* Englewood Cliffs. N.J.: Prentice-Hall, 1969.

Goldbeck, Willis. "Seen But Not Heard." *Motion Picture Classic,* October 1922.

Green, Abel, and Joe Laurie. *Show Biz: From Vaude to Video.* New York: Henry Holt, 1951.

Hampton, Benjamin B. *History of the American Film Industry: From Its Beginnings to 1931.* New York: Dover Publications, 1970.

Hano, Arnold. "How Skippy Finally Grew Up." *Coronet,* January 1961.

Harmetz, Aljean. "Jackie Coogan Looks Back with Pride." Los Angeles *Times,* April 2, 1972.

Hatterer, Lawrence J. *The Artist in Society.* New York: Grove Press, 1965.

Havoc, June. *Early Havoc.* New York: Simon and Schuster, 1959.

Hawley, Renée Dunia. "Los Angeles and the Dance, 1850–1930." Master's thesis, University of California at Los Angeles, 1971.

Howe, Herbert. "What's Going to Happen to Jackie Coogan?" *Photoplay,* December 1923.

Hurrell, George, and Whitney Stine. *The Hurrell Style.* New York: John Day, 1976.

Janis, Elsie. *So Far, So Good.* New York: E. P. Dutton, 1932.

Lahue, Kalton C. *Kops and Custards: The Legend of the Keystone Films.* Norman: University of Oklahoma Press, 1968.

————. *Mack Sennett's World of Keystone: The Man, the Myth and the Comedies.* New York: A. S. Barnes, 1971.

————. *World of Laughter: The Motion Picture Comedy Short.* Norman: University of Oklahoma Press, 1966.

Lamparski, Richard. *Whatever Became of* ——? New York: Crown Publishers, 1967.

————. *Whatever Became of* ——? Second Series. New York: Crown Publishers, 1968.

————. *Whatever Became of* ——? Third Series. New York: Crown Publishers, 1970.

————. *Whatever Became of* ——? Fourth Series. New York: Crown Publishers, 1973.

————. *Whatever Became of* ——? Fifth Series. New York: Crown Publishers, 1974.

————. *Lamparski's Whatever Became of* ——? First Giant Annual. New York: Bantam Books, 1976.

————. *Lamparski's Whatever Became of* ——? Second Giant Annual. New York: Bantam Books, 1977.

Lee, Gypsy Rose. *Gypsy.* New York: Harper & Brothers, 1957.

Lewis, Phillip C. *Trouping, How the Show Came to Town.* New York: Harper & Row, 1973.

Lloyd, Harold. *An American Comedy.* New York: Dover Publications, 1971.

Maltin, Leonard, and Richard W. Bann. *Our Gang: The Life and Times of the Little Rascals.* New York: Crown Publishers, 1977.

Marion, Frances. *Off with Their Heads!* New York: Macmillan, 1972.

Marx, Samuel. *Mayer and Thalberg: The Make Believe Saints.* New York: Random House, 1975.

Morris, Lloyd. *Curtaintime.* New York: Random House, 1953.

Parrish, Robert. *Growing Up in Hollywood.* New York: Harcourt Brace Jovanovich, 1976.

Pearsale, Ronald. *Night's Black Angels: The Many Faces of Victorian Cruelty.* New York: David McKay, 1975.

Pickford, Mary. *Sunshine and Shadow.* New York: Doubleday, 1955.

Powdermaker, Hortense. *Hollywood: The Dream Factory.* Boston: Little, Brown, 1950.

Ramsaye, Terry. *A Million and One Nights.* New York: Simon and Schuster, 1926.

Ronnie, Art. "The Kid Is Still Going Strong: Jackie Coogan De-

fines Attributes of Child Stars." Los Angeles *Herald-Examiner,*
TV Weekly, October 28–November 3, 1962.

Rooney, Mickey. *i.e.: An Autobiography.* New York: G. P. Putnam's Sons, 1965.

Ross, Ishbel. *Uncrowned Queen: Life and Times of Lola Montez.*
New York: Harper & Row, 1972.

Rourke, Constance. *Troupers of the Gold Coast, or The Rise of
Lotta Crabtree.* New York: Harcourt Brace, 1928.

Rubin, Jay. "Jay Rubin Interviews Jackie Coogan." *Classic Film
Collector,* October 1976.

St. John, Adela Rogers. "The Kid Who Earned a Million. The
Real Story of How Jackie Coogan Was Discovered." *Photoplay,*
February 1923.

Sangster, Margaret. "How They Raise Jackie Coogan." *Photoplay,*
May 1923.

Sennett, Mack. *The King of Comedy.* New York: Doubleday,
1954.

Wagner, Walter. *You Must Remember This: Oral Reminiscences
of the Real Hollywood.* New York: G. P. Putnam's Sons, 1975.

Wilson, Thane. "A Wonder Child Who Is Just a Natural Boy."
American Magazine, August 1923.

Windeler, Robert. *Sweetheart: The Story of Mary Pickford.* New
York: Praeger, 1974.

Yallop, David. *The Day the Laughter Stopped.* New York: St.
Martin's Press, 1976.

Zierold, Norman J. *The Child Stars.* New York: Coward-McCann,
1965.

———. *The Moguls.* New York: Coward-McCann, 1969.

Index

Actor's Equity, 256
Agar, John, 259, 260
Ah, Wilderness!, 239, 245
Alexander, Little Benny, 46
Alice in Wonderland, 220
American Expeditionary Force (A.E.F.), 191–92
Anne of Green Gables, 227
April Fool, 172, 220
Arbuckle, Roscoe "Fatty," 53, 54, 66, 109, 117; scandal surrounding, 114, 115
Attol Tryst, Mary Ann and Lotta Crabtree's, 26, 27, 266

Baby Burlesks, 84, 202–3
"Baby Face," 146, 262
Baby Gladys Smith, *see* Pickford, Mary
Baby Helen Parrish, *see* Parrish, Baby Helen
Baby June, *see* Havoc, June
Baby Lillian, *see* Coogan, Lillian
Baby Lillian Gish, *see* Gish, Lillian
Baby Marie Osborne, 125, 165, 218, 232, 233
Baby Peggy, 102; *Ah, Wilderness!*, 245; and animals kept at Century Studio, 80–81, 84–87; *April Fool*, 172, 220; auctioning off of movie memorabilia of, 240; birth of, 72; booking of, in Fort Worth, 174–78; *Captain January*, 142, 143, 169; changing of her name, 262; comeback efforts of, 207–8, 214–19; comedies of, 91, 120; contract offer from Century Studio for, 76–77; and Jackie Coogan, 126, 204–5; dangerous situations faced by, while filming, 83–84; *The Darling of New York*, 136; decline in her career, 166, 168–72; at Democratic National Convention (1924), 146–47; discovery of, by Fred Fishback 69–70, 74–76; dude ranch purchased by her father, 205–8; education of, at Lawlor's, 222–31 *passim*; *Eight Girls in a Boat*, 220; embezzling of her movie earnings, 169; failure of her marriage to Gordon Ayers, 258, 262; her feelings of responsibility for her family, 246–47; fifth birthday party of, 143–44; future of, 188–89; hard times suffered by, 250–51; *Heidi*, 142, 169; *Helen's Babies*, 142; intelligence quotient of, 92; and Elsie Janis, 191–94, 247–48; and later years of her mother, 269–71; her life at Century Studio, 77–83, 119–20; Los Angeles *Herald Tribune* on, 93; marriage of, to Gordon Ayers, 249–50; melodramas of, 136; musical play written by (1938), 247–48; her occupational hazards, 183–84; one-night stands of, 145–46; on-the-road vaudeville act of, 180–82; painful adolescence of, 232–35; *Peg o' the Movies*, 203; *Playmates*, 76; her recollections of her parents, 122–25, 127–29; her relationship with Gordon Ayers, 246, 247, 248; her relationship with her parents, 120–21; her retreat to Catholic Church, 262; and Ginger Rogers' departure with Jack Pepper, 190; royalties from her products, 136–37; salary of, 110, 136; second marriage of, to Bob Cary, 263; self-hatred of, 251–52; settling of, in San Diego area, 269; and seventieth and last birthday of her father, 268; uniqueness of, 125; her visit to New York, 143, 144–45; her visit to Pickfair, 138–39
Baby Peggy Corporation, 137, 138, 142; embezzling of funds of, 169
Baby Peggy Fan Club, 144
"Baby Take a Bow," 204
Baggot, King, 136
Bara, Theda, 165
Barker, Bobby, 93
Barry, Wesley, 92, 125
Barrymore, Lionel, 225
Barthelmess, Richard, 108
Bartholomew, Freddie, 104–5, 233; adult life of, 256; *David Copperfield*, 224, 243; family squabble over income of, 242–43; *Little Lord Fauntleroy*, 224; and Mickey Rooney, 239
Bateman family, 5

Baxter, Grandmother, 71
B.B.B.'s Cellar, 223
"Beautiful Baby" contests, 92–93
Beery, Wallace, 100
Belasco, David, 31–32, 35, 266
Belcher, Ernest, 230, 251; School of Dance of, 200
Belmore, Lionel, 136
Benton & Bowles, 256
Berkeley, Busby, 182
Berlin, Irving, 41
Bernhardt, Sarah, 191
Bernstein, Arthur, 131, 137, 139, 241–42; his contract offer for Baby Peggy, 140–41; and Jackie Coogan's Children's Crusade, 147; death of, 242; and death of Jack Coogan, 238; his divorce, 189–90; marriage of, to Lillian Coogan, 240; and Shirley Temple, 210–11, 260
Bernstein, Mrs. Arthur (first), 189
Bernstein, Mrs. Arthur (second), see Coogan, Lillian (Dolliver)
Bicycle Thief, The, 253
Bierbower, Elsie Janet, see Janis, Elsie
Bierbower, Jenny Cockrell, see Janis, Jenny
Bierbower, John, 22, 23, 24
Bierbower, Percy (Percy Janis), 22, 24, 38, 160
Big Jim, 74, 77
Billboard, 226
Biograph Company, 34–36
Black, Charles, 260–61
Black, Shirley Temple, see Temple, Shirley
Black Pirate, The, 205
"Blue Moon," 229–30
Booth, Edwin, 4
Bosworth, Hobart, studio, 38
Boy's Life, 133
"Break the News to Mother," 23
Brewster Hotel (Boston), 27, 147
Bright Eyes, 227
Brockwell, Gladys, 136, 165
Broken Blossoms, 108
Brownie the Wonder Dog, 67, 74, 76, 80; death of, 91
Browning, Elizabeth Barrett, 235
Brownlow, Kevin, 267
Buckwheat, 224
Burroughs, Edgar Rice, 170
Bye, George T., 143

California Stock Company, 256
Canadian War Loans, 42
Cantor, Eddie, 176, 182, 214
Captain January, 142, 143, 169
Captains Courageous, 239
Carroll, Lewis, quoted, 15
Carter, Fern, 224
Carter, Joe, 93–94
Carter, Nell, 93–96, 153, 154, 239, 258
Cary, Bob, 268, 269

Cary Diana Serra, see Baby Peggy
Cary, Mark, 268–69, 272
Casting Director's Album of Screen Children, The, 151, 219–20
Castle, Irene, 41, 113
Castle, Vernon, 41
Central Casting, 220, 222, 244, 256, 265, 266
Century Studio, 64–65, 66–67, 74, 200; animals kept at, 80–81, 84–87; Baby Peggy's life at, 77–83, 119–20; contract offered to Baby Peggy by, 76–77; fire at, 87; scenery and supplies at, 81
Champion, Gower, 223, 229
Champion, Marge, 229
Chaplin, Charlie, 139; and Little Benny Alexander, 46; childhood of, 52–53; criticism of Jackie Coogan's later films by, 135; and Marion Davies, 116; A Day's Pleasure, 57; discovery of Jackie Coogan by, 52, 53–55, 67, 195; The Gold Rush, 115; The Idle Class, 64; The Kid, 54, 57, 58–61, 62–64, 76; and Lilita McMurray (Lita Grey), 61–63, 64, 115; and Mary Pickford, 44, 99, 266–67; reputation established by, 51–52
Chaplin, Sydney, 53, 64, 139
Chapman family, 5, 7–8
Charley (elephant), 80–81, 84, 85–86
Chase, Charlie, 131, 132
Chevalier, Maurice, 191
Chink and the Child, The, see Broken Blossoms
Circus Days, 135
Clemenceau, Georges, 147
Cobb, Irvin S., 90, 210
Cocoanut Grove, 139, 140
Cohan, George M., 47
Cohn, Harry, 244
Coleman, Ronald, 172
Columbia Pictures, 244
Combs, Jackie, 153
Coogan, Jack, 49–51, 52, 57–58, 77, 134; and Arbuckle scandal, 114; and Baby Peggy Corporation, 137; and Bernsteins' divorce case, 189; and Charlie Chaplin, 53–54, 59; death of, in automobile accident, 236–38; difficulties imposed on, by son's success, 123–24, 125, 142; on endorsements, 134; estate of, 239–41; and Douglas Fairbanks, 139, 205; and Jackie's Children's Crusade, 147; and Jackie's million-dollar contract, 141; joke-telling by, 139–40; and The Kid, 64; separation of, from his wife, 189–90; setting up of Jackie Coogan Productions by, 135; signed by Roscoe Arbuckle, 53, 54; on his son's success, 92
Coogan, Jackie, 68, 77, 102, 109; adult life of, 255–56; and Roscoe Arbuckle, 117; auto accident of, 134; and Baby Peggy, 126, 204–5; birth of, 49; Chil-

dren's Crusade of, 147; *Circus Days*, 135; *Daddy*, 135; *A Day's Pleasure*, 57; and death of Arthur Bernstein, 242; death of his father, 236–38; discovery of, by Charlie Chaplin, 52, 53–55, 67, 195; early years of, in vaudeville, 50–51; earnings of, 204; effect on, of first appearance in studio world, 56–57; endorsements of, 134; estate of his father, 239–40; his father's comments on success of, 92; Golden Cross of the Order of Jerusalem received by, 147; *Huckleberry Finn*, 220; *The Kid*, 57, 58–61, 63–64, 134, 135, 255; listing of, as has-been, 232; marriage of, to Betty Grable, 240-41, 254; million-dollar contract awarded to, 141, 168; *My Boy*, 135; *Oliver Twist*, 135; *Peck's Bad Boy*, 134–35; popularity of, 90–91; praise for, 60–61; quoted, 56, 130, 255; salary paid to, by Chaplin, 76; schedule of, 91–92; his separation from Betty Grable, 241; suing of his mother by, 240–41; *Tom Sawyer*, 204, 214, 220; *Trouble*, 135; uniqueness of, 125
Coogan, Leslie, 255
Coogan, Lillian (Dolliver), 48, 50–51, 92, 139, 147; at Baby Peggy's fifth birthday party, 143–44; Jack Coogan's estate willed to, 240; and death of Arthur Bernstein, 242; and death of Jack Coogan, 238; difficulties imposed on, by son's success, 124, 125; marriage of, to Arthur Bernstein, 240; marriage of, to Jack Coogan, 49; named in Bernsteins' divorce suit, 189; present status of, 256; separation of, from Jack Coogan, 189–90; suing of, by her son, 240–41
Coogan, Robert, 256
Coogan Act, 242, 261
Cooper, Jackie, 133, 233, 242, 254-55; *Skippy*, 133
Cooper, Barbara (Kraus), 255
Cosmopolitan, 133
Cowboys, clique of, in Hollywood, 109–10
Crabtree, George, 17, 19, 26
Crabtree, John Ashworth, 13–14, 20, 22; birth of his son, 10; his life with wife Mary Ann, 1–4, 5–6, 16–17; retirement of, to England, 20–21
Crabtree, John Ashworth, Jr., 19, 20; birth of, 10; death of, 26, 38, 160
Crabtree, Lotta, 2, 3, 4, 38, 60, 90; attitude of, toward films, 27–28; and Attol Tryst, 26, 27; her climb to fame, 17–20; death of, 147; description of, 5, 6; formation of traveling company around, 13–17; fortune of, 20; honoring of her mother's memory by, 271–72; and Elsie Janis, 22, 24; and Jenny Janis (Jenny Bierbower), 21; last visit of, to New York, 145; and Lola Montez, 6–7, 11; performance of,

before miners, 11–13; retirement of, 26–27; special talent of, 191
Crabtree, Mary Ann, 10–11, 26, 29, 194; and Attol Tryst, 26, 27, 266; her daughter Lotta's performance for miners, 11–13; death of, 27; formation of traveling company around Lotta by, 13–17; honoring of memory of, by Lotta Crabtree, 271–72; and Jenny Janis (Jenny Bierbower), 21, 24–25; land speculations of, 20; her life with John Ashworth Crabtree, 1–4, 5–6, 17; and Lotta's climb to fame, 17–19; and Lola Montez, 4–5, 6–7, 17; her passion for the theater, 4
Crosby, Percy, 133
Curry, Dave, 127
Curwood, James Oliver, 123

Daddy, 135
Daddy Long Legs, 159
Dainty June, *see* Havoc, June
Dancing schools, 198–99; proliferation of, 199–202
Daniels, Bebe, 99
Daniels, Mickey, 132, 134
Darling, Jean, 132, 134, 153, 233
Darling of New York, The, 136
Darmour, Larry, 95
Darro, Frankie (Frankie Johnson), 100, 225–26, 229, 256
Darro, Mrs. Frank Johnson, 100, 226
David Copperfield, 224, 243
Davies, Marion, 116
Day's Pleasure, A, 57
Dear Brutus, 27
De Mille, Cecil B., 156, 200, 225; *The Little American*, 46; *Ten Commandments*, 136
Depression, Great, 207, 208, 209
"Destiny," 99
Dianando Studios, 165
Dickens, Charles, 53, 60, 209; *Great Expectations* (quoted), 236; *Nicholas Nickleby*, 8; *The Old Curiosity Shop*, 19; *Oliver Twist*, 9
Dickens, Charles, Jr., 19
Dolliver, Baby Lillian, *see* Coogan, Lillian (Dolliver)
Dolliver family, 48, 49
"Don't Wait Too Long," 41
Downs, Johnny, 132, 134
Dressler, Marie, 66, 109
Duffy, Kathryn, 199
Duke, Patty, 252
Duncan Sisters, 176
Durbin, Deanna, 214, 233, 254, 263; marriages of, 258–59; quoted, 249
Durkin, Gertrude, 236
Durkin, Grace, 236
Durkin, Trent "Junior," 220, 236, 238–39; death of, 237; funeral of, 238

Eames, Peggy, 134
Earle, Jack, 120, 127
Earp, Wyatt, 110
East Lynne, 22, 23
Educational Films, 202
Education of movie children, 222–29
  passim
Eight Girls in a Boat, 220
Evansmith (photographer), 151
Every Pearl a Tear, 46

Factor, Max, 216
Fairbanks, Beth, 41, 42
Fairbanks, Douglas, 61, 99, 155, 160; and
  Baby Peggy, 139, 216; *The Black Pirate*,
  205; his divorce from Mary Pickford,
  266; estrangement between Mary
  Pickford and, 215; first meeting between
  Mary Pickford and, 41, 42; marriage of,
  to Mary Pickford, 98, 113, 116; and
  Charlotte Pickford's death, 161;
  Charlotte Pickford's jealousy of, 159;
  ratings on, 204
Family Affair, A, 239
Fanchon (producer), 201
Faust, 229
Fellows, Edith, 102–4, 132, 223; disappear-
  ance of earnings of, 261; family squabble
  over income of, 242, 243–44; her first
  break, 157; her Jewel song from *Faust*,
  229; and Jane Withers, 245
Fellows, Elizabeth, 102–4, 157–58, 243–44;
  death of, 261
Film Daily, 133
Film Test Laboratory, 152
First National, 43, 63, 142
Fishback, Fred, 66–67, 139; and Arbuckle
  scandal, 114; discovery of Baby Peggy
  by, 67–70, 74, 75–76; and *Playmates*, 76
Fisher, Gloria, 158
Flying Johnsons, 100
Flynn, Errol, 271
Forty-second Street, 218
Fox, Fontaine, 95, 96
Fox Kiddies, 125
Fox Studio, 210–11
Fraser, Phyllis, 218
Freud, Sigmund, 121
Furness, Betty, 218
Fyfe, David T., quoted, 1

Gable, Clark, 225, 234, 253, 257, 270;
  Manhattan Melodrama, 239
Gardner, Ava, 257
Garland, Judy (Frances Gumm), 102, 118,
  270; attempt of, to enroll at Hollywood
  High, 223; dancing lessons of, 202; death
  of, 268; early career of, as Frances
  Gumm, 101–2, 201–2; education of, at
  MGM, 224; enrollment of, at Lawlor's
  Professional School, 229–30; income of,
  handled by mother, 242; on men in her

life, 213; tragic relationship between her
  mother and, 267–68; *The Wizard of Oz*,
  268
Gay, Charlie, 87
Gay's Lion Farm, 80, 86
Gibson, Hoot, 110
Gilmore, William, 267
Gish, Dorothy, 32, 33, 112, 113; and
  Biograph Company, 36; *Hearts of the
  World*, 46
Gish, Lillian, 30, 32, 112, 113; and Bio-
  graph Company, 36; *Broken Blossoms*,
  108; *A Good Little Devil*, 35; her hatred
  for hardships on the road, 33; health of,
  33; *Hearts of the World*, 46
Gish, Mrs. James Leigh, 32–33, 46
"Give My Regards to Broadway," 192
Gleason, James, 216
Gleason, Lucille, 216
Goldbeck, Willis, *Motion Picture Classic*,
  92
Gold Rush, The, 115
Goldwyn, Samuel, 43
Good Little Devil, A, 35
Goulding, Alf, 126–27, 202
Goulding, Alfie, 126, 127
Grable, Betty, 223; marriage of, to Jackie
  Coogan, 240–41, 254
Gracian, Baltasar, quoted, 71
Grant, Ulysses S., 17
Green, Mitzi, 191, 194–95, 227; and *Tom
  Sawyer*, 214
Green, Rosie, 191, 227
Grey, Lita (Lilita McMurray), 61–63, 64,
  115
Grey, Zane, 123
Griffith, David Wark, 36, 43, 115; *Broken
  Blossoms*, 108; *Hearts of the World*, 46;
  and Mary Pickford, 34–35
Growing Pains, 219–20, 236, 239
Gumm, Ethel (Virginia Lee), 101–2, 201–2,
  229; death of, 267; and Judy Garland's
  income, 242; tragic relationship between
  Judy Garland and, 267–68
Gumm, Frances, *see* Garland, Judy
Gumm, Frank (Jack Lee), 101–2, 201; death
  of, 242
Gumm, Jane, 101–2, 201–2
Gumm, Virginia, 101–2, 201–2

Hallem, Basil, 39–40, 41, 248; death of, 40,
  191, 192
Hal Roach Studio, 131, 157–58, 199–200,
  214
Hampton, Dorothy, 268
Hampton, John, 268
Hanson, Earl, 174–75, 176, 178
Hardy, Andy, 219, 220, 239, 257
Harris, Mildred, 51, 63
Hart, Neal, 110
"Has-beens," 232–34

Havoc, June (June Hovick), 96–99, 164; changing of her name, 97n, 187; discord between her mother and, 184–87
Hayes, Helen, 27
Hays, Mr. (banker), 207
Hays, Will, 117
Hearst, William Randolph, 115–16
Hearts of the World, 46
Heidi, 142, 169
Helen's Babies, 142
Henry, Charlotte, 220, 223
Herbert, Victor, 145
Hickman, Darryl, 132
Hickok, Wild Bill, 110
"Hinky Dinky Par-lez Vous," 192
Hippodrome Theatre (New York), 145
Hobart Bosworth Studio, 38
Hollytown Theater, 218
Holmes, Guy, 237–38
Holmes, Leon, 220
Hood, Darla, 84, 199–200, 213–14; earnings of, spent by her parents, 261–62; education of, 224; and Elizabeth Taylor, 234
Hood, Arthur, 199, 200, 213–14, 262
Hood, Mrs. Arthur, 199–200, 214, 262
Hopper, Hedda, quoted, 148
Horner, Robert, 236, 237–38
Hovick, June, see Havoc, June
Hovick, Louise, see Lee, Gypsy Rose
Hovick, Rose, 96–99, 164; discord between daughter June and, 184–87
Howard, Little Cordelia, 8, 26, 60; death of, 253; first stage appearances of, 9–10
Howard, George C., 8, 9–10
Howard, Mrs. George C., 8, 9
Howe, Herbert, 60–61
Hula Hut restaurant, 108–9, 173
Hurrell, George, 212
Hutschnecker, Arnold, The Will to Live, 255

Idle Class, The, 64
IMP Films, 36
Ince, Ralph, 100
Ince, Thomas, 66, 116
Intelligence quotients, growing interest in (1920s), of movie children, 92

Jackie Coogan Productions, Inc., 135, 141, 236; Lillian Coogan becomes president of, 240; value of, 241
Jackson, Mary Ann, 132, 171
Jacobs, Paul, 67
Janis, Elsie (Elsie Janet Bierbower), 24–25, 27, 58, 77, 112, 113; appearancce of, at White House, 23; and Baby Peggy, 192–93, 194, 247–48; birth and early years of, 22; career of, launched by her mother, 23–24, 29; death of her brother Percy, 38; and death of her mother, 195–96; entertaining of servicemen by, 191–92; her first movie contract, 38–39; and Basil

Hallem, 39, 40, 248; impact on, of sinking of Lusitania, 39; Manor House of, 40–41; and Mary Pickford and Owen Moore, 39; popularity of, 38; quoted, 29; rowdy audience's displeasure with, 176; talent of, 22–23, 191; her tours of Orpheum circuit, 164
Janis, Jenny (Jenny Cockrell Bierbower), 21–23, 58, 112; and Baby Peggy, 192–93, 194; backstage career of, 164; her crossing to England on Lusitania, 39; death of, 195–96; death of her son Percy, 38; and Elsie's first movie contract, 38–39; formidable presence of, 29–30; launching of daughter Elsie's career by, 23–25; Manor House of, 40–41, 266; popularity of her daughter, 38
Janis, Percy, see Bierbower, Percy
Jessel, George, 182
Jewish community, Hollywood's, 110–11
Johnson, Dick Winslow, 220, 236–37, 248, 265
Johnson, Frankie, see Darro, Frankie
Johnson, Frank, 151
Johnson, Wynonah, 151, 152, 220, 237, 264; voted Hollywood Movie Mother of the Year, 265
Jolson, Al, 176, 182
Jones, Charlie, 237–38
Jones, Frieda, 150–51, 159, 264–65
Jones, Macon, 151
Jones, Marcia Mae, 132, 151, 159, 264
Jones, Margaret, 151, 158–59
Jones, Marvin 151
Jones, William Macon, 150, 151, 265
Journey for Margaret, 252
Judgment of the Storm, 100

Karno Company, 53
Kellerman, Annette, 50, 54
Kellogg Corporation, 133
Keno, Joe, 191
Kid, The, 54, 76, 115, 128; Chaplin's rights to, 63; Jackie Coogan's role in, 57, 58–61, 63–64, 134, 135, 255; Lilita McMurray's role in, 62–63
King, Henry, 172
Kipling, Rudyard, 123
Kornman, Mary, 132, 134, 233
Kosloff, Theodore, 200
Kraus, Barbara, see Cooper, Barbara (Kraus)

Lacy, Philippe de, 102, 232
Laemmle, Carl, 36–37, 43, 65–66, 79; and Baby Peggy's comeback efforts, 217, 219; and The Darling of New York, 136; negotiations over Baby Peggy's salary with, 135–36; profits made by, 110–11
Laemmle, Recha (Stern), 65
Lamont, Charles, 202–3
Lasky, Jesse, 194
Laurel, Stan, 109

Laurel and Hardy, 131
Lawlor, Viola F. (Mom), 225–26, 229, 230, 238
Lawlor's Professional School, 222–31 passim
Leatherneck, 165
Lee, Gypsy Rose (Louise Hovick), 96–97, 97n, 164, 184, 187
Lee, Jack (Frank Gumm), 100–102. See also Gumm, Frank
Lee, Jane and Katherine, 165
Lee, Virgina (Ethel Gumm), 100–102. See also Gumm, Ethel
Lehrman's Knock-Out Comedies (L-KO), 64, 78
Lesser, Sol, 131, 135; and Baby Peggy films, 168, 169; and Captain January, 142; his contract offer to Baby Peggy, 141–42, 167; severing of relations between Baby Peggy and, 170
Lewis, Sheldon, 136
Liberty, 133
Liberty Bonds, 41–42, 45
Little American, The, 42, 46
Little Annie Rooney, 159, 161
Little Cordelia Howard, see Howard, Little Cordelia
Little Elsie, see Janis, Elsie
Little Lord Fauntleroy, 224, 239
Little Miss Marker, 210
Little, Princess, The, 212
Little Red Schoolhouse, The, 30, 33
Littlest Girl, The, 25
Little Women, 214–15
L-KO, see Lehrman's Knock-Out Comedies
Lloyd, Harold, 61, 99, 131, 204
Loew's State Theater, 201, 202
London, Babe, 57
Lord Jeff, 239
Los Angeles Herald Tribune, 93
Los Angeles Orpheum, 202
Los Angeles Times, 189, 242
Los Angeles Tribune, 99
"Lover Come Back to Me," 205
Luft, Sid, 267
Lusitania, sinking of, 39, 42
Lyman, Mike, 242
Lynn, Mr. (of RKO), 250
Lyon's Van and Storage Company, 240

McAvoy, J. P., 210
McAvoy, May, 117
McCoy, Tim, Colonel, 110, 117
MacDonald, Cordelia Howard, see Howard, Little Cordelia
McDonald, Mary, 224
McDowall, Roddy, 224
McFarland, Spanky, 132–33, 224
McGuire, Micky, see Rooney, Mickey
McKinley, William, 23
McMurray, Lilita, see Grey, Lita

Maguire, Tom, 17
Manhattan Melodrama, 239
Manor House, Jenny Janis's, 40–41, 266
Marco (producer), 201
Martin, Joe (chimpanzee), 80, 84–85
Mayer, Louis B., 111, 133, 267
Meglin, Ethel, 230; dance studio of, 200–201, 202, 227
MGM, 133, 156, 219; Little Red Schoolhouse at, 224, 228; mutiny at, 257; profits of, on Andy Hardy films, 239
Miller, Joaquin, 123
Miller, Sidney, 229, 230
Mills, Hayley, 252
Minter, Mary Miles, 115
Mitchell, Maggie, 22
Mix, Tom, 73, 76, 99, 137; My Pal, the King, 153
Modjeska, Helena, 22
Montez, Lola, 4–5, 17; and Lotta Crabtree, 6–7, 11, 20
Montgomery, Jack, 72–73, 82–83, 86; and Baby Peggy's one-night stands, 145–46; and Baby Peggy's on-the-road vaudeville act, 181; Baby Peggy's plans for happiness of, 235, 246–47; Baby Peggy's recollections of, 123, 127–29; and Arthur Bernstein, 141; and booking of Baby Peggy in Fort Worth, 174–78; and contracts offered to Baby Peggy, 76–77, 141–42; and daughter's mental crisis, 262; death of, 269; and decline in Baby Peggy's career, 170–72; difficulties imposed on, by Baby Peggy's succcess, 124–25; and discovery of Baby Peggy by Fred Fishback, 69–70, 74–76; and embezzlement of Baby Peggy's movie earnings, 169; employment of, at Hollywood studios, 73–74; his friendship with the Coogans, 139, 140; grandson of, 268–69; illness and depression of, 167, 173–74; investments of, 137; and invitation to Pickfair, 138–39; last birthday celebration of, 268; lawsuit filed against RKO by, 250–51, 265; marriage of, to Marian Baxter, 71–72; and negotiations over Baby Peggy's salary, 135–36; new life for, 265, 266; and profit made on Baby Peggy, 110–11; purchase of dude ranch by, 205–8; his quarrels with his wife, 120–21, 138, 187–88; return of, to Hollywood, 221; sum of money loaned to Baby Peggy by, 270–71; on theme of genius and obedience, 124–25, 143; and The Winning of Barbara Worth, 172–73
Montgomery, J. G., 138, 169
Montgomery, Mrs. J. G., 138, 169
Montgomery, Louise, 72, 74, 75, 82, 121, 139; Baby Peggy's feeling of responsibility for, 246; and Baby Peggy's on-the-road vaudeville act, 181; and booking of Baby Peggy in Forth Worth,

175, 176, 177; dance contest entered by, 166, 178; dancing school enrollment of, 207, 208; dude ranch purchased by her father, 206; her father's illness, 174; and Ginger Roger's departure with Jack Pepper, 190; sensitivity of, 122; her work as an extra, 220–21
Montgomery, Marian (Baxter) (later Peggy Montgomery), 72–73, 82–83, 84; her advice to parents of would-be child stars, 92; assumes name of Peggy Montgomery, 266; attitude of, toward Baby Peggy as grown woman, 270–71; on Baby Peggy's future, 188–89; and Baby Peggy's on-the-road vaudeville act, 181; Baby Peggy's plans for happiness of, 235, 246–47; Baby Peggy's recollection of, 122–23; Arthur Bernstein's conversation with, about Baby Peggy's contract, 140–41; and booking of Baby Peggy in Fort Worth, 174–78; and contract offered to Baby Peggy, 77; and daughter's mental crisis, 262; and decline in Baby Peggy's career, 170–72; and discovery of Baby Peggy by Fred Fishback, 68–70, 74–75; and embezzlement of Baby Peggy's movie earnings, 169; enters Motion Picture Home, 269–70; her friendship with the Coogans, 139; grandson of, 268–69; and husband's illness and depression, 167, 174; and invitation to Pickfair, 138–39; and Elsie Janis, 191; marriage of, to Jack Montgomery, 71–72; her meeting with her mother, 188; new life for, 265–66; her quarrels with her husband, 120–21, 138, 187–88; quoted, 163; and Ginger Roger's departure with Jack Pepper, 190; her happiness living on dude ranch, 206; her work as an extra, 220–21
Montgomery, Peggy, see Baby Peggy. See also under Montgomery, Marian
Moore, Colleen, 153
Moore, Dickie, 214, 225, 256
Moore, Lola, 153, 154–55
Moore, Richard, 214
Moore, Owen, 41, 159; end of his marriage to Mary Pickford, 42, 116; as leading man opposite Mary Pickford, 34, 35, 36–37; his marriage to Mary Pickford, 37, 39
Moran, Polly, 66
Mosconi brothers, 207, 208, 230
Mother's Trust, 5
Motion Picture Home, 269–70
Motion Picture Relief Fund, 122
Murphy, Mrs. (tutor), 224
Murray, Mae, 91
Music Master, The, 50
Mutiny on the Bounty, 237
My Best Girl, 215
My Boy, 135

"My Buddy," 136
My Pal, the King, 153

Nation, Carrie, 107
National Press Association, 143
National Theater (Washington), 17
National Vaudeville Artists' Association, 182
Negri, Pola, 91
New York Evening Journal, 239
New York Sun Globe, 143
"Nobody Knows Me Number," 184
Normand, Mabel, 115

O'Brien, Margaret, 224; Journey of Margaret, 252
O'Day, Dawn, see Shirley, Anne
Olcott, Chauncey, 36
Oliver Twist, 135
Olson, Rose Smith, 144
O'Neal, Tatum, 252
Oneida (Hearst yacht), 116
Only Yesterday, 217–18, 219
Open City, 253
Orchids and Ermine, 153–54
Osborne, Baby Marie, see Baby Marie Osborne
Our Gang comedies, 91, 94, 95, 102, 157, 199; birth of idea for, 131; children of, 132–34, 153, 171; Darla Hood's career with, 261–62; original members of, 132, 232; safety factors involved in making, 83, 84
"Over There!," 192

"Pack Up Your Troubles in Your Old Kit Bag," 192
Paramount on Revue, 195
Paramount Pictures, 132, 133, 210
Parents' Magazine, 211
Parrish, Beverly, 150, 159
Parrish, Gordon, Sr., 150, 264
Parrish, Gordon, Jr., 150, 264
Parrish, Baby Helen, 132, 150, 159, 264
Parrish, Maxfield, 123
Parrish, Reesie, 150, 151–52, 159, 264, 265
Parrish, Robert, 150, 264, 265
Parsons, Louella, 116
Pasadena Playhouse, 219-20
Passing Show of 1915, The, 39
Paul, Vaughn, 259
Pavlova, Anna, 97
Payson, Blanche, 120, 127
Peck's Bad Boy, 134–35
Pepper, Jack, 190, 218
Pershing, John J., 46
Philipse, Frederick, 40, 41
Photoplay, 133
Pickfair, Mary Pickford's, 98, 113, 266, 267; Baby Peggy's invitation to, 138–39

Pickford, Charlotte (Charlotte Smith), 25, 64, 113; changing of her name to Pickford, 32; her contract negotiations with Adolph Zukor, 37–38, 42–43; and daughter Mary Pickford's work in films, 36; death of, 161, 163; description of, 29–30; her efforts to break up Mary's relationship with Owen Moore, 36–37; estate of, 160–61; on Lillian Gish's health, 33; and Jenny Janis, 195; launching of daughter Baby Glady's career by, 30–31; and Mary and Doug Fairbanks, 41, 42; as shining example of movie motherhood, 159; and suicide of son Jack's wife, 115
Pickford, Gwynne, 160, 161
Pickford, Jack (Jack Smith), 29, 31, 32, 161; chaperoning of sister Mary Pickford by, 36; death of, 160; on location in Cuba, 37; suicide of his wife, 115
Pickford, Mrs. Jack, see Thomas, Olive
Pickford, Lottie (Lottie Smith), 29, 31, 32, 160, 161; death of, 162; on location in Cuba, 37
Pickford, Mary (Gladys Smith), 25, 64, 102; and Baby Peggy, 139, 215; changing of her name, 32; and Charlie Chaplin, 43–44, 46, 53; her contract with Adolph Zukor, 37–38, 42–43; on Jackie Coogan, 61; Daddy Long Legs, 159; death of her mother, 161, 163; her divorce from Douglas Fairbanks, 266; early career of, as Baby Gladys Smith, 25–26, 27, 29, 30–31; estrangement between Douglas Fairbanks and, 215; first meeting between Douglas Fairbanks and, 41, 42; her hatred for hardships on the road, 33; and June Havoc, 99; image of, 43; and Elsie Janis, 39, 195; The Little American, 41–42; Little Annie Rooney, 159, 161; marriage of, to Douglas Fairbanks, 98, 113, 116; marriage of, to Owen Moore, 37; marriage of, to Charles "Buddy" Rogers, 266; and her mother's estate, 161–62; My Best Girl, 215; and Pickfair, 98, 113, 139, 266, 267; real estate holdings of, 204; Rebecca of Sunnybrook Farm, 159; and suicide of brother Jack's wife, 115; The Warrens of Virginia, 31; 266; work of, for Biograph Company, 33–36
Playmates, 76
Pollard, Snub, 126, 131
Polly Tix in Washington, 203
Powdermaker, Hortense, 112
Powell, Dick, 218
Previn, Dory, quoted, 88
Purviance, Edna, 62

Quigley, Juanita, 223

Rappé, Virginia, 114
Rebecca of Sunnybrook Farm, 159

Redbook, 194
Reed, Virginia Ann, 152
Reid, Walter, 115
Reynolds, Sir Joshua, The Age of Innocence, 61–62
Rich, Larry, 181
Riesner, Chuck, 61
Rin Tin Tin, 225
RKO, 132, 214–215, 227; law suit filed against, by Baby Peggy's father, 250–51, 265
Roach, Hal, and Our Gang comedies, 91, 94, 131–34
Roach, Jack, 131, 132
Roach, Mrs. Charles, 131–32
Roberts, Theodore, 136
Robinson, Dr. William, 5, 11, 12, 13, 17
Robinson, Little Sue, 7, 11, 13
Robinson family, 5, 7–8
Rogers, Charles "Buddy," 215, 266
Rogers, Ginger, 164, 188, 190; Charleston contest entered by, 166, 178; her departure with Jack Pepper, 190; early life of, 165–66; Forty-second Street, 218; impact of her mother on career of, 178–79; her rise to fame, 218–19
Rogers, John, 165–66
Rogers, Lela, 164–66, 188, 247; her advice for Baby Peggy, 218–19; impact of, on Ginger's career, 178–79; her penchant for comparing others with Ginger, 191; quoted, 180; reaction of, to daughter's departure with Jack Pepper, 190
Rogers, Roy, 262, 271
Rooney, Mickey (Joe Yule, Jr., "Sonny"), 118, 220, 229, 247; Ah, Wilderness!, 239; An Autobiography (quoted), 222; Captains Courageous, 239; early career of, as Joe (Sonny) Yule, Jr., 93–96; education of, 224; enrollment of, at Lawlor's Professional School, 223, 225, 229, 230; A Family Affair, 239; Little Lord Fauntleroy, 239; Lord Jeff, 239; Manhattan Melodrama, 239; My Pal, the King, 153; Orchids and Ermine, 153–54; passed over for Our Gang comedies, 132; stormy career and personal life of, 257–58; use of name Mickey McGuire by, 153; A Yank at Eaton, 239
Roosevelt, Franklin D., 146–47, 212–13
"Roses of Picardy," 136
Rothafel, Mr. (Roxy), 185–86
Rouverol, Auriana, 219, 239
Rouverol, Jean, 220

San Diego Union, 237
Saturday Evening Post, 79
Scandals, Hollywood, of 1920s, 114–17, 189–90
Schenck, Joseph, 143
Screen Actors Guild, 250
Sels Floto Circus, 100

Sennett, Mack, 51, 53, 66, 109; and Ethel
    Meglin, 200–201; and Blanche Payson,
    120
Serra, Father Junípero, 262
Service, Robert W., 123
Shea, Mike, 23–24
Sheehan, Winfield, 204
Shirley, Anne (Dawn O'Day), 220, 223,
    234; name changed from Dawn O'Day
    to, 227–28; retirement of, from films, 261
Shootist, The, 265
Shoulder Arms, 51
Singer, Mr., midgets of, 145
Skelton, Red, 256
Skidding, 219, 239
Skippy, 133
Smith, Alfred E., 147
Smith, Charlotte, see Pickford, Charlotte
Smith, Baby Gladys, see Pickford, Mary
Smith, Jack, see Pickford, Jack
Smith, John, 25
Smith, Lottie, see Pickford, Lottie
Sparrows, 155, 159
Sperry, George I., "Budge," 104
Sperry, Maye, 104
Sperry, Ray, 104–5, 224–25
Standard Casting Directory, The, 152–53,
    166, 171
Stand Up and Cheer, 203–4, 210
Steamers, transatlantic, 112–13
Stecker, Curley, 80, 84–86
Stecker, Mrs. Curley, 80, 84
Sterling, Ford, 66
Stern, Abe, 65, 66, 67, 110, 111; and ani-
    mals at Century Studio, 84–85; Baby
    Peggy's father's conflict with, 135; and
    Baby Peggy's life at Century Studio,
    77–79; contract offered to Baby Peggy
    by, 76; and fire at Century Studio, 87
Stern, Julius, 65–66, 67, 110, 111, 117;
    animals kept by, at Century Studio, 80–
    81, 84, 86–87; Baby Peggy's father's
    conflict with, 135; and Baby Peggy's
    life at Century Studio, 77–79; contract
    offered to Baby Peggy by, 76; and fire
    at Century Studio, 87; and Blanche
    Payson, 120; and Tarzan films, 170
Stowe, Harriet Beecher, 60
Streisand, Barbra, 112
Sullavan, Margaret, 217
Sun, Gus, 164
Sunday, Billy, 107
Sunshine, Sammy, 132
Swain, Mack, 66

Taylor, Desmond, 115
Taylor, Elizabeth, 118, 252; education of,
    224; her penchant for movielike solu-
    tions to problems, 234
Taylor, Mart, 10–11, 12; and formation of
    traveling company around Lotta Crab-
    tree, 13–16

Teddy (Great Dane), 80
Temple, George, 197–99, 203, 211, 213;
    investment of Shirley's income by, 242;
    uniqueness of, among movie parents,
    260
Temple, Gertrude, 197–98; on Arthur
    Bernstein, 210–11; on bringing up
    Shirley, 211–12, 213; and dancing les-
    sons for Shirley, 198–99, 202; and dis-
    covery of Shirley, 202–3; investment of
    Shirley's income by, 242; quoted, 197;
    on Shirley's rendition of "Baby Take a
    Bow," 204; uniqueness of, among movie
    parents, 260
Temple, Shirley, 214, 228, 233, 259–60;
    Baby Burlesks, 84, 202–3; Arthur Bern-
    stein's offer to handle affairs of, 210–11;
    birth of, 198; Bright Eyes, 227; dancing
    lessons for, 198–99, 202; discovery of,
    202–3; intelligence quotient of, 211;
    investment of income of, 242; Little
    Miss Marker, 210; The Little Princess,
    212; marriage of, to John Agar, 259, 260;
    marriage of, to Charles Black, 260–61;
    passed over for Our Gang comedies,
    132; Polly Tix in Washington, 203;
    quoted, 209; role of mother in career
    of, 211–13; Stand Up and Cheer, 203–4,
    210; as symbol of optimism, 209–10
Ten Commandments, 136
Thomas, Olive (Mrs. Jack Pickford), 115
Thomason, Barbara, 267
"Three O'Clock in the Morning," 173
Tolstoy, Leo, quoted, 119
Tom Sawyer, 204, 214, 220
Toyland, 145
Tracy, Spencer, 270
Trouble, 135
Try Later, 256
Tucker, Sophie, 182
Turpin, Ben, 66
Twain, Mark, 134
Twentieth Century-Fox, 259

Uncle Tom's Cabin, 10, 26
United Artists, 159, 216, 266
Universal Pictures, 65, 66, 96, 217, 219
Us Bunch, The, 95

Valentino, Rudolph, 91, 101, 111, 204
Variety, 226, 248, 253
Vaudevillians, former, in Hollywood, 109

Wagner, Walter, 262
Warfield, David, 50
Warner Brothers, 132, 218
Warrens of Virginia, The, 31, 266
Waterhole, 73
Wayne, John, 265, 271
Weber, Harry, 153, 178, 225
Weidler, Virginia, 223, 228

Weidler family, 228
West, Mae, 203
West, Mrs. (tutor), 224, 225
White, Pat, 93
White Cargo, 250
Winchell, Walter, 250
Winning of Barbara Worth, The, 172–73
Winslow, Dick, see Johnson, Dick Winslow
Withers, George, 226
Withers, Jane, 158, 223, 228, 233; and Edith Fellows, 245; mother's handling of in-

come of, 242; successful career of, 226–27; tap numbers of, 229
Withers, Lavinia Ruth, 226, 227, 242
Wizard of Oz, The, 268

Yank at Eton, A, 239
Yule, Joe, 230, 257
Yule, Joe, Jr., see Rooney, Mickey

Zanuck, Darryl F., 212
Zierold, Norman, The Child Stars, 249
Zukor, Adolph, 37–38, 42–43